WHY SETTLE
FOR MORE

AND MISS
THE BEST?

Linking your life to the purposes of God

WHY SETTLE FOR MORE AND MISS THE BEST?

TOM SINE

Author of *The Mustard Seed Conspiracy*

WORD BOOKS
PUBLISHER
WACO, TEXAS

A DIVISION OF
WORD, INCORPORATED

WHY SETTLE FOR MORE AND MISS THE BEST?

Scripture quotations in this book are from the following sources:

The King James Version of the Bible (KJV).
The New American Standard Bible (NASB), © The Lockman Foundation 1960, 1962, 1963, 1968, 1971, 1972, 1973, 1975, 1977.
The Holy Bible, New International Version (NIV). Copyright © 1973, 1978, 1984 International Bible Society. Used by permission of Zondervan Bible Publishers.
The Revised Standard Version of the Bible (RSV), copyrighted 1946, 1952, © 1971, 1973 by the Division of Christian Education of the National Council of the Churches of Christ in the U.S.A., and are used by permission.
The New Testament in Modern English (PHILLIPS) by J. B. Phillips, published by The Macmillan Company, © 1958, 1960, 1972 by J. B. Phillips.

Library of Congress Cataloging-in-Publication Data:

Sine, Tom.
    Why settle for more and miss the best? : linking your life to the purposes of God / Tom Sine
        p.   cm.
    1. Christian life—1960   I. Title.
BV4501.2.S47254   1987
248.4—dc19   87-31728
                                                          CIP

Printed in the United States of America
8 9 8   BA   9 8 7 6 5 4 3 2 1

*To those Christian leaders
in the Third World
who work so tirelessly for God's kingdom
with such limited resources*

*My prayer, as we
approach the twenty-first century,
is that thousands of Christians
will join hands with them
in seeing God's kingdom reign
established in every land and nation
by the power of His Spirit.*

contents

acknowledgments

This book had its inception at Wheaton '83, a conference on the nature and mission of the church sponsored by World Evangelical Fellowship. At the conclusion of the conference, leaders expressed a desire to present in more popular form some of the scholarly insights derived from our Bible study—and the result was *Why Settle for More and Miss the Best?* This book, therefore, is offered with gratitude to the hundreds of sisters and brothers from all over the world who participated in this important convocation.

I am also deeply indebted to many friends who read, commented and helped this project along, including: Lorraine and Arek Shakarian, Mark and Sheri Mahle, Theron and Robin Miller, Phil Wegner, Steve Hayner, Les Steele, Glen Saul, Kathy Giske, Louise Engstrom, Kent Hill, Rodney Clapp, Andrew and Maya Jeffrey, Paul Pierson, Mike McGregor and many others.

I am particularly grateful to JoAnne Whitney for her helpful reflections—and for tirelessly typing and retyping this manuscript. Anne Buchanan's patient and insightful editing of this book has helped tighten it in its stated purpose. And I am appreciative of all the encouragement I received from my friends at World Concern and the Seattle chapter of ESA.

Of course, I could not have completed this task without the support of my parents, my sons, and those with whom I live in Christian community. Finally, I feel a growing sense of indebtedness to all those who have gone before us in the Story of God, particularly those who participated in the Celtic Christian movement in the sixth through the tenth centuries.

foreword

Subconsciously, I always believed that the Sermon on the Mount was not meant for ordinary Christians. It seemed to me that the teachings set forth by Jesus in the fifth, sixth, and seventh chapters of Matthew were okay for the Mother Teresas of the world, but were beyond what could be expected of the rest of us.

The Beatitudes set forth by Jesus in Matthew 5 seem to be opposed to what the dominant culture has prescribed as a normal, happy lifestyle. Jesus says, "Blessed are the poor"—or, as Dietrich Bonhoeffer suggests, blessed are those who have become poor as they have responded to the needs of the poor and the oppressed. We have been brought up to believe that it is the wealthy who are the happy people.

Jesus tells us that people who cry because their hearts are broken over the things that break the heart of God are the ful- filled people in this world. We have been trained to believe that fulfillment comes to those who make their lives an endless round of partygoing with plenty of laughs.

The "will to power" is viewed as a positive personality trait in a competitive world in which only the fittest survive. But Jesus tells us that the meek are the blessed.

In our attempts to bolster law and order, we are convinced that capital punishment is an essential deterrent to crime. Conse- quently, Jesus' call to be merciful seems like unrealistic softness.

We have come to accept national policies which are designed to further our economic self-interests, even when such policies re- quire that we bolster the regimes of totalitarian dictators. Over and against such policies, we read that Jesus blesses those who hunger and thirst for justice. To those of us who have come to believe that social ethics are complex if not paradoxical in nature,

Jesus declares that those who live with pure hearts and accept truth in its simplicity are the ones who will see God.

In a world arena where the accepted logic is that the only way to prevent war is to prepare for it, Jesus calls us to be peacemakers. The implications of such a simple lifestyle would set us up to be persecuted and reviled, and would make us vulnerable to those who would "do all manner of evil against." Yet Jesus says that if such should come from our radical commitment to His values, we should rejoice.

It is no surprise that Christianity has taken the values prescribed by Jesus and inverted them. It should shock no one that the church should restate the message of the Master in such a way that it often comes out meaning just the opposite of what the Lord intended. For the sophisticated members of the world's intelligentsia, the Sermon on the Mount comes across as foolishly naïve.

There are those, like Tom Sine, the author of this book, who are not so convinced that the wisdom of this world is all that wise. He and other aliens in this strange and distant land called America probingly ask whether those who have followed the "reasonable" ways of the world have ended up happy. Sine and his friends are quick to ask if Yuppies have really found a way to happiness and if the pot of emotional riches lies waiting to be found at the end of the corporate rainbow. They sense a lack of joy among those down-to-earth, realistic executive-types who have bought into the American dream. They discern an absence of joy among the children who live in the affluence which their parents have provided.

Sine and his counterculture associates contend that what Jesus taught two thousand years ago in the Sermon on the Mount is a viable lifestyle that will produce joy and personal ecstasy in the midst of modern America. These voices, crying in the wilderness, call young people to abandon the temptation to live out their lives in the pursuit of the reasonable goals prescribed by the dominant culture and, instead, seek vocations wherein they can be instruments for the propagation of the values of another kingdom, the kingdom of God.

This book is a call to abandon the comfortable, pleasant, attractive, reasonable form of slavery that has come to typify so many of our lives. It is a call to recognize that the foolishness of the gospel is more reasonable in the end than the wisdom of this world. *Why Settle for More and Miss the Best?* offers help for those who have begun to doubt the validity of conventional values and are looking for a better way to find joy and meaning in life.

TONY CAMPOLO

start here . . .

Rushing! Running! Ripping around. From the first bell to the final test pattern, life for too many of us is just one frantic dash after another.

Every place I go, I meet people whose lives are busier and more frenetic than ever before. And they're honestly not sure what it's about anymore.

Most of these good folks are serious Christians. They are trying to do what's best for their families. They are responsible and committed to their jobs and to their homes. You will find them faithfully serving on church boards and committees. They are trying to do more and more.

But at the same time, these people are troubled because they live virtually without any larger sense of purpose that calls them beyond themselves, and they live without that quiet center that provides direction in every new situation.

Julie, for example, had no idea of what she wanted to do with her life. She was in the mad whirl of her final quarter as a sociology major at Seattle Pacific University. And Julie had been taking a course I taught in social work. We had talked several times about her uncertainty about future direction.

As graduation rapidly approached, I asked, "Julie, what are you going to do when you graduate?" She replied, "I've just found a job selling clothes in the basement of Nordstrom's department store." She continued, "This must be God's will for my life because it was the only job I could find." I thought to myself, "Not necessarily, Julie. I happen to know that you have only been looking for three weeks!"

I have heard from Julie from time to time. She has changed jobs several times and leads a very busy life, but she has never found direction. She is deeply frustrated. Julie's story could be repeated a thousand times over. I travel the United States speaking at Christian colleges, conferences, and churches. My heart aches as I meet hundreds of young people who are bright, highly gifted, and energetic but have absolutely no sense of purpose for their lives.

But this lack of purpose and direction is not just a young person's problem. Art came up to me after a creativity workshop I conducted in his church in Portland. He told me that for twenty years he had worked at a job he hated and his schedule had him on the run every waking minute of the day. He asked me, "What is it all for?"

Sharon was obviously frustrated when she talked to me at a conference in Wheaton. She and her husband had gone with the flow of other people's expectations. They had gotten the house in the suburbs, two cars, a camper, and a mountain of debt. And they both had to work full time just to stay even. I noticed how tired Sharon looked as she told me her story and how obviously trapped she felt in a way of life she really didn't want.

Julie, Sharon, and Art's profound frustration could have easily been expressed by Bruce Cockburn's ironic lyrics, "Let's hear a laugh for the man of the world who thinks he can make things work. . . . tried to build the New Jerusalem and winds up with New York. . . ."

Do you know what Bruce Cockburn is talking about? Do you know what it's like to start building towards New Jerusalem and wind up with New York? Do you ever wonder if there's life beyond the gerbil wheel? Does God have any purpose for our lives beyond our knocking ourselves out in the stress race?

Absolutely! God not only wants to liberate us from stressed-out living and help us catch our rhythm; He longs to fill our lives with direction and purpose. And nothing will give our lives greater purpose than linking up to the purposes of the One who is making all things new.

That's what this book is about—*enabling you to discover a better way of life. A way of life filled with purpose. A way of life that is more festive and celebrative than anything the rat race can offer. A way of life that makes a difference in the world around us.*

recovering our story

I am finding numbers of people who are beginning to look for that kind of life. Christians and non-Christians alike are fed up with the gerbil wheel. They instinctively sense they are on earth for something better—and they're right. But they don't really know how to find it.

At World Concern, the Christian mission organization where I work, we are receiving a growing number of calls from people who are hungry for a larger purpose that calls them beyond themselves. Young and old alike are searching for a way to make their lives count. They really want to be a part of what God is doing in history. But they don't know how.

How did we ever get to this point? How did we lose our way? In Elie Weisel's book of Hasidic tales, there is a story of a rabbi who throughout his life maintained a weekly ritual.

Every week he would go to a special place in the forest near his home. He would light a fire and say a prayer that told the story of God's salvation.

The rabbi's students, deeply influenced by the old man, continued his ritual for years after his death. However, little by little they changed the tradition. First they lost the sacred place in the forest. Then they failed to light the fire. They forgot the prayer. And eventually all they could do was tell the story.

It seems to me that what has happened in American Christianity is exactly the opposite. We haven't lost our sense of place. In our many traditions we have maintained our institutions and rituals. And we still pray. But I think there is convincing evidence that many of us in our individual and collective lives have forgotten our story. And without our story it shouldn't be surprising to any of us to find ourselves caught in the mad whirl of purposeless living.

By failing to have our lives and churches captured by the compelling story of the salvation of God, we have been satisfied by a superficial faith. We have been content with an institutionalized Christianity that demands a share of our allegiance and a compartment of our time, but has very little power to infuse our lives with compelling purpose. And many have settled for a private piety that is largely disengaged from the rest of life and the larger world.

Significant living begins with the recovery of the Story of God. And if we can begin to comprehend something of God's Story, then we can begin to discover what role God expects us to play in His cosmic drama. Then our Christian faith becomes something more than a little religious activity worked in around the edges of an already time-congested life.

Now, please understand that in speaking of "story" and
"drama," I am not talking about anything fictional or superficial.
I am talking about the fundamental values to which we give our
lives. I am talking about the dreams and visions for the better
future that captivate our lives, energy, and resources.

In this book we are going to thoughtfully examine stories we
have embraced and stories we have forgotten. And we are going
to pay particular attention to God's Story for our lives and His
world. For in reconnecting with God's Story, we discover not only
who we are, but what God's purposes are for our lives.

You see, it's no accident that you are living at the turbulent
close of the second millennium since the birth of Christ. God has
called you onto life's stage for such an hour as this. You can be
sure He has a very important role for you to play in His historical
drama. The Lord of history invites you to join Him in the remarkable adventure of seeing the world changed—of seeing a little
of His joy, hope, and jubilation come to the growing number of
broken and hurting places that surround us.

God isn't looking for the luminaries—the prestigious and the
powerful—to advance His cause. He is looking for ordinary people
like you and me. He invites you and me to the extraordinary adventure of seeing the world changed.

a look ahead

If we are going to take this journey together towards a more
meaningful way of life, we will need a road map. So let me outline
where we are going in this book.

In chapter 1, I would like to look at some reasons why our lives
seem to lack direction and begin to explore some new possibilities.

Then, in chapter 2, we will do a little diagnostic work. We will
analyze the half-truths and false stories to which many of us have
unwittingly given our lives. It is important to note that even
those of us who are committed Christians have often subscribed
to very limited views of the Christian Story which in turn have
had very limited power to give direction to our lives—or have
even led us off track.

Chapter 3 is the launch pad of the entire book. Here we will
attempt to recover something of the sweep of the Story of God as
told in the Bible. As we begin to discover the breadth of God's

redemptive initiative in history, I believe we will hear God call us out of our institutionalized, privatized Christianity into a cause that is quite literally changing the world. And we will discover more fully God's purposes for our lives and His world.

It is essential to realize the drama of God doesn't end with the Book of Acts. So in chapter 4 we will witness a few scenes of the ongoing saga of God's acts in history—from the early Christian era down to the present day. Here we will meet ordinary people like you and me who radically committed their lives not only to God, but to the purposes of God in the world. And they lived with a rich sense of meaning and fulfillment. They can be models for those of us who are struggling to find direction today.

You and I come on stage in chapter 5. God calls us to choose whether we are going to put His purposes first in our lives. He invites us to become the living presence of His Story in the world. Together we will discover ways through prayer, community, and worship to allow His values to become our values.

In chapter 6 we will discover that God expects us to be not only the presence, but also the agents of His new order. Here we will outline specific steps in active listening to help you discern your role in the drama of God. We will learn how to more fully link our lives to the purposes of God.

In chapter 7 we look beyond ourselves—to the world that God loves and Christ died for. We will discover how we can connect our congregations more fully to the purposes of God . . . and move mission back to the center of our congregational lives. We will discover an array of creative ways that we can be involved in whole-life mission for God's kingdom.

Finally, chapter 8 is a creativity tool kit. In this chapter we will call for a renaissance of Christian imagination in life and missions. More than that, we will seek to help you create imaginative new ways you can follow God's call in your life by actually creating new forms of celebration, timestyle, nontraditional vocations, community, and mission. In this final chapter we will try to help you break out of the constraints of the conventional and move more creatively towards the life to which Jesus Christ is calling you—a life filled with meaning.

Why Settle for More and Miss the Best? is designed to be used as a text in seminaries and colleges as well as a study book for adult groups and Sunday School classes. Questions are included at the end of each chapter to stimulate thought and discussion. Special emphasis is put on applying what is discussed. And a little visual summary called "Life Links" is featured at the end of each chapter to emphasize the central thrust of that chapter.

In this journey together we will be sharing biblical principles on redemptive theology, missions, and ethics—but we will be doing this through a story form. I am convinced that we can more fully engage biblical insights for our life through a narrative approach to theology and ethics. So again, don't allow our storytelling mode to distract you from the serious theological and ethical issues with which we are struggling. Remember, the One who calls us to follow Him is a Storyteller.

And in view of the way of life He promises us, why would any-one settle for more and miss the best—the opportunity to link our lives to the purposes of God?

for thought and discussion

As we begin this journey together, try to answer the following questions:

1. What are those pressures that you are facing that are making your life more frenetic than you would like it to be?
2. What is your sense of God's call on your life?
3. In what specific ways are you seeing God's call on your life realized or frustrated?

introducing link

welcome to

WHY SETTLE FOR MORE AND MISS THE BEST?

I've discovered in both my writing and speaking that I am not always as clear as I would like to be. For that reason I have asked for some help from a friend. I would like to introduce you to my friend, Link.

Any similarity to my other friend, Tony Campolo, who generously did the foreword for this book, is purely coincidental. Link has never taught sociology, worn glasses, or won the Campus Crusade for Christ Theologian of the Year award.

But Link is given to definite opinions.

At the end of each chapter he will join us and explain what I was really trying to say. Usually he will answer three questions:

(1) What are our life directions?

(2) How are we connected to those life directions?

(3) What are likely to be the consequences of following different life directions?

I think you will find Link a very agreeable companion on your journey through this book. I hope he will help make the thrust of each chapter a little clearer. However, if you have no difficulty interpreting what I am saying, please feel free to skip over the Life Links pages. I assure you Link will not be offended.

discovering life

Life! This book is about life . . . it's about having the time of your life. It's about those who have discovered the secret of living life fully and festively—and about those who are missing it.

Do you ever sense deep down that life must be more than you are experiencing? Do you ever long to live life more deeply, more significantly—to feel you have caught stride with the very rhythm of God and are participating in His dreams, to feel your life counts?

Then join us on this journey together as we seek to learn how to live full, significant, satisfying lives that God will use to transform the hurting world around us. Join us as we climb a new mountain, discover a new city, and participate in a new celebration—the wedding feast of the Lamb. You are invited to a better way of life.

But first, in this chapter, I want to take a candid look at the lives most of us are leading now. We will explore the peaks of other people's expectations that demand our attention—the mountains we climb every day of our lives, along with all the busy people around us. And, then I want us to look toward a better mountain—the mountain of God that offers us life instead of draining it from us.

The purpose of this chapter, quite simply, is to help us examine some reasons our lives are so incredibly busy and yet so lacking in direction and purpose.

movin' on up

King of the Mountain was a terribly popular game when I was growing up. I can still remember struggling to the top of a huge mountain of dirt, only to have a big guy at the top send me hurtling to the bottom again. Spitting dirt, I would turn and begin my climb all over again, only to discover a new way to the bottom. On one of those repeated ascents, exhausted and caked with dirt, I got stuck halfway up. I can still see myself stuck on the side of that hill, my friends climbing over me and using my skinny body for a ladder. (We really knew how to have good times in those days!)

There's a children's story called *Hope for the Flowers* that reminds me a little of that game. It's about an ambitious caterpillar named Stripe who decided to climb a different sort of mountain—a huge mountain of caterpillars, all climbing over one another, trying to get to the top. As Stripe plunged into the pile and began his ascent, he asked, "What's at the top?" Another climber responded, "No one knows, but it must be awfully good because everybody's rushing there. . . . "

Stripe soon found that moving up the mountain was a struggle. He was "pushed and kicked and stepped on from every direction. It was climb or be climbed." But Stripe disciplined himself neither to feel nor be distracted as he continued to push his way up. "'Don't blame me if you don't succeed! It's a tough life. Just make up your mind,' he yelled to any complainers."

Finally, Stripe neared the top of this humongous mountain of caterpillars. And as he looked ahead, he saw something disturbing: a tremendous pressure and shaking was sending many at the top crashing to their death below.

"Stripe felt awful with this new knowledge. The mystery of the pillar was clearing—he now knew what always must happen on the pillar. Frustration surged through Stripe.

"But as he agreed that this was the only way 'up' he heard a tiny whisper from the top: 'There's nothing here at all!' It was answered by another: 'Quiet, fool! They'll hear you down the pillar. We're where they want to be. That's what's here.'

"Stripe felt frozen. To be so high and not be high at all. *It only looked good from the bottom.*"[1]

What must it be like to discover there's nothing at the top, that "it only looks good from the bottom," particularly after one has invested enormous energy in climbing? What must it be like to discover the mountain we've been climbing is absolutely meaningless?

In my travels, I have met so many people who are struggling to climb mountains made up largely of other people's expectations.

---

1. Trina Paulia, *Hope for the Flowers* (Mahwah, NJ: Paulist Press, 1978), 21–94.

Like Stripe, they know they have to get to the top, but often *they don't know why.* They don't even know if what they are looking for is at the top of their caterpillar pillar. And they often climb at tremendous cost to themselves and their loved ones.

I encounter so many folks who are overworked, overbooked, overcommitted, and completely stressed out. Sound familiar? These people aren't finding life very satisfying, even when they are acquiring everything they are supposed to want.

Christian friends told me about Mr. and Mrs. Rose, a retired couple who live in a huge mansion on a two-hundred-acre estate near Salem, Massachusetts. They have spent their entire lives seeking to expand and protect their multimillion dollar fortune. Their estate is ringed with security devices. But they constantly worry that rats will eat through the electrical system, leaving them unprotected. So, they have hired a Canadian couple to augment their security systems and to watch their house, particularly when they are gone. And then they have people come by periodically and drop in on the couple they hired to check up on them. They trust no one, and they live with chronic fear.

The Roses live on a pinnacle of prosperity that many Americans would covet. But they are in absolute bondage to their wealth, and their lives are filled with fear and isolation.

In fact, Mrs. Rose is deeply envious of other multimillionaires, such as J. Paul Getty, who have more wealth than she does. She declares, "If we just had more money, then we would be happy." In other words, if we could only climb a little higher we would find what we are searching for.

Ironically—and tragically—the Rose's only son was recently murdered in a small town near where they lived. All of their wealth and concern for security failed to protect him. And they discovered in the midst of this crisis that they had so distanced themselves from other people that they had no one to turn to—not even each other. Mrs. Rose would sit alone by the hour in her large sitting room, rocking and hugging their old dachshund Solo—the only consolation she could find. Often, all people find at the top is that they are alone.

In London I met Bryan, a thoroughly likable chap who, in his efforts to get to the top, had lost his executive position in advertising, gone through bankruptcy, and was struggling to start over at age thirty-five. And as he took me on a tour around London for his new employer, I quickly discovered that Bryan wasn't cut out for the "climb or be climbed" rat race. He seemed too gentle, sensitive, and distracted to ever succeed in that world—although he kept trying valiantly. (For those who saw the 1986 film *The Gods Must Be Crazy,* Bryan is almost a clone of the white biologist.)

I have never been with anyone who experienced as many calamities in a single day as Bryan. It seemed as if every fifteen minutes something would happen to him. He lost his briefcase on the Underground, banged his shin as we sat down for coffee. Then, as we left the hotel, I heard screams behind me, and looked back to see Bryan still going around in the revolving door; somehow he had gotten his finger caught at the top. He went around four or five times before he was able to pull free.

After half a dozen such incidents, I concluded that my amiable friend must be accident prone—that he brought it all on himself. I was wrong. We had lunch in a charming outdoor cafe on Carnaby Street. After some predictable confusion, we finally got our food and found a table in the sun. No sooner had we seated ourselves than Bryan discovered that the huge stuffed baked potato he ordered for lunch was ice cold. With a look of composed stoicism, he dug in and took a large bite, but no sooner had that bite reached his mouth than an overflying pigeon scored a direct hit on the cold potato on his plate. Without saying a word, he quietly folded his napkin over the potato (careful not to bump his injured finger) as though these kinds of events happened every day. For Bryan they probably do.

We sat across from each other while taking the Underground back to Bryan's office at the end of a very eventful day. At the next stop a very large woman got on. She ignored the open seats and targeted her expanse for the six inches between Bryan and the guy sitting next to him. As she ominously backed in, Bryan's entire left side was jammed into the air and his right side was crunched pitifully into the metal panel next to him. He stared straight ahead without blinking for the entire thirty-minute ride, looking as if he had gotten painfully caught in someone's garbage compacter.

As we separated, Bryan said, "You may not believe this, but last week I was hit by an ambulance." I replied, "Bryan, I have no problem at all believing that."

Many of us in our mad scramble to the top really spend much more time in garbage compacters and on the front end of ambulances than we need to. I think we would be surprised how a change in direction could change our whole way of life.

Lost in America, circa 1985, is a film that thoughtfully asks the question, "What are we living for?" Unfortunately, it fails to come up with an answer. David and Linda Howard, two high-living young professionals, decide the corporate system asks too much

from them, and so they drop out. They scuttle it all, buy a Win-
nebago®, and set off to experience America—"I want to touch Indians," says David. Unfortunately, while they drop out physically,
they take their upwardly mobile values with them. And so it's only
a question of time until the film comes full circle and they wind
up right back where they started.

steep slopes and tough questions

Let me tell you about some other people—some Christians I
know who are more than a little exhausted climbing somebody
else's mountain and are asking some tough questions. They are
wondering, "Will I really be satisfied when I get to the top? Buy
the house? Purchase all the things I want? Get the promotion?"
And unlike David and Linda in the movie, these people are determined to get some answers.

For example, I met a Christian dentist in Eugene, Oregon, who
was working his tail off trying to create the kind of life and practice that was expected of an up-and-coming health professional.
He found himself continually struggling to expand his practice because he believed expansion was synonymous with success. He
continued to expand even though he already had more work than
he could handle, and he was working more and more evenings.

He had bought a large expensive home on a huge acreage outside of town for his family because that was expected of health
professionals like himself. Of course, he and his wife had bought
everything on time to tastefully furnish the home, and this, with
the mortgage payments, had significantly increased his sense of
economic pressure.

When I met this man, he was under a great deal of stress. He
spent most of his waking hours either at work or on his long com-
mute to or from work. He had little free time, and he wasn't able to
spend much of that with his wife and two kids because he used that
time to fix up their new home and keep his huge acreage mowed.

Now, you can be very sure this dentist was well respected in the
community and at church, though he obviously had precious little
time to be involved with either. He had the prestige and prosperity
that others only dream of. He was climbing the mountain and by
all external indicators doing very well. But he was beginning
to question if this was really a mountain God had asked him to
climb, or if he was simply trying to satisfy other people's
expectations.

Janet talked to me after I spoke in chapel at a Christian college she attended. I had challenged the students to put Christ and His mission at the center of their lives, and Janet told me she really wanted to respond to the challenge. She said that for years she had done everything her parents expected of her. She had gone to the college they had picked and majored in business, as they had recommended.

Now she was graduating, and she felt God was calling her to spend two years working in a refugee camp in Thailand. So she had gone home at spring break of her senior year to tell her folks. Their response had been immediate and unbending. "We didn't spend fifty thousand dollars sending you to college for that. You get your career established, get your IRAs started, and then you can travel to Thailand on your vacation if you are still interested." Janet found herself stuck halfway up her parent's mountain, asking herself some very tough questions.

As soon as Tom and Sue decided to get married, they immediately found themselves in a pressure cooker. They discovered themselves confronted by a whole new set of expectations from their fellow "baby boomers"—expectations to move to the suburbs, buy a split-level, and get into serious "nesting."

Tom and Sue had met while they were working in their church's ministry with Laotian refugees. They had wanted to buy a home in the inner city near their Laotian friends and continue working with them. But their peers at church strongly urged them to give up their plans. "Property values are terrible in the inner city. You'll never make any money on your investment. And that's certainly no place to raise kids. We will help you find a nice house in the suburbs and you can still drive into the inner city when you want."

Tom and Sue found themselves stuck at the bottom of somebody else's mountain trying to decide what they really wanted.

the mountains of madison avenue

It's amazing the number of mountains we are expected to climb in every area of our lives as employees, parents, students, church workers—and, of course, as consumers. Listen to the confessions of Erma Bombeck:

> I did as I was told. I was fussy about my peanut butter, fought cavities, became depressed over yellow wax buildup. . . . I was

responsible for my husband's underarms being protected for twelve hours. I was responsible for making sure my children had a well-balanced breakfast. I alone was carrying the burden for my dog's shiny coat. . . . We believed if we converted to all the products that marched before our eyes we could be the best, the sexiest, the freshest, the cleanest, the thinnest, the smartest and the first in our block to be regular. Purchasing for the entire family was the most important thing I had to do.[2]

In our upwardly mobile lifestyles, being good consumers is for many of us the most important thing we do. Shopping has become a major leisure-time activity for many. Increasingly, our sense of identity and self-worth is integrally connected to what we buy. We have come to really believe we are what we own—and that the more we own, the more we are. Our entire view of the better future is seen largely in materialistic terms of what we consume.

The folks on Madison Avenue have done a remarkable job of tantalizing us and persuading us to scale their illusory peaks and buy into their empty dreams. They have tried to convince us that an ever-increasing level of consumerism is synonymous with happiness. And they constantly seek to convince us we have new needs that we didn't know we had and that can only be satisfied by the new products they offer. As a consequence, when they tell us to "move on up," "grab the gusto," and "have it our way," most of us obediently begin to lockstep up their mountain together—non-Christian and Christian alike.

For example, while doing dorm inspections for homecoming in a Christian college, I was amazed to see virtually every room sporting the "sex appeal" toothpaste. Apparently the students had succumbed to the ridiculous illusion that a particular brand of toothpaste could actually make a person more appealing. A whole new generation has become even more coopted by slick advertising and seductive claims than their parents were.

Listen to this little jingle for Michelob beer—it sounds like what caterpillars must have been singing when they began their scramble up the caterpillar hill: "You're on your way, moving up. You were always the one . . . eager to try. You're on your way to

2. Erma Bombeck, *Aunt Erma's Cope Book* (New York: Fawcett Crest, 1979) 47–53.

the top." *Newsweek* predicts that Michelob's new light beer promo will become the battle cry of this generation: *"You can have it all."*[3]

Essentially what my dentist friend, Janet, Tom and Sue, Erma Bombeck, the student, and all the rest of us keep hearing from friends, society, and Madison Avenue is: *CLIMB THAT MOUNTAIN!* We are pressured persistently and intensely from all sides to scale those peaks because the good life is waiting for us at the top with "rich and famous" and "we can have it all!" "You're on your way, moving up. . . . You're on your way to the top."

But exactly what is waiting for us at the top? Is it indeed the good life, or is it something else? Is it worth the sacrifice? Is it worth a little ruthless climbing over our peers to attain? Or have we been sold a bill of goods? Will we find the same thing at the top that Stripe the caterpillar did?

the summit revisited

Just what is the good life so many Americans are climbing to achieve? Frankly we Americans tend to see the good life almost exclusively in economic and materialistic terms . . . with a little freedom of expression tossed in. It's how much we can accumulate in our bank accounts, store in our garages, and consume in one small lifetime. Cultural anthropologists affirm that for Americans "achievement and success are measured by the quantity of material goods one possesses."[4] Too many of us have really come to assume that consumption is synonymous with happiness, that we will really find the good life on the "wheel of fortune."

Someone has written that "communism says all there is is matter, and capitalism says that all that matters is matter" but the fact remains that they are *both* inherently materialistic world views. And they both lack any sense of transcendence.

Paul Wachtel's analysis is helpful in enabling us to understand how materialism and economic growth has reached such ascendancy in American society:

---

3. "Special Report: They Live to Buy," *Newsweek*, 31 December 1984, 28.
4. Conrad M. Arensberg and Arthur N. Niehoff, "American Cultural Values" from James P. Spradley and Michael A. Rynkuwich, *The Nacirema: Readings on American Culture* (Boston: Little, Brown, 1975), 367.

For most of human history people lived in tightly knit communities in which each individual had a specific place and in which there was a strong sense of shared fate. The sense of belonging, of being part of something larger than oneself, was an important source of comfort. In the face of dangers and terrifying mysteries that the lonely individual encountered, this sense of connectedness, along with one's religious faith, which often could hardly be separated from one's membership in the community, was for most people the main way of achieving some sense of security and the courage to go on.[5]

Over the past several centuries, the sense of rootedness and connectedness in Western society has markedly declined. In its place has appeared a kind of isolation in which separate individuals function more or less autonomously in the larger society. At the center of the lives of these persons, we find no shared faith or common cause. Instead, we find an attempt to remedy their sense of aloneness and spiritual alienation with economic growth and technological progress. "Our present stress on growth and productivity is, I believe, intimately related to the decline in rootedness. Faced with loneliness and vulnerability that come with deprivation of a securely encompassing community, we have sought to quell the vulnerability through our possessions."[6]

In other words, we are a people possessed by fear. Henri Nouwen charges, "Fear dominates every part of our being. We think fearfully, we act and react fearfully. Fear has often penetrated our inner selves so deeply that it controls, whether we are aware of it or not, most of our choices and decisions."[7] In our isolation we live in fear and insecurity. In our materialism we seek to achieve security for ourselves and our families. And it doesn't work.

Of course, when we stop to think about it, we *know* our possessions will never satisfy our deepest longings or provide any real security. They will no more overcome our fears than they did for the wealthy couple described earlier in this chapter. But the problem is that we *don't* stop to think about it—at least not long enough to let the reality sink in. We simply put on our clamps, grab pickaxes and ropes. And then we begin climbing mountains

---

5. Paul L. Wachtel, *The Poverty of Affluence: A Psychological Portrait of the American Way of Life* (New York: Free Press, 1983), 61.

6. Ibid., 61–65.

7. Henri Nouwen, "Creating True Intimacy," *Sojourners*, June 1985, 15–16.

that have been erected not only to satisfy others, but to pacify our
deepest fears and gratify our deepest longings.

the high price of
high climbing—for participants

For those who believe that ever-increasing levels of consumption
will make us happy, Wachtel has a disquieting word. He reports
that, according to social surveys, Americans were much more satisfied with life in 1958 than they are today . . . even though we
have much more in the way of consumer products today.[8]

Not only is there serious question about whether the destination
is worth the trip, there is growing evidence that the climb itself
isn't doing us a whole lot of good either! Our humanity is certainly
not enhanced by being stepped on or by climbing over others to
make it to the top!

In our high-growth, high-efficiency society, our use of time, for
example, has become absolutely manic. We have really come to
believe "time is money"—or at least we live as though that must
be true.

I run into so many Christians who are living lives of hyper-
stress and chronic burnout. What we are doing to ourselves and
our children in this frenetic high-tech society is absolutely criminal. We are working so hard to get to the top that we are making
life along the way unbearable.

Stress has become a national illness whose impact is reflected
in troubling mental-health statistics, growing alcohol and drug
abuse, breakdown of family life, and escalating suicide rates.
Robert Anderson, a physician who has written about stress, says
he used to think that 35 to 40 percent of the problems presented by
patients were stress induced. Now he thinks it could be as high as
90 percent.[9]

Even young children are under growing stress to achieve and get
ahead. "The daily schedule of some children, especially those in the
suburbs, is fuller than that of a business executive." Children are

8. Wachtel, 546.
9. Robert Anderson, *Stress Power: How to Turn Tension into Energy* (New
York: Human Sciences Press, 1978), 18.

under pressure to grow up fast socially and excel academically. "A lot of children's anxiety is associated with the current preoccupation with testing. Standardized testing is now a regular part of school life for 90 percent of American school children. Test scores are often an excuse to brand low-scorers as 'unteachables' and relegate them to lower track or slow classes, where they fall even farther behind."[10]

Added to this is the tremendous parental pressure on many youngsters not only to go to college, but to go to a prestigious university, whose academic standards may exceed the ability of the student. And on top of everything, the fear of nuclear war often looms much larger in children's minds than it does in the minds of many adults.

Increasingly, ways are being created to hook children on the rat race at an earlier age. For example, at a posh resort in Florida, youngsters play a game called "Money Management Mania," learning how to start scrambling up the slopes of greed and acquisition. Or for $1450 children can spend a week at Howard Ruff's "Young Americans Success Camp." "Kids are being taught that the secret to happiness is to have money" says psychologist Lee Salk.[11] And of course this all adds to the tremendous pressure to make it.

In light of the mounting stress that the young are facing, it should surprise no one that alcohol abuse among children and young adults has climbed steeply. Nor should we be surprised by the tragic increase in youth suicide.

We could, of course, spend an entire chapter outlining the hidden health care costs of living in the midst of our affluent environments. High-fat, high-sugar, and high-salt diets that accompany our affluence are making us sick and sending us to early graves. Many communities are living on toxic waste sites—time bombs that will go off before we reach the twenty-first century. We are living in the midst of the garbage of our technological society, and that is making us sick, too. It is reported that 75 percent of our cancers are environmentally caused—they come from what we eat, drink, breathe, and are exposed to in our workplaces and neighborhoods.

It's becoming clearer all the time that the rat race—the frantic climb up the mountain of upward mobility—isn't really the good life. It isn't good for us. It isn't good for our children or our

---

10. Pauline Rhiner, "Pressures on Today's Children," *PTA Today*, February 1983, 43.

11. "Greed on Sesame Street," *Newsweek*, 20 July 1987, 38–39.

environment, and we need to say so. We are the wealthiest, most powerful nation in the world. But we are discovering not only that our ever-increasing levels of consumption haven't made us happy, but that maintaining and protecting these consumptive lifestyles is one of the major causes of stressing us out!

"To be so high and not to be high at all! It only looked good from the bottom."

Let's bring it right home. How are you doing? What pressures do you live with? What symptoms of stress are you struggling with in your own life? Have you gotten close enough to the top of your mountain to learn whether what's waiting at the top is worth the struggle? Deep down have you ever suspected that there is another mountain, a different dream, a more satisfying way of life? A way of life with more compelling purpose?

What a tragedy to spend an entire life—like Willy Loman in *Death of a Salesman*—laboring for a false dream. How sad to discover when it's too late to change, that "it only looked good from the bottom."

the high price of high climbing—for nonparticipants

The American rat race is not only taking its toll on those who are participants; it isn't doing a whole lot of good for the other people with whom we share the planet! By the year 2000, we will share our global habitat with 6.2 billion people. And all the statistics I see indicate that the gap between the planetary rich and the planetary poor is widening dramatically as we approach the twenty-first century. In addition, as I will illustrate in chapter 7, there are signs that we are going *backward,* not forward, with the Great Commission.

Well, what does this have to do with our struggle for upward mobility? Everything! To the extent that we are caught up in our own lives, we aren't available to the mission of the church to help others. At a time when the American church should be initiating a program of massive mobilization to carry out both the Great Commission and the Great Commandment, we are using the vast majority of our individual and institutional resources on ourselves.

I believe a major reason so little of our total resources or time are invested in the mission of the church is that we have such heavy demands on our lives to carry out another mission. Other peaks and mountains have our attention, resources, and commitment. Even many of our churches have developed upwardly mobile lifestyles of extravagant—or at least comfortable— affluence.

I am convinced our limited commitment to Christ's mission in the world can be directly traced to a limited biblical vision for the human future and a limited understanding of God's redemptive plans in history. Over the past two decades, Christian theologians throughout the world have been doing some excellent biblical work on the nature and mission of the church, but unfortunately, few pastors and laity are in touch with this work. As a consequence, we often tend to work with a vision for the future that is more influenced by culture than by Scripture. And our lives tend to be more involved in "movin' on up" the cultural mountain than in the advance of the kingdom of God. Not surprisingly, mission, discipleship, and stewardship tend to get shoved to the periphery of our congested lives and our bureaucratized churches.

My hope—indeed, my conviction—is that we can find in Scripture a new sense of purpose for our lives and God's world. We need our sense of Christian responsibility sharpened and our commitment to Christ and His kingdom radically deepened. Above all, I pray we will indeed discover that more significant life to which our Lord calls us—a way of life that will never disappoint us and will be used by the power of God to transform His world and redeem His people.

climbing another mountain

Expansive blue skies stretched above Jerusalem as I walked up Mount Zion toward the gates of the Old City. I was traveling in the Middle East on a fact-finding mission talking to Jews and Arabs, Muslims and Christians . . . trying to understand the complex problems of that troubled region.

We had been given the day off. Not having been to Jerusalem before, I decided to spend my day as a pilgrim. I visited the Via Dolorosa and could almost hear the crowds calling for our Lord's life. As I entered the church of the Holy Sepulchre, said to be the site of Christ's entombment and resurrection, I was deeply moved.

Then, as I climbed Mount Zion something surprising happened. I suddenly found myself surrounded by a vast throng pressing its way up to Jerusalem. Singing. Dancing. Children on shoulders. Banners streaming. Horns blaring. Outrageous joy. Unspeakable worship. To this day I don't fully understand the experience. But I found myself swept away by the throng and caught up in their song.

Since that remarkable experience I have found a number of others drawn up to Jerusalem—that place where God chose to dwell. We do indeed have a better dream and a better mountain to climb. In Isaiah 2 we are told that Mount Zion, the hill of the Lord, will transcend all other mountains.

Isaiah shares many compelling images of God's festive future. Listen to Isaiah 35:

> The desert and the parched land will be glad;
>   the wilderness will rejoice and blossom.
> Like the crocus, it will burst into bloom;
>   it will rejoice greatly and shout for joy.
> The glory of Lebanon will be given to it,
>   the splendor of Carmel and Sharon;
> they will see the glory of the Lord,
>   the splendor of our God.
> Strengthen the feeble hands,
>   steady the knees that give way;
> say to those with fearful hearts,
>   Be strong, do not fear;
> your God will come,
>   he will come with vengeance;
> with divine retribution
>   he will come to save you.
> Then will the eyes of the blind be opened
>   and the ears of the deaf unstopped.
> Then will the lame leap like a deer,
>   and the tongue of the dumb shout for joy.
> Water will gush forth in the wilderness
>   and streams in the desert.
> The burning sand will become a pool,
>   the thirsty ground bubbling springs.
> In the haunts where jackals once lay,
>   grass and reeds and papyrus will grow.

And a highway will be there;
  it will be called the Way of Holiness.
The unclean will not journey on it;
  it will be for those who walk in that Way;
  wicked fools will not go about on it.
No lion will be there,
  nor will any ferocious beast get up on it;
  they will not be found there.
But only the redeemed will walk there,
  and the ransomed of the Lord will return.
They will enter Zion with singing;
  everlasting joy will crown their heads.
Gladness and joy will overtake them,
  and sorrow and sighing will flee away.

(Isa. 35:1–10, NIV).

It's time for Christians to discover that we have a new song of ascents, a new way of life, and a new mountain to climb that shades into insignificance the piddling peaks of this world. God calls us to life. A life made whole in realization that we are deeply loved. A life made full in the paradoxical discovery that losing is finding. A life made powerful in discovering God uses the foolish to confound the mighty. A life made significant in the incredible realization that God chooses to use broken, ordinary people like you and me to join Him in transforming His world.

The first step we take down the mountains we are scaling will be the first step up toward Jerusalem. Remember the dentist, the student, and the young couple? They not only asked tough questions regarding the peaks they were struggling to scale; they also took that critically important first step down, which has placed each of them on a new journey up.

The young dentist told me that he had, with difficulty, made it through my book, *The Mustard Seed Conspiracy,* which outlines some ways Christians can participate in God's future. And finally he and his wife had reached a hard decision. They had decided to sell their large, expensive home and buy a more modest home near his work.

This Christian dentist was clearly exuberant when I talked to him that second time. He had not only been set free from other people's expectations; he had also been set free to follow his sense of God's dream for his life. He reported that as a consequence of significantly reducing his commuting time and the time he invested in maintaining his huge acreage, he had much more time to spend with his family and to invest in ministry to others in Eugene.

(By the way, his nine-year-old daughter wasn't as impressed by the decision as the rest of the family. She suggested that they burn the book "before it causes any more trouble.")

And then there was Janet. After talking and praying with leaders in her church, Janet reported that they confirmed God's call on her life for short-term service in Thailand. Janet, deeply respecting her parents, spent a great deal of time trying to help them understand that God's call on her life had to come first.

Subsequently, she learned about a new Masters of Business program at Eastern College which was designed to train persons to start small businesses among the poor overseas and at home. That program presents a real possibility to Janet, when she returns from her service in Thailand, to further her business education in a way that is consistent with God's call on her life.

And remember Tom and Susan? As they struggled with the decision of where to live, they realized they were struggling with fears—fears of what other people would think, fears of not living up to other people's expectations. But Henri Nouwen's article about fear helped set them free. Nouwen points out that "fear is one of the most effective weapons in the hands of those who would seek to control us."[12] But the first words of the messengers who announced the coming of Christ were, "Don't be afraid." After much thought and discussion, Tom and Susan decided to buy a house in the poorer part of the city where they can be close to their ministry. And as they work, they are learning that "perfect love casts out all fear."

I should say a word about Stripe the caterpillar, too. As the story turns out, Stripe also decided to descend from the top of his mountain. And eventually, through the miracle of metamorphosis, he found a new ascendant life soaring in beauty in the brilliance of God's creation.

The formula is always the same. Our journey up begins with coming down, with turning away from our frantic climb and turning instead towards the mountain of God. If we are going to discover life with purpose, we must in earnest prayer turn to the Source of life and devote ourselves to His agendas in place of our own—or those our culture imposes on us. As you begin this book,

---

12. Nouwen, 15.

I encourage you to do so with prayer, giving God all your dreams, aspirations, fears and desires, opening yourself to His dreams and visions for your life. We can trust our Father's love to lead us to a new significant level of purposeful living within His new community of ascent.

God created us and God calls us to meaning—to lives lived fully and significantly. Those who have tasted something of the goodness and purposes of God can never again be satisfied with the "fleshpots of Egypt" or the "splendor of Babylon." We are called to something more—to climb a better mountain.

Because God's love is expressed so compellingly to us in incarnation, we discover we are deeply loved. Because God's grace is communicated so mercifully to us in crucifixion, we discover that our lives do indeed have meaning. And because God's call to us is expressed so powerfully in resurrection, we discover our lives do have purpose. He invites us to join with sisters and brothers all over the world to set aside lesser agendas and become a part of what He is doing in history to transform His world and redeem His people—to become a part of His Story. That, my friend, is significant living—joining the Lord of history in seeing His world changed.

for thought and discussion

As you prepare to examine in more detail in the next chapter the false stories to which we have given our lives, you may want to ask the following questions:

1. What are those specific expectations that are keeping you climbing?
2. What is it costing you in terms of your time, your relationships, and your own mental or physical health to scale your peak? What motivates you to keep climbing?
3. Describe the longing within you to be a part of a larger cause, longing to see God use your life in a way that makes a difference. Describe your sense of what God's purpose for your life might be.

life links

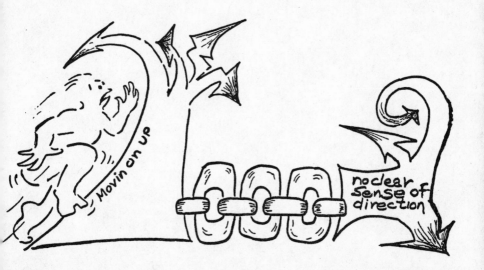

Movin on up

no clear sense of direction

life direction	linkages	consequences
For many, life has never been so busy, so frenetic, so totally lacking in direction, except for the mad scramble to scale the mountain of other people's expectations—getting and possessing.	Many seem content simply to connect their lives to other people's expectations and the cultural aspiration of moving on up—without ever questioning what they are climbing for.	Often people *do* succeed in their scramble up the Mountain of Evermore, only to discover there's nothing at the top. Belatedly they find their lives have no sense of meaning or purpose.

discerning half-truths and false visions

Discerning! From the moment we arrive on planet earth, we begin struggling to discern who we are and what we are here for. We are all born into families, churches, and cultures with many different stories and expectations that early begin shaping the direction and character of our lives. Most importantly, they teach us what is the better future to which we should give our lives.

Implicit in all our lives are certain images, values, and assumptions which influence our actions and the decisions we make. When we become Christians, we begin the process of sorting out which of these are genuinely part of the Story of God and which we have simply absorbed from the world around us.

Frankly, this discerning business isn't easy, and most of us aren't very good at it—we may not even know it is something we need to do! But discernment is necessary if we are to be clear about where we are going and what values we are working from.

And that's the purpose of this chapter—to enable us to discern more fully the half-truths and full fictions that have become a part of our lives. We want to begin to clear the decks so that we will be able to embrace more fully God's purposes for our lives and His world.

But let's be honest. There's nothing tougher than trying to sort through the images and illusions we have unconsciously incorporated into our own stories, and it's very easy to become confused as we do this. Therefore, I hope we can be particularly prayerful in this chapter, asking God's Spirit to help us honestly identify dreams, assumptions, images, and values in our lives that aren't really consistent with God's loving purposes.

a step beyond confusion

Some people seem to have almost a genetic predisposition towards confusion in this business of finding direction. I have had to come to terms with this predisposition in my own life. (Actually, I have come to think of it as something of a gift. A little well-placed confusion does wonders to keep life from becoming boring, predictable, and ordinary.)

Last spring, for example, I was traveling from Amsterdam by train to a speaking engagement in a church in Basel, Switzerland. Such a clear-cut assignment should provide very little opportunity for confusion—but I managed it!

I confidently climbed on a train marked "Geneva" and arrived, after an enjoyable ride, at about two in the afternoon. But then, as I stepped down from the train, I was surprised to see a friend of mine from Lausanne, Switzerland, running to meet me.

"Hurry! You can still make it," she exclaimed in rushed tones.

"Make what?" I responded.

"The next train to Basel. You're not supposed to be in Geneva. You're supposed to be in Basel!"

I just looked at her, dumbfounded. She was right. What was I doing in Geneva?

As Elaine pushed me on board the train to Basel, she yelled, "You can still make your seven o'clock speaking engagement, so nothing is lost." As the train pulled out of the Geneva station, I waved and called out my thanks—grateful that I have learned to wire my travel plans to a friend in each country where I travel. Elaine had received my wire, discerned my confusion, and come to my aid.

Some time later, as the train was pulling out of Zurich, I asked the conductor if we were near Basel—I was determined not to give my proclivity towards chaos any more opportunity to display itself. He replied, "Basel is not far now."

About fifteen minutes later, two Swiss gentlemen sitting across from me got up to get off the train at the next stop. One turned to me and said, "This is your stop. This is where you want to get off."

I quickly shouldered my garment bag and followed them obediently off the train. I found myself in the most modern receiving area I had ever seen—red and blue tile covered the walls, reaching transcendently four to five stories above. I looked around for my hosts, whom Elaine had promised to call and inform about my new arrival time. I would barely have time to get cleaned up a bit before speaking. But no one was there to meet me.

For some thirty minutes I tried to call my hosts without success. Finally, I asked at Visitor Information how much it would cost to take a cab to my destination in Basel. She responded with, obvious incredulity, "Well, over a hundred marks."

"Where am I?" I asked.

"At the Zurich International Airport," my informant responded. (Sometimes all I need is a little outside help to become even more confused than usual!)

I quickly found when the next train was headed for Basel. Then I called my hosts, explained the entire fiasco, and told them my train to Basel wouldn't arrive until around nine. I apologized for missing my speaking assignment and thanked them for their hospitality.

Frankly, as I boarded my third train to Basel, I was more than a little relieved I wouldn't have to speak. I hadn't had an opportunity to sleep in almost twenty-four hours. I hadn't had a shower for three days. I needed a shave, my hair was a mess, and I really wasn't prepared to speak because I didn't know who my audience was.

When I finally arrived in Basel a little after nine, every cell in my body was looking forward to a hot shower and a clean bed. And there were my hosts. I began bubbling all over myself with apologies, but Johann exclaimed, "Not to worry. We sent the congregation out for coffee and told them to be back by a quarter after nine."

I stood dazed, not quite believing my ears. There wasn't even time to shave, comb my hair, or write down a little outline. On the way to the church I found my Bible, selected a verse, and prayed.

But I've discovered that once you're on a roll nothing can stop you. I shouldn't have worried about my message. The young woman they asked to translate for me had never done it before. I am convinced to this day that the very gracious congregation had no idea what I was trying to say, and I must have been a rumpled, bedraggled delight to look at.

Even if you don't have my remarkable predisposition to confusion, it still seems to be endemic to the human condition. And there is no area in which confusion plays greater havoc than in the ways we seek to direct our lives. Remarkably, many of us are unaware of our confusion because we haven't even noticed the stories to which we have given ourselves or the futures toward which we are working. We simply seem to dance to someone else's tune and never question the melody.

If we want to move beyond confusion and embrace more fully the Story of God, we must first identify the stories we are living for.

And we need to examine the visions of the better future that are a part of these stories to see how they line up with God's vision.

some false visions of the better future

We live in a world that is filled with thousands of stories that promise a wide variety of visions for the good life and the better future and reflect very different value systems.

For example, when I was in Nepal three years ago, a young man driving a truck in front of us inadvertently hit a cow and killed it. The local pastor explained to me that from the young man's perspective, it would have been better if he had hit a person, because the penalty for killing a cow—even accidentally—is life imprisonment.

That may seem like an outrageous penalty to you and me. But given the Hindu story of how the world runs, it makes perfectly good sense. Hindus believe cows are the most sacred animals— that they symbolize humankind's link to the rest of nature. Hindus also believe a human being can look forward to other lives in other life forms. Therefore, from their point of view, spending this life in prison is not such a calamity.

Of course, such a reincarnational view is clearly in conflict with the Christian understanding of how God designed His creation and the future He intends. So is the vision espoused by the so-called "New Age" movement, a pop collection of Eastern and animistic religious themes that is rapidly gaining popularity in the United States.

Perhaps the best-known apostle of the New Age movement is actress Shirley MacLaine, whose popular book, *Out on a Limb,* recounts her pilgrimage into New Age religion. She asks us to believe, for example, that her guru was tutored by an extraterrestrial who commuted to earth via a flying saucer. She tells all about her experiences in "previous lives." And she invites us to go "out on a limb" with her in her New Age beliefs. Tragically, thousands are setting aside their reason and buying into this pop New Age vision of reincarnation.

Not quite so blatant, but still clearly in conflict with Christian views, are the claims of futurist Willis Harmon, who several years ago shared his vision for the human future with a group of evangelical leaders. Harmon predicted that the human spirit would arise like the phoenix out of the ashes of a decaying world to create a new and transformed society. But the evangelical leaders were quick to realize that his ideas, though expressed in religious language, were not Christian. They pointed out that the Bible teaches the future is in the hands of God and God alone; the New Age expectation that humans can create a new, transformed world through their own goodness or initiative is a fraudulent one.[1]

Marxism espouses another false vision of the future which captures the imaginations of many throughout our planet. Marxism views the better future in singularly economic and political terms, envisioning a new society of liberated workers. But there is no transcendence to the Marxist vision—no place for God.

More than twenty years ago, Dale Vree was one of many young people around the world who bought into the Marxist fiction. Dale traveled to East Germany in 1965 to live among the communist working class and experience firsthand the fruition of the promised grand, new Marxist age. Instead, he was confronted by a pervasive materialism as "corrupt" as anything in the West.

Disillusioned, Dale visited an East Berlin church early on an Easter morning. That morning a would-be communist stumbled onto another Story. He turned his back on Marxism and committed his life to a new Master and a new vision of the future.

Today, Dale is the editor of the *New Oxford Review* in Berkeley, California. He tells the moving story of his journey from Marxism to Christianity in the book, *From Berkeley to East Berlin and Back.*[2]

false visions within the american society and church

If we are to find life, we must join Dale and thousands of others in turning away from the half-truths and full fictions that would possess our lives. But to do that we must first identify those dominant illusions and false visions for the better future that fill our society and our churches. Some of them are so familiar that they are not as easy to spot as Hinduism, New Age ideology, or Marxism.

In order to help us examine familiar stories that are closer to

---

1. For a responsible Christian analysis of the New Age movement, write: Gordon Lewis, Denver Theological Seminary, Box 10,000, Denver, CO 80210. Or pick up a copy of Douglas Groothuis's book, *Unmasking the New Age* (Downers Grove, IL: Inter-Varsity, 1986). Also see pp. 40–41 and 83 of my book, *The Mustard Seed Conspiracy,* (Waco, TX: Word, 1981).
2. Nashville: Thomas Nelson, 1985.

the lives of most American Christians, I want to introduce four
hypothetical couples who are typical of certain people I meet in
my travels.

Let me emphasize that these couples are *not* representative of
all secularists, mainliners, evangelicals, or fundamentalists. They
simply represent some of the outlooks of folks from those groups I
have gotten to know in my travels. And they are overstated a bit to
make the point. As a consequence, these examples will probably
not fully connect with your own visions and values. I hope, however, that they will help you discern some areas where your assumptions and outlook may differ from the biblical story without
your even realizing it. At the very least, I hope they provoke some
questions.

In introducing each family, I will tell you a bit of their story, and
I will tell something about the images and values to which they
seem to subscribe—consciously or unconsciously. In each story, I
will particularly emphasize their vision for the better future, because I believe that a person's vision for the future is instrumental
in shaping his or her direction in life. But I will also examine something of these people's assumptions about God, creation, and humanity, and their notions of how to achieve their vision of the better
future. I would urge you to read carefully and try to identify any
elements in their stories that may also be a part of yours.

couple #1: brent & vivian hightower
catching the escalator to the land of evermore

Brent Hightower and Vivian Michaels met while completing
their MBAs at UCLA, and they married shortly after graduation.
Vivian took a position in public relations for a chemical company,
and Brent went to work in new business research for a major aeronautics firm. Hardworking, conscientious, and responsible people,
they typically work sixty-plus hours a week—and often meet for
dinner after work, just to have a little recovery time.

The Hightowers live in a condo in downtown Los Angeles with
pool, sauna—the works. What leisure time they have is spent cruis-
ing up and down the coast in a Chris Craft they're leasing. They
love beautiful things and support the arts, and they are both very
active in community fund-raising organizations as well.

Though the Hightower's condo is close to their work and has a
number of conveniences, the nesting years are beginning to sneak

up on them, and they are thinking of starting a family. So they are beginning to look for a place in the suburbs in Brentwood, Beverly Hills, or Malibu. They want what's best for their anticipated offspring, and they're willing to pay for it—the homes they are considering are four hundred thousand dollars and up.

Viv and Brent consider themselves Christians—she was raised a Lutheran and he a Methodist. But the church plays virtually no role in their lives. In fact, the last time they were in a church was seven years ago, when they got married. In their very busy lives, there simply isn't time for everything!

what is the better future?

Brent and Viv are obviously working very hard for what's important to them. And what they are working for is probably the dominant dream of many Americans—a dream that has its roots deeply embedded in our common past.

This young couple has bought into the number-one popular vision in America—that the better future is to be found in ever-increasing levels of affluence, consumerism, and success—and they have never questioned its validity.

This particular story has its origins three centuries ago in the period of history known as the Enlightenment, or Age of Reason (1648–1789), a seminal time that influenced our modern society in a variety of ways. Many influential thinkers of that age— philosopher John Locke, and even American founding fathers such as Thomas Jefferson and Benjamin Franklin—together spun a new tale about how the world works. And implicit in this tale were a whole new set of assumptions about God, creation, humankind, and the better future.

The emphasis of the Enlightenment was on reason, science, human potential. God was acknowledged as the creator of the natural order, but not as actively involved in history. The basic emphasis was on the scientific, the material, and the secular, rather than the spiritual.

One important aspect of Enlightenment thinking was that progress is built into the very structure of the natural order. It was assumed that if people simply cooperated with natural law, they would inevitably move up—almost like riding up an escalator of progress to the Land of Evermore. And once again, this progress was seen largely in economic and material terms.

This belief in inevitable progress and this basically secular and materialistic world view have permeated our society. We are promised a future of economic and technological progress if we play by the rules—that is, work hard and support the system. And the better future is still seen almost exclusively in economic and materialistic terms.

(Remember the question asked during the 1984 presidential election: "Are you better off?" Were we being asked about the quality of our family relations or prayer life? Of course not. We were being asked if we could materially consume more than before. And that kind of thinking is basically a product of the Enlightenment.)

I believe that viewing the better future in predominantly economic and materialistic terms is in direct contradiction to the biblical vision of the better future. As Christians, we must base our vision for the future and our world view on scriptural principles, not economic theories. Even our economic views must be derived from the study of Scripture.

Now, let me be clear. I am not saying it is wrong to be concerned about finances and economics. And I am certainly not advocating an overthrow of our basic economic structure! I personally favor an economic system in which there is a free exchange of goods and services. In my opinion, socialism hasn't worked very well in those countries where it is the operational economic system.

But what has happened is that millions of people—Brent and Viv, as well as many more active Christians—have elevated their economic system, rooted in Enlightenment thinking, to the status of their dominant world view. They have come to see the *entire world* in predominantly economic and material terms. Their world view is born primarily from their economic theories, not biblical principles. Regardless of what they *say* they believe, their actions reveal that their ultimate values are economic—not biblical—and that's idolatrous.

Listen again to the words of Jesus: "No one can serve two masters. Either he will hate the one and love the other, or he will be devoted to the one and despise the other. You cannot serve both God and Money" (Matt. 6:24, NIV). Neither can we concurrently embrace two world views. We cannot embrace a world view primarily committed to the pursuit of material gain and at the same time subscribe to a world dedicated to the service of God and others. We cannot "serve God and Money" . . . because these two visions are based on totally different value systems.

Now, this discussion is probably of little interest to Brent and Viv, since they have no investment in issues of faith. They and

millions like them simply scale the peaks that others have
erected. They have come to accept the illusion that the good life
is largely synonymous with how much one can acquire and consume in one lifetime.

And Brent and Viv also share another assumption about the
good life—one that I believe is largely unexamined by most Christians and non-Christians alike. They want the best for the children
they plan to parent—and "the best" is seen almost exclusively in
terms of economic advantage. The Hightowers assume that "the
best" is most likely to be found in the most expensive suburban
community they can afford. They want the best schools and all the
advantages for their children.

However, there is mounting evidence that affluent suburbs may
not be the best place to live or to raise children you care about. For
example, Mill Valley, California, is nationally touted as one of the
most desirable suburban communities in the United States. The
prestigious residences are priced at a million dollars and up.
Driveways display a sparkling array of Porsches, BMWs, and
Winnebagos. The schools are equipped with state-of-the-art computers, lab equipment, and video units. And every Christmas looks
as if the department store blew up in the living room.

But recent research shows a very different side of Mill Valley.
Those fabulous dream homes mask one of the highest levels of
drug and alcohol abuse in the nation. Teen suicides and family
breakups are also critical problems. And, of course, young people
in the "burbs" are all expected to dress alike, hit the slopes on the
same weekends, and subscribe to the same values regarding sexual
morality, drug use, and upward mobility. (While similar pressures
exist in small towns, cities, and rural areas, the pressures are especially relentless in the suburbs, because generally there is only
one adolescent peer group.)

These problems are, of course, larger than the suburbs. They
reflect the reality that middle- and upper-middle-class people in
the United States have bought into a notion of the better future
that isn't really good for us or our kids. We need a little more
reflective discussion on what the good life is and where we are
likely to find it.

Listen to the indicting analysis of psychologist Robert Cole:

> Very little is asked of a lot of American children with regard to
> compassion and thinking of others. The emphasis is to cultivate the
> individuality and self importance of a child. One sees home after

home where children are encouraged to look out for themselves and get what they can. Very little emphasis is put on pointing the child's eyes and ears away from himself or herself and towards others.[3]

For eighteen years, Alexander Astin has studied college freshmen nationwide, and his research confirms Cole's indictment. Fifteen years ago the dominant value among college freshmen was "finding a meaningful philosophy of life." Today that value has dropped to number eight on the list. And predictably, "being well off financially" has soared to the top of the list for 70 percent of all freshmen.[4]

Most of us can probably recognize a little of ourselves in the Hightowers' life and values. Never in American history has there been a greater commitment to materialism as a way of life or extravagance as a supreme good. We have given preeminence to economic gain and lifestyles of personal extravagance.

Robert Bellah describes this counterbiblical attitude in his insightful book, *Habits of the Heart:*

> What is good is what one finds rewarding. The ultimate ethical rule is simply that individuals should be able to pursue what they find rewarding, constrained only by the requirement that they do not interfere with the "value systems" of others.[5]

The so-called "Yuppies" and "Boomers" are point people for this movement. They are busy exchanging their Baskin-Robbinses for Italian ices, and they are trading in their French poodles for Andean llamas. And their homes are bulging with the latest gadgets our high-tech culture can generate.

Charles Colson, in discussing the Yuppie phenomenon, tells the story about one very egocentric young man who was throwing a prolonged tantrum in a car rental agency. All they had was a blue Lincoln Continental and he wanted a black one. Colson reports that the young man turned away in disgust from the patient rental agent. "The man faced in my direction for the first time. Emblazoned across his shirt was a motto that puts the

3. Robert Cole, "Our Self-Centered Children—Heirs of the 'Me' Decade," *U.S. News and World Report,* 15 February 1981, 80.

4. Alexander W. Astin, "Student Values: Knowing More about Where We Are Today," American Association of Higher Education Bulletin, May 1984, 10–12.

5. Robert Bellah, et al., *Habits of the Heart* (New York: Harper & Row, 1985), 6.

whole affair in perspective: 'The one who dies with the most toys wins.'"[6]

But the Yuppies aren't the only materialists around; we're all involved. Inside the church as well as outside, many of us have come to view the better future in terms of catching the escalator to the Land of Evermore . . . pursuing success, affluence, and economic progress. And in many cases this preoccupation—clearly idolatrous—is almost unconscious.

Now, I am not arguing that people shouldn't seek to excel in their lives. But we must ask *why* we are seeking to excel—for God's purposes or for our own gain. We have unwittingly embraced the materialistic dreams of our culture without comparing them with the transcendent visions of our faith.

where does God come in?

When Brent and Vivian bought into this story about how the world runs and what the future will be, they also bought into certain assumptions about God, His creation, and humankind.

For one thing, in this tale of inevitable progress and material values, the initiative is clearly ours and not God's. It's up to us to erect the skyscrapers, grow the food, and heal the sick. The dream of ever-increasing levels of economic and technological growth can only be realized through take-charge human initiative: "God helps those who help themselves." And that leaves very little room for God in this particular story. Of necessity, He becomes something of a passive bystander—an anachronistic hangover from a bygone culture.

If you asked the Hightowers, they would probably tell you they believe in God. But given the mountains they are scaling, God seems pretty irrelevant to the realization of their dreams.

This view of God is pervasive in our culture. Practically speaking, instead of a divine providence, we tend to depend on a secular one—"the invisible hand of the marketplace." This concept was promoted by Adam Smith in the eighteenth century and has become basic to our economic thinking. We are assured that if we trust our future to this impersonal providence, it will impartially determine winners and losers. Furthermore, if left free to operate, this "secular providence" will cause the escalator to operate

---

6. Charles Colson, commencement address at Bethel College, 1984.

efficiently. Continued economic progress will be assured for the successful—and hopefully a little will trickle down to the poor.

Furthermore, in our essentially scientific, economic world view, creation is no longer understood in sacred terms—as pervaded by the presence and purposes of the living God. It is reduced to being the place where we dig our oil and set up our campers. God's creation then becomes nothing but a grab bag of passive, malleable resources—the "stuff" out of which we fashion our escalator to the Land of Evermore. And our young couple in their work and their leisure relate to God's creation in starkly utilitarian terms. Like millions of others, they live in a universe freed from any sense of divine presence and purpose.

what does it mean to be human?

Since in Brent and Vivian's world the better future and the created order are seen in largely materialistic and economic terms, it shouldn't be surprising that persons are seen in the same way. In a world freed of divine presence and purpose, there's no basis to assume persons have any kind of transcendent purpose or personal immortality. Persons are seen simply as the sum of their organic cores and behavioral surface.

Furthermore, when the world is seen largely as an arena for economic and commercial activity, individuals tend to derive both their sense of identity and their sense of worth from what they produce and consume. We identify ourselves by where we work, what we live in, and what we drive—the more we own, the more we are. Brent and Viv have certainly connected their entire identity to what they do and what they own.

Again, the roots of this viewpoint are deeply embedded in the seventeenth and eighteenth centuries. In fact, Benjamin Franklin quite deliberately offered himself as the new model of the new humanity . . . pursuing success and prosperity.

Franklin, a deist (one who believes God is unable to intervene in His universe), even did a revisionist job on Christian ethics in order to develop a new set of values and to promote his vision of an upwardly mobile America. His revisionist ethics were marketed under the label of *Poor Richard's Almanac.* And in his day it was second in popularity only to the Bible.

Franklin's values encouraged efficient, conforming, and acquisitive behavior. For example, he said that the Puritans were right— virtue is important—but that they were a little confused. They thought virtue was an end in itself. Wrong! Franklin explained that virtue isn't an end in itself; it's a means. If you are virtuous, then you get to be successful. Success, not virtue, is the goal of life.

Today, the gospel of success and prosperity has thousands of apostles and millions of disciples. And whether they realize it or not, they are much more indebted to the writings of Benjamin Franklin than to the gospel of Jesus Christ.

John Locke and Thomas Jefferson added still another wrinkle to the way our culture looks at persons. Throughout history, most cultures have traditionally given ascendancy to the community over individuals. But Locke and Jefferson helped turn that way of thinking upside down. They advocated a radical individualism and a largely autonomous view of self—popularly conceived today as individuals' "doing their own thing."

This emphasis on individualism and autonomy was based on the belief that individuals were essentially good. In fact, this whole view of Western progress was based on a fundamental belief in the goodness of human nature. This led naturally to the belief that if persons were given maximum personal and political freedom, they would do what's right. They could be trusted with power.

Adam Smith took individualism one step further. He asserted that individual pursuit of self-interest would not only benefit the individual economically, but also work for the common good.

In this remarkable teaching, self-interested living was transformed from an absolute evil to an absolute good. Accordingly, many American Christians who have inherited this way of thinking have turned a deaf ear to Christ's call to "lose life." They have joined everyone else in the mad race to seek life and pursue happiness. And many have willingly embraced Adam Smith's teaching that the pursuit of economic self-interest is the way we most effectively help those around us.

This ideology of radical individualism and the pursuit of self-interest has taken strong root in America. Brent and Viv, for instance, have very little community beyond their own relationship. Most of their friends are other professional young people with whom they work, and for the most part those friendships are based on their position in the company—when their position changes, their friendships change, too.

The Hightowers are away from home so often they have not had time to develop relationships with their neighbors; besides, they plan to move soon. They live many miles from their families and don't see them very often. In Brent and Viv's highly mobile, affluent world, relationships are largely disposable and certainly secondary to one's private economic scrambling.

In my view, this ideology of radical individualism and the pursuit of self-interest has been the single most potent force in the breakdown of family, morality, and community in all levels of our society. Tragically, it is even unusual to find much real community in churches in the United States. Christians don't seem to realize that the Scripture emphasizes that participation in community is absolutely essential to Christian living.

We have fostered a society of autonomous individuals like the Hightowers, whose sense of identity and self-worth is tied largely to their success as producers/consumers on the slippery slopes up to the Land of Evermore.

which way is up?

If the better future in the Hightower's story consists of material abundance—a prosperous Land of Evermore—how is that better future supposed to come about? We are told we will only achieve the heady highlands of this future by catching the escalator of technological progress, economic growth, and economic self-interest. Clearly, the realization of this tale is dependent on human and not divine initiative.

And frankly, success demands the most aggressive levels of personal initiative and highest levels of personal sacrifice. Brent and Viv are heroically investing the initiative and they are making the sacrifices. Of course, with many of the rest of us, they are reaping the material benefits. But they are doing it at tremendous cost to body, mind, and soul. They are both stressed out most of the time. Brent copes with the stress by drinking more than he should, and Vivian has over the last three years begun to take too many pills. And their chaotic schedules have all but destroyed relationships with several of their best friends.

In this tale, the way up means placing outrageous pressures on ourselves, our families, and our friends to make it materially. And this press for success is not only "maxing us out"; it is also causing us to miss the good life of God and compromising those with whom we share the planet.

For the facts are that millions of people in our country and around the world are denied even the most basic elements of human existence. The "magic of the marketplace" doesn't work as well for them as it does for Brent and Viv, and the material benefits seldom trickle down. The result is a kind of economic Darwinism that favors the strong and affluent over the weak and powerless.

So now, what about you? I am sure your life probably differs from the Hightowers in a number of ways. But can you recognize any of yourself in them—their aspirations or their values? What is the good life you want for yourself or your kids? What kind of pressure are you placing on yourself, family, and friends to make it to the top?

The Hightowers represent one set of hopes, dreams, and aspirations that is widespread in America. But now let's look at another couple who are giving themselves to a little different version of the Western Dream—one that includes their faith.

couple #2: ernest and fran liberman
catching the mainline to progress town

Ernest and Fran Liberman live in urban Philadelphia. Ernest is retiring from thirty years of teaching choral music at a local university. Fran is a social worker for a local mental-health organization.

This couple have lived in the same ancient but comfortable house in an older section of Philadelphia since their four kids were tiny. Now the kids are all grown and dispersed, and Ernest and Fran are enjoying having time to devote to their own interests.

The Libermans have always attended First Mainline Church, but they have become even more involved as their children grew up and left home. Now they are very active in the political action committee of the church and the struggle for inclusive language in worship. (Of course, Ernest also directs the choir.) They are also active in their community, and have served on a number of task forces on environmental and social issues.

The Libermans are a very relaxed, congenial couple who value tolerance, humanity, and learning. And they care very deeply about those who are less fortunate than themselves—that is why they spend so much time supporting legislation to help the poor.

In fact, Ernest and Fran are proud to call themselves liberals, and they would be shocked if we told them that in some ways they are like the Hightowers, whom they would see as selfish, shallow, and a little crass.

But in the first place, Ernest and Fran and their friends are not immune from the individualism, materialism, and upwardly mobile trekking that consume the Hightowers, although they do their climbing with more restraint and subtlety. They live very comfortably. They have both worked hard to climb up the ladder of their respective careers, and they have been very concerned that their children attend the best colleges.

what is the better future?

More important, the Libermans are like the Hightowers in their view of the future. They, too, have bought into the Enlightenment idea of progress, but their interest is in *social* as well as economic progress. According to some of the Enlightenment thinkers, society will gradually improve if we just help it along a little. And this is exactly what the Libermans are trying to do.

The Libermans dream of a society with equal opportunities for the poor, tolerance toward alternative lifestyles, and peace for everyone—and they are working hard to achieve it. In other words, instead of fundamentally questioning the "escalator to Evermore," they are content with making sure everybody gets on board—with a high degree of personal freedom. Their image of the better future is the desire to see society operate more humanely.

Perhaps nowhere is the Liberman's progressive image of the better future more compellingly presented than in Edward Bellamy's nineteenth-century classic, *Looking Backwards*. In the book, the hero, Jeremy West, goes to sleep in 1887 and wakes up abruptly in the year 2000. He finds himself in an advanced, high-tech society. But the most remarkable thing about this society isn't its technology, but its humanity; it has been planned as if people mattered.

Edward Bellamy envisioned a future in which all people are treated with dignity and equity—a future in which everyone has an opportunity to participate in the society. And that opportunity is assured primarily through state planning.

Of course, the Liberman's concerns for the poor, social justice, and peace are biblical concerns. But they and many of their compatriots tend to see the better future almost exclusively in terms of social and economic change; there's virtually no transcendent spiritual character to their visions. Accordingly, there's little discussion at First Mainline of bringing people to faith in Christ—the emphasis is almost entirely on improving the larger society and helping people "become more fully human"—because for them salvation is synonymous with "humanization."

Not surprisingly, the Libermans' view of a life beyond this life is somewhat ambiguous. While their church has seminars on death and dying, eternal life is something that isn't discussed very often. Ideas about human immortality cover the waterfront in their congregation.

The Libermans have been mainline Christians and liberal Democrats all their lives. And, to be honest, they tend to see very little distinction between the agendas of their church and their party. Essentially, they have bought into stories of both organizations as though they were one.

For the Libermans as well as some other mainline Christians, there is almost a congenital need to be advocates for any agenda that is considered politically and socially "progressive," regardless of what Scripture may have to say on a given issue. As a consequence, it's not surprising to find the Libermans and some of their friends becoming advocates (out of a progressive political vision) for abortion on demand, sanctioning of gay lifestyles, and so on. However, they often seem to have little to say on issues viewed as conservative—such as family life, pornography, and sexual immorality. As a consequence they tend to see evil almost exclusively in terms of political structures and multinational corporations and seldom in terms of personal morality.

where does God come in?

Since Fran and Ernest's political and theological liberalism has its origins in the Enlightenment—the so-called Age of Reason—they tend to view God and His creation from a largely intellectual standpoint. As a result, Ernest and Fran's relationship to God often seems pretty cerebral, impersonal, and remote.

For the Libermans, the initiative for church life and social action clearly is with the people in the church and society, and their God plays a relatively passive role. Unlike some of my Catholic friends, who emphasize spirituality, the Libermans tend to relate to God as more of a theological abstraction and a cultural necessity than a personal reality. (Similarly, the Bible is treated as a rich historical, literary, and religious source, but seldom is seriously consulted for making personal life decisions or formulating public policy.)

The Libermans even tend to be somewhat pantheistic in their view of the divine. In other words, they tend to see God as largely inseparable from His creation and therefore largely amorphous and impersonal.

In explaining this way of looking at God, C. S. Lewis observed,

The religious options open to humanity are limited: We can believe in no God and be atheists. We can believe in one God and be theists. Or we can believe that all is God and be pantheists. Of these three, pantheism has been humanity's major preoccupation through history—not because it is the final stage of enlightenment, but because it is the attitude into which the human mind falls when left to itself. In the absence of revealed religion, humanity gravitates towards natural religion.[7]

Those of pantheistic inclinations tend to see nature in less utilitarian terms (they are less likely to see creation as something to be exploited). But they are *more* likely to make creation synonymous with the Creator. That is, they may tend to vaguely equate God with the "Forces of Nature." Like the New Agers, they tend to see Nature (with a capital *N*) as a beneficent force that is actually directing the course of human history—a force that can be trusted.

what does it mean to be human?

Since they assume that nature is essentially good, the Libermans also tend to see persons as innately good (although large structures run by people are seen as innately evil). Like Edward Bellamy, they tend to believe that people left to themselves will do what's right—their doctrine of sin is rather vague and impersonal.

And while they emphasize human dignity, their emphasis seems to have little to do with persons being image bearers of God or a transcendent part of His creation. Accordingly, there is very little emphasis on personal immortality.

In essence, then, Ernest and Fran Liberman have a rather kindly, guardedly optimistic attitude toward their world and their fellow human beings.

At First Mainline, there is no shortage of committees, but there is nothing that approximates real Christian community—community where people are known, loved, and held accountable. There is no teaching on the importance of common life. Therefore going to church is a much more individualistic and autonomous activity than in many evangelical congregations.

---

7. Quoted in Robert Burrows, "Americans Get Religion in the New Age," *Christianity Today,* 16 May 1986, 17.

which way is up?

Ernest and Fran Liberman seem to believe society will gradually improve if we simply tinker with the system a bit, advocate progressive legislation, and try to help the poor as we are able. And since they tend to view salvation as humanization, they tend to assume this process for change can be brought about through human initiative.

Since their vision has little transcendent spiritual quality, it should not be surprising that there is little emphasis on world evangelization. Instead, the emphasis is on increasing dialogue and cooperation between major world religions, which are seen as having essentially common goals. In their high commitment to tolerance, they tend to abandon the historic Christian teaching that God chose to disclose himself fully in Jesus Christ—and Jesus Christ alone.

And of course, the Libermans like the rest of us give a major share of their time and resources scaling the peaks of Evermore—perhaps they do it with a bit more class and a little more compassion. But while this dream for the human future is indeed more humane, it fails to seriously consider a biblical vision.

couple #3: rich and piety duellway
waiting for soul rescue and working for fat city

Rich and Piety Duellway live in a middle-class suburban community in Portland, Oregon. They have two teenage children. Mark excels in basketball and in getting to know the opposite "species" but has very little interest in school. Sarah works very hard on her schoolwork but has few friends outside her church youth group.

Rich owns and operates a small rug-cleaning business, and Piety teaches fifth grade at a local Christian school. Rich and Piety became Christians about ten years ago and are loyal members at the Independent Bible Church. Piety teaches Sunday school, and they both enjoy attending Wednesday night Bible studies.

Recently, however, Rich has had to cut back on some of his church involvement because he has increased his workload to almost seventy hours a week. The reason for this is that he and Piety have their eyes set on a larger home in a more exclusive part of southwest Portland. Piety is even looking into selling cosmetics on the side to help make the down payment. And, of course, they are praying for God's help in getting their new home.

what is the better future?

Unlike both the Hightowers and the Libermans, whose interest focused largely on the material side of life, the Duellways are very interested in the spiritual matters. They are very serious about their Christian faith, which to them primarily means a private, personal relationship with Jesus here and an assurance of eternal life beyond.

But at this point something interesting happens. For when it comes to their view of the better future, Rich and Piety seem to have split vision. At the same time that they are reaching for a life beyond this life, they are also working hard to get a solid "piece of the rock" right now. I call this schizophrenic view of the future "waiting for soul rescue and working for fat city."

Let me be clear as I describe this schizophrenia that the Duellways aren't hypocrites. In fact, like thousands of others who think this way, they are very sincere. But they are unwittingly writing a story for their lives that is based on two very different visions for the future.

On the one hand, Rich and Piety tend to view the future of God pessimistically and spiritually. Theologically speaking, the Duellways and their friends have a very fatalistic view about the future of the earth and a deterministic view of history. Their own Bible study and a number of popular books have convinced them that the end is very near, that things will get worse and worse and nothing can be done about it.

My greatest concern with this viewpoint is that it causes many people to psychologically and actually withdraw from working for the kingdom now because they are convinced they can't make a difference. Remarkably, the powers of darkness seem to have conspired through end times eschatology to convince a number of the most affluent, best educated Christians in history that God can't really use our lives or resources to make much of a difference.

Of course, Rich and Piety are still looking forward hopefully to an eternal life with God. But they seem to have some serious confusion—as do many Christians—in understanding the nature of that eternal life.

Recently, speaking at a leading Christian college, I asked students what their image was of the ultimate future of God. They responded, "Heaven." I asked, "What images come to mind when you think of heaven?" In both cases they responded, "Clouds, harps, and angel wings."

They were surprised when I suggested to them that this view of the future of God came more from Greek writings than Judeo-Christian teachings. Greek philosophers such as Plato insisted that the material world is bad and a disembodied unification with the spiritual world of ideas is good. Unfortunately, by embracing this dualistic view of the world, many evangelical Christians have bought into a nonmaterial view of the future of God and a faith narrowly preoccupied with one's private spiritual life.

The dominant hope of these Christians is that God will rescue our disembodied souls here and take them out there somewhere to plunk on harps. While Rich and Piety would intellectually endorse the biblical doctrine of the physical resurrection of believers, their images are all caught up with a disembodied existence in a nonmaterial heaven in the clouds.

But as Leslie Newbigin declares, such a disembodied existence is simply not biblical: "For the biblical writers, continued existence as a disembodied soul is something not to be desired, but to be feared with loathing."[8] As Newbigin points out, when the Bible speaks of salvation, it's not speaking in terms of disembodied survival, but in terms of the resurrection of the body—a new creation.

(Of course, when we die we are absent from the body and present with the Lord. But that is only an interim state awaiting the bodily resurrection of all believers at the return of Christ.)

Recently, students at a Christian high school questioned me at length regarding the biblical teaching that we are going to be resurrected as whole persons. This was a startling new teaching to them. They asked, "What are we going to do with bodies in heaven? How can we walk on clouds?" I explained that the Bible says nothing about walking on clouds. Istead, it says we are going to be bodily resurrected to participate with our God in a new heaven and a new earth. And I encouraged them to reread Isaiah 65:17-25, Ezekiel 37, and 1 Corinthians 15, which give a vivid picture of what God's future will be like . . . the fusing together of heaven and earth. God intends to complete His creation, not destroy it.

Although the Duellways view the future of God pessimistically and spiritually, they see their future here and now optimistically and materialistically. It's evident in their lives that they, like the Hightowers, are caught up in the belief that the better future

---

8. Leslie Newbigin, "Cross Currents in Ecumenical and Evangelical Mission," *International Bulletin of Missionary Research*, October 1982, 149.

here on earth is to be found in getting, having, and possessing.
And because they believe God is only interested in "saving their
souls," they never imagine there is a contradiction between
their two views of the future.

Even though they sincerely believe the end is near, they also
believe the American Dream is getting four percent better every
year. They want a piece of the action while the getting is still
good. And they believe that God will become a co-conspirator,
insuring that they successfully ascend the escalator to the Land
of Evermore.

The extent of this kind of schizophrenic thinking and view of
the future is strikingly illustrated by the example of an author
of prophecy books who predicts that everything is going to end
tomorrow, and the only thing we can hope for is the rescue of our
disembodied souls in the nick of time. Reportedly, this author has
invested the profits from his prophecy books in long-term American growth bonds. That's schizophrenia!

where does God come in?

Perhaps the most troubling feature of the Duellway's double
thinking is that it reveals a frighteningly narrow view of God's
redemptive work in history—and a very limiting view of God
Himself.

For example, since the Duellways assume that God's concern is
narrowly limited to souls, they tend to see His activity as limited
exclusively to the spiritual realm. God is expected to show up at
their prayer meetings, worship services, and evangelistic campaigns. But in that larger world beyond the doors of the church,
He is seen as largely impotent—or at least uninterested. For example, He seems to have little to do with the problems of terror-
ism in Central America or homelessness in the United States.

According to this view, all God really cares about is rescuing
our disembodied souls for the clouds. This view tends to cause
those who buy into it to subscribe to a very private view of piety, a
very narrow view of Christian mission, and a restricted view of
God's activity in history. And they tend to view evil only in terms
of personal morality while being largely oblivious to the activity of
evil in large organizations and structures—just the opposite of the
Libermans' view.

David Bosch, an evangelical theologian, asserts that "evangelicals
tend to regard salvation history as something quarantined from

world history."[9] Essentially, many evangelicals such as the Duellways seem to view God as an impotent bystander who only gets to bring down the final curtain at the end of history.

In this story, then, like the others, we wind up with a deity who is passive and largely without power in the world He created. And into this vacuum the Duellways, like the Hightowers, are dependent largely on their own initiative to achieve their materialistic image of the better future here on earth.

That is why folks like the Duellways can be seriously committed to their God while maintaining a high level of confidence in the secular providence of the marketplace to make the secular world work smoothly and assure them economic success.

But our young couple tend to look dualistically not only at God's activity, but also at His creation. They have been conditioned to divide the spiritual from the natural. And so, like their secular counterparts, they relate to creation in very utilitarian terms. They have joined the Hightowers and all those who look at God's world as nothing but a grab bag of "resources"—the place where we dig our oil and set up our campers.

Unwittingly, the Duellways and others like them have wound up with a creation that seems to know little of the presence or purposes of our Creator. They look forward to a future in which God's creation is destroyed and we all head for the clouds. Not surprisingly, they have very little concern for the environment, "because this world is not our home . . . we are just a-passing through."

what does it mean to be human?

Not surprisingly, if the Duellways see God's future and His creation in dualistic terms, they see persons that way too. Of course, Rich and Piety believe in the immortality of the soul. But since in their story the spiritual is largely divorced from the natural, once again they see God's interest and activity as being limited to the spiritual side of a person's life.

For example, while Piety strongly emphasizes in her Sunday school class that human beings are the image bearers of God, it's a whole different story when she and Rich participate in the larger society. Like their non-Christian neighbors, they tend to value

---

9. David Bosch, *Witness to the World: The Christian Mission in Theological Perspective* (Atlanta: John Knox, 1980), 230.

people more by what they produce and consume than by what they are in God's sight. In their Christmas newsletter, for example, they focus almost exclusively on their family's successes at work and school and on the fancy new things they have been able to purchase.

And while Rich and Piety enjoy the fellowship of the midweek Bible study and many church meetings, they are certainly no less individualistic than the other couples. Their church almost always targets the needs of individuals. Rarely does their church ever foster the development of community over the nurturing of individuals.

And the values of the upwardly mobile culture are accepted by Rich and Piety and their church as an unquestioned given, including the radical emphasis on personal autonomy. Even their quest for God's guidance is individualistic; it never occurs to them to involve others in their church fellowship in major life decisions.

which way is up?

How do the Duellways hope to attain their two very different visions for the future? Clearly, the initiative is still with Rich and Piety in every area but the spiritual compartment of their life. In that area, God is seen as the initiator, actively directing their lives—and He will save them. And while they are hoping for His help to get their new home, essentially it's going to take their energy and initiative and resources to get all the things they want in the Land of Evermore. And they also trust the secular providence of the marketplace to help them get ahead. Autonomous individualism is given very high value in this story, as is the belief that if we each pursue our own economic self-interest, our efforts will somehow work for the common good.

Orlando Costas asserts that the content of this kind of Christianity is "another worldly kingdom, a private inwardly limited spirit, a pocket God, a spiritualized Bible, and an escapist church. Such a gospel makes possible the 'conversion' of men and women without having to make any drastic change in their lifestyles and value systems."[10]

Please understand the Christian commitment for people like the Duellways is genuine. They honestly believe that following Jesus is almost exclusively tied up with one small spiritual compartment of their lives. As a consequence, both their quest for soul rescue and their labor for fat city become very self-involving

---

10. Orlando Costas, *Christ Outside the Gate* (Maryknoll, NY: Orbis, 1981), 80.

and self-centered activities—even though carried out with the most sincere motivation.

couple #4: chuck and liberty amright erecting a super state for Jesus

Chuck and Liberty Amright recently moved from Atlanta to Arizona because they wanted to raise their kids in a more wholesome environment, away from the problems of the city. They settled right outside of Scottsdale in a rural area, and at first they were pretty isolated, but every day the suburban development edges closer. Still, they own a dozen head of cattle and a couple of horses and manage to live a fairly comfortable life.

Chuck is manager of a truck repair business. Liberty stays home and takes care of their three preschoolers. She has set up a home schooling program for the five-year-old. They plan to educate all their kids at home to keep them away from the "humanistic influences" of the public schools.

The Amrights are deeply concerned about the future of the United States—they see many changes as threats to the American way of life. They love their kids deeply and want to protect them from negative influences. And they care passionately about their country and want to preserve it.

Chuck spends a lot of his free time fencing the property to keep out "bad elements." But he and Liberty have not holed up on their property waiting for problems to come to them. They have both become involved in crusading for issues they believe in. They are actively involved in picketing an abortion clinic in Scottsdale, for example, and in campaigning for prayer in public schools.

These folks were raised Southern Baptist. But when they moved to Scottsdale, they joined the Freedom Bible Church because it was committed to "returning our society to traditional American values and strengthening our country."

The Amrights are using every extra penny to try to buy additional land around their property as a buffer against those moving in. They place a high value on privacy and family life and are willing to do a lot to protect it.

what is the better future?

Chuck and Liberty share many common values with the Duellways—including a schizophrenic view of the future. And their vision of the future is certainly no less pessimistic than Rich and Piety's. If anything, Chuck and Liberty approach the future with even more apprehension; as we approach the third millennium, they see Armageddon as even more imminent and menacing.

However, Chuck and Liberty are not content to simply get a little bigger piece of the American pie themselves—though that's certainly a part of their agenda, too. Their vision is much larger. They and those they go to church with are absolutely driven by the obsession of erecting a "super state" for Jesus. They genuinely believe they are called by God to make America great because America has been chosen by God to carry out His redemptive work in the world. And when it comes to this brand of messianic nationalism, they are bullishly optimistic.

(Let me be very clear here. I am very grateful to God that I was born in America. The opportunities and the constitutional freedom make our country unique. But I still believe we need to ask what the Bible teaches about an individual nation's role in His agenda on earth. And I believe the Amrights are seriously mistaken in their particular vision.)

To understand Chuck and Liberty's story, we first have to understand what they are afraid of. For more than any of the other stories we have looked at, this one is deeply rooted in fear. These folks live under a constant sense of threat—fear of the Soviet menace without and the "humanist conspiracy" within.

At the very center of Chuck and Liberty's fear is the expectation that someone will somehow create a one-world government that will come under the control of the anti-Christ. Since communists do aspire to establish an international order and the Soviets are clearly expansionistic, they are given top nomination for such a conspiratorial takeover. But there are any number of other candidates, including the Trilateral Commission, Zionist bankers, the Vatican, and so on. And true believers will tell you it is only a question of time before those holding the reins of power make their final move and take over.

Chuck and Liberty also live in fear of a "secular humanist" takeover and see signs of this menacing conspiracy at every turn. They are especially afraid that the nation's school system is being taken over by humanists. That is one reason they have chosen to educate their kids at home. (Undeniably, there are people in our society who work for godless secular agendas, and we must strongly oppose them. But I have seen no convincing evidence that they have even bought into the same brand of secularism, let alone that they are consciously working together.)

Chuck and Liberty's fear stems in part from the conservative culture in which they were raised and in part from their own particular view of the end times. Generally, they see the last chapter's being written with a Soviet invasion of Israel, which in turn will trigger an American response, which in turn will trigger World War III and nuclear conflagration.

But it is here that their vision of the future takes a different kind of schizophrenic twist. For even though, theologically, they see these events as inevitable and even desirable, they also seem to believe God has chosen America to step in and be His agent of redemption on earth!

In other words, the end of the world is near—but it is up to America to make a final stand against the forces of the Antichrist. Therefore, they believe, we must make America strong.

Essentially, what those like the Amrights have unwittingly done in subscribing to this epic of messianic nationalism has been to rewrite the biblical doctrines of creation, fall, and redemption. Their revisionist story of creation begins with a second creation—the creation of America.[11] They believe that God created the American state as a special act of providence through which God could work in the world.

Jerry Falwell is certainly a spokesperson for this point of view. "I believe that America has reached the pinnacle of greatness unlike any nation in history because our founding fathers established America's laws and precepts on the principles recorded in the laws of God."[12]

Mark A. Noll, Nathan O. Hatch, and George M. Marsden, three leading evangelical historians, convincingly refute this claim. In their important work, *In Search for Christian America*, they state:

> We feel that a careful study of the facts of history shows that early America does not deserve to be considered uniquely, distinctly or even predominantly Christian, if we mean by the word "Christian" a state of society reflecting the ideas presented in the Scripture.[13]

---

11. Gabriel Fackre, *The Religious Right and the Christian Faith* (Grand Rapids, MI: Eerdmans, 1982), 50.
12. Jerry Falwell, *Listen America* (New York: Doubleday, 1980), 25.
13. Mark A. Noll, Nathan O. Hatch, George M. Marsden, *In Search for Christian America* (Westchester, IL: Crossway Books, 1983), 17.

Those who subscribe to a messianic nationalism place America at the very center of God's redemptive activity in the world. Again, the idea is that we must make America strong so that America can play out its redemptive role in the consummation of history.

I believe this notion is dangerous and even idolatrous. While I believe Christians must indeed labor to call America and every nation to the righteousness before God, I find not a scrap of biblical evidence that God has singled out the United States to be the agent of His redemptive mission in history. I believe Robert Webber is right; this tale simply "baptizes Americanism and politicizes the church."[14] In fact, in a real sense, America becomes a substitute for the church. And as a consequence, Christian religion is replaced by American civil religion.

Gabriel Fackre asserts,

> Perhaps the greatest departure from Christian doctrine by the religious right is its transfer of the special covenant from the elect of God in the particular history of the children of Israel to another people. The functional elevation of America to the place of a chosen nation adds to the Christian story a chapter which is not in the book—the United States shares with all peoples the universal covenants of Adam and Noah. But there is only one covenant stream in the Christian narrative through which God does the special work of redemption.[15]

In other words, committing ourselves to work for a vision of messianic nationalism is committing ourselves to work for an agenda that is as secular as anything the humanists have dreamed up. If we are to discover God's Story for His people and His world, we must go not to the founding documents of America but to the Scriptures. We need to help Chuck and Liberty and their friends relinquish some of their fears and rediscover God's transnational vision for all peoples, tribes, and nations.

where does God come in?

Of course, in things spiritual, God is seen by Chuck and Liberty as active and initiating. But in their political agenda God is seen as essentially passive, though enthusiastically sanctioning their

---

14. Robert Webber, *Church in the World* (Grand Rapids, MI: Zondervan, 1986), 226.
15. Fackre, 62–63.

activity. They see themselves as called by God to take initiative at His bequest to turn America around and protect their loved ones. It's really up to activists like them to save the day. They also tend to invoke the secular providence of Adam Smith to run the larger economic world while evoking the God of the Bible to strengthen them in their spiritual lives. And like the Duellways, they just don't perceive any contradiction.

Chuck and Liberty, like the Hightowers and the Duellways, tend to see creation in very utilitarian terms. And they add to this attitude an assumption that the United States, because of its chosen status and superiority, has a stronger claim on global resources than other countries.

what does it mean to be human?

Like Rich and Piety, Chuck and Liberty also tend to see humanity in largely schizophrenic terms. On the one hand, persons are seen as primarily spiritual beings made in the image of God. On the other hand, they are treated as largely economic beings— producers/consumers—who vote.

Those people they view as "good" or "moral" are the ones who subscribe to what they call "traditional American values"—pay their taxes, work hard, and get along with their neighbors.

But Fackre argues convincingly that in this thinking they have presumed to abolish the biblical concept of original sin and rewrite the doctrine of Christian morality:

> The dividing line between all sinners in their fallen state and God the righteous judge is moved: It becomes the line between the morally upright and the immorally fallen. The human problem is no longer the controversy God has with the rebellious race as a whole, but the controversy the moral majority has with the immoral minority.[16]

Tim LaHaye has even started an organization not to call the fallen to be transformed by the grace of Christ but to call Americans to return to "traditional American values." But while there are some positive values in our culture, traditional American values also enslaved blacks, slaughtered Indians and took their land, and oppressed the poor.

Again, this idea of returning to some notion of traditional

---

16. Ibid., 46.

American morality is directly in contradiction to a biblical view of morality that insists that all must come to the cross: "All have sinned and fallen short of the glory of God." I doubt that Chuck and Liberty have any awareness of this contradiction.

Interestingly enough, while the Amrights are strongly committed to the American individualism in a sense, they have rediscovered a form of community. They identify strongly not with the transnational community of the people of God, but with the national community of America, since nationalism is very much at the center of their particular story.

which way is up?

The Amrights are of course waiting expectantly for the last days and their rapture to a heaven in the clouds by God's power. But like those espousing the agendas of the left, however, Chuck and Liberty and their compatriots rely heavily on political action to achieve their dream for their nation now.

But as Robert Webber charges, such politicization

> gives America a religious veneer and the church a political character. America is thought to be the center of God's activity in the world and the church is supposed to become a political power base, a special agent of capitalism economics, a champion of western liberty and a defender of messianic Americanism. Thus the churches are made the servants of a particular ideology.[17]

While I believe there is a place for Christians to influence their country and world through political action, I fear that this politicization of the church has seriously sidetracked it from its biblical mission—the proclamation and demonstration of the gospel of Jesus Christ. In fact, many Christians are finding that the rigid conservative political agenda of the religious right is undermining efforts in evangelism. Growing numbers of people believe that to become a Christian they must accept not only Christ into their hearts, but the political agenda of the religious right into their lives. The cross is enough of a stumbling block! In my mind, it is a serious mistake for us to add our own cultural and political baggage to the acceptance of Jesus Christ as Savior and Lord.

If we can recover a biblical view of redemption in which God acts

---

17. Webber, 218–219.

in history through His church—not through a nation—then we can recover a biblical view of mission. And while a biblical view of mission includes concern for politics, it is not primarily political. It is God working supernaturally through His Spirit and empowering His church to see His reign established in hearts, communities, and nations throughout His world. Chuck and Liberty's tale, while exciting passions of patriotism, fails to offer such a transcendent vision that draws on every dimension of our lives and moves us towards the transnational vision of God's future.

getting our stories straight

Clearly, the key to connecting with God's kingdom purposes lies beyond the stories of the Hightowers, the Libermans, the Duellways, and the Amrights. All four couples—and the groups they represent—have based their lives on half-truths and full fictions that keep them from being fully linked to God's loving purposes that are changing the world.

If we are going to get our stories straight, we have to discover a story that transcends the trivial tales of upward mobility, social gradualism, soul rescue, and messianic nationalism.

If we are to discover a story that is powerful enough to transform both our lives and God's world, we must go back to the Bible—and we must ask one question of the Bible if we are to find clearer direction for our lives: "What are God's purposes for the human future?"

for thought and discussion

None of these stories fully match any reader's life situation. But let's discuss the following questions:

1. Which of the values or images in these stories are possibly a part of your life and story? Do you identify with any particular couple—or with more than one of them? Do you find yourself defending one particular couple? Why?
2. What is the better future you want to achieve for yourself and your loved ones?
3. If you are in a group, try role playing the four different couples introduced in this chapter, advocating from their viewpoint the future you want for yourself and your family.

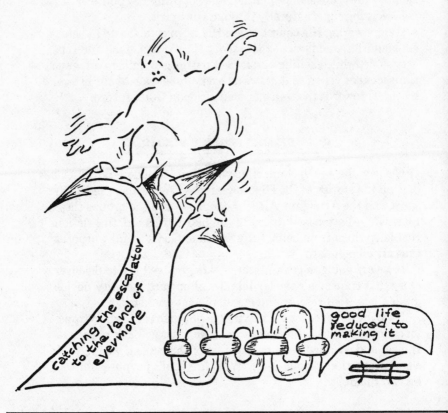

catching the escalator to the land of evermore

good life reduced to making it

life direction ▶	linkages ▶	consequences
Many Americans believe they will find the better future in the high and precarious elevations of the Land of Evermore. They have really come to believe the good life is synonymous with "movin' on up" in careers, buying power, and status.	A number of people have, with very little reflection, linked their lives to the dream of ascending the escalator to the Land of Evermore—perhaps with church on Sundays. And then they wonder why their lives lack purpose.	In this scenario, the good life is reduced to "making it." But many who *do* make it to the slippery summits of Evermore are discovering that getting, achieving, and consuming are not synonymous with happiness, and that the climb is not worth what it costs in terms of physical and mental health, relationships, and spirituality.

catching the mainline to progresstown

life direction ▶	linkages ▶	consequences
Some liberal Christians have a very humane vision for the future—a vision of society slowly progressing and improving itself as we push it up the steep slopes of history. For them, salvation is virtually synonymous with humanization—"becoming more fully human." God has little to do with this process of social gradualism. It's really up to us.	Many have linked their lives to this vision of gradual humanization because it is consistent with their larger world view. They believe that since persons are essentially good, all that is required is a little tinkering with the sociopolitical environment to allow persons to progress as nature intended. There is little emphasis on any kind of personal transformation.	One problem with this vision is that it simply doesn't work! While there is modest progress in certain areas of society, other areas are rapidly going downhill—perhaps because sin isn't taken seriously. Also, though this vision claims to have a Biblical premise, it is more directly connected to a "progressive" political philosophy and as a result lacks any serious eternal dimension—it's for this world only.

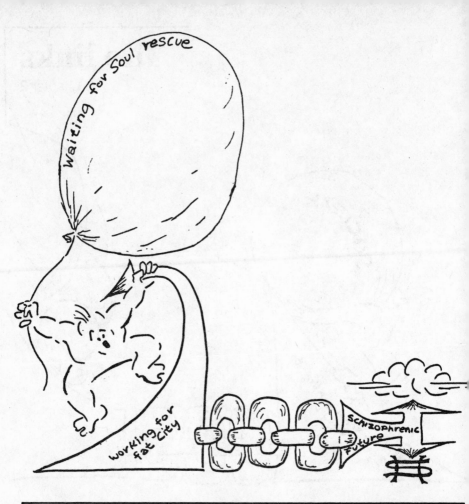

Waiting for Soul rescue

Working for fat City

schizophrenic future

life direction	linkages	consequences
Many evangelicals seem to hold two very different visions for the future at the same time. On one hand, they look forward to God's future as a nonmaterial existence in the clouds. But they are also looking forward to getting as big a piece of the great American pie as possible while they are still here.	Seldom do those who connect their lives to these two very different visions ever check either one against the biblical vision, and as a result they live largely unexamined, "schizophrenic" lives. They don't seem to realize they have linked their lives with two very different world views that really aren't compatible.	The scramble up the slopes of Evermore gives these Christians no more sense of purpose than it does their secular counterparts. And while the vision of a nonmaterial existence does give many an eternal hope, it tends to provide little sense of direction in this life and to disconnect them from any sense of social responsibility or concern for others.

erecting a super state for Jesus

fostering civil religion

life direction ▶	linkages ▶	consequences
Some on the religious right have bought into a highly nationalistic vision for the future. They believe God has somehow chosen the United States to be His agent on earth—working as a nation to carry out His purposes. Therefore the task of Christians is quite simply to make America as strong as possible so it can carry out its mission in the world.	Fundamentalist Christians who link their lives to this vision of messianic nationalism do so with the utmost sincerity. But while claiming to be people of the Book, they don't seem to recognize that there is not a shred of biblical material to support the view that the United States has been chosen by God to replace His church as His agent on earth.	This vision of the better future tends to "baptize Americanism and politicize the church"—to create a new civil religion that seriously departs from a biblical faith. More tragically, it draws lives and resources of believers away from proclaiming and demonstrating the gospel to be invested in various political causes.

connecting with the Story of God

Connecting! Deep within every person is a longing to be connected to a story larger than ourselves. We sense it isn't enough simply to buy into the stories that make up our small world—stories that we have discovered are filled with distortions, illusions, and half-truths. Even when we invest every ounce of energy scaling the illusory peaks these stories call us to, they end up disappointing us. As we have discovered, even some of our religious stories are inadequate.

At the very center of our beings we sense there is something more. We want our lives to count for something. And the only way we are going to get there is to connect our lives to a dream that is bigger than we are—a dream that is big enough for the times and the world in which we live. We will find that connection only when we merge our lives and our stories with the Story of God.

The intent of this chapter, then, is to help us understand something of the scope, drama, and redemptive purposes of the Story of God as shown in the Bible—in order to discover how we can link our lives to what He is doing in history right now.

But why all this emphasis on "story"—and especially "the Story of God"? It is only as we begin to comprehend the Story of God in its entirety and understand something of God's loving purposes for His people and His world that we find direction for our lives and our congregations. The God who made us knows that a story is one of the best ways for us to connect with truths that are larger than ourselves.

Garrison Keillor, who used to tell his engaging yarns on the National Public Radio program, *A Prairie Home Companion*, has helped us understand the compelling power of stories to connect us with the larger world. His homely recollections of his mythical hometown of Lake Wobegon, Minnesota, somehow remind us of our common past, the poignancy of the everyday, the seasons of our lives. For example:

> The Sons of Knute Ice Melt Contest starts on Groundhog Day, when they tow Mr. Gerge's maroon 1949 Ford onto the lake, park it forty yards off shore with a long chain around the rear axle and wait for spring. You guess the day and the hour she will go down, at a dollar per guess. The winner gets a boat, and the profits go to the Sons of Knute Shining Start Scholarship Fund to send kids to college. . . .
>
> The first week of April is a good guess, though the car has sunk as early as late March and as late as the third week of April. Once it never went down. They parked it off the end of the long sandbar that comes off the point. The Ford sat there in four inches of water, a sort of buoy, and the scholarship fund earned hundreds of dollars. . . .
>
> On the first real warm day, you can sit on the back steps in your P.J.s before church, drink coffee, study the backyard, which was such a dump a week ago you wouldn't have wanted to be buried there, but with the tulips coming up and a faint haze on the lilacs, a person can see this is not the moon but earth, a planet named for its finely ground rock containing organic material that, given sunlight and moisture, can produce plant life and may support advanced life forms such as Catholics and Lutherans. School windows open and faint wisps of talk drift out and choral music. Rototillers start up, and the first whap of a ball in a glove is heard . . .
>
> On the first real warm Sunday, attendance is down at church, people deciding God being everywhere they can worship Him anywhere—what Fr. Emil calls "the Protestant fallacy." He strolls around after mass, surprising some absentees who were busy worshipping with rakes and didn't see him coming.[1]

As Garrison Keillor spins his tale, we find ourselves getting involved, reconnecting with the smells, tastes, and renewal of spirit that come with the thawing of winter and coming of spring. And I am convinced that is the way we need to connect with the Creator and His Story of redemption for His people and His world.

reconnecting with The Story

But of course, we're talking about something with much more grandeur than springtime in Minnesota! We're talking about

---

1. Garrison Keillor, *Lake Wobegon Days* (New York: Viking, 1985), 276–279.

something that's large enough to live and die for—that challenges every dimension of our lives.

Growing up in northern California, I quickly learned that when people in my part of the state said they were going to "the city," they meant San Francisco—even though there were a number of other cities in the vicinity. In the same way, although there are many stories that seek to explain the human experience and describe the human future (we've looked at a few of them), the epic of God is in a class by itself. It is THE Story. Its sweep ranges from creation to consummation and remarkably embraces your life and mine.

Now, I want to stress that in referring to God's acts in history as a "Story," I certainly am not suggesting they aren't true! I hold a very high view of Scripture; I join my conservative friends in affirming that the Bible is fully authoritative for faith and life. In fact, I go beyond some of them in insisting that Scripture is fully authoritative for *all* of life—including the social, political, economic, and environmental issues of God's world as well.

But I think it's important to remember that our faith doesn't come to us as "theology"—in the sense of a set of systematic precepts. No, our faith comes to us as a Story—*The Story*. And in "losing the story," says Robert McAfee Brown—"we have lost both the power and the glory. We have committed the unpardonable sin of transforming exciting stories into dull systems. We must recover the story if we are to recover a faith for our day."[2]

To "recover the story," to reconnect with what God is doing and how we can have a part in His redemptive purposes, we need to go back to Scripture and read it with new eyes, a new sense of anticipation and involvement. We need to listen to The Story as if we are hearing it for the first time.

We must also be aware that the many other stories with which we have been raised can become a distorting filter through which we see The Story. For example, I can still remember how upset I was the first time I read Ron Sider's *Rich Christians in an Age of Hunger.* I kept saying over and over to myself as I read the book, "I've read the Old Testament a number of times and I never saw all these passages Sider keeps referring to about justice and God's concern for the poor!"

---

2. Robert McAfee Brown, "Starting Over: New Beginning Points for Theology," *Christian Century,* 14 May 1980, 547–548.

But of course, when I checked Sider's references, I discovered those passages had been in the Bible all the time; I simply had never seen them. And that was because I had been taught that The Story was a narrow, private, pietistic story about how God wanted to bless me and my personal spiritual life—period.

If we really want to recover the power and the glory of God's Story, we need as much as possible to put all those other stories we have been told (including those we examined in the last chapter) on the shelf. And then we need to let the Word speak to us with all the freshness of a spring morning. We need to learn what it must have meant to those who first heard it.

And we must try to grasp The Story in its entirety. Many of us have focused on fragments of Scripture. But while the Bible is indeed comprised of a diverse collection of history, poetry, and letters, there is only one Story—that of the Creator God's taking initiative over and over to redeem His people and transform His world.

welcome to the drama of God

Perhaps it's easiest to visualize this Story as a vast drama covering the sweep of history. Picture the incredible range of locations—from the pyramids of Egypt to the Hanging Gardens of Babylon; from the teeming streets of Jerusalem to the imperial palace at Rome. Nothing can match this epic for pure panoramic sweep. It is more variegated and compelling than any other human drama—absolutely filled with stories of heroism, romance, tragedy, comedy, rebellion, and restoration.

Christopher Wright helpfully breaks this enormous drama down into nine segments, and this breakdown can serve as a useful guide as we reexperience the drama of The Story from opening curtain to the dimming of the final footlights:

Act 1: The Creation
Act 2: The Fall
Act 3: The Call of Abraham and Sarah
Act 4: The Exodus Experience
Act 5: The Life and Ministry of the Messiah
Act 6: The Crucifixion and Resurrection of Jesus
Act 7: Pentecost and the Church Age

Act 8: The Return of Christ

Act 9: The Creation of a New Heaven and a New Earth[3]

As you can see from this outline, The Story doesn't conclude at the end of the first century A.D. with the writings of the apostles. This story, because it is The Story, stretches across the Dark Ages, Middle Ages, the Renaissance, the Enlightenment, the Industrial Revolution, the Electronic Age, and through your life and mine into the unfinished future. We are living in the middle of Act 7—between Pentecost and the return of Christ.

Given this perspective, you and I have an important role in this drama. Like it or not, we are called upon to be a part of the Story of God. As John Dunne suggests about the stories of the New Testament,

> Perhaps the special character of the stories . . . lies in the fact that they are not told for themselves, that they are not only about other people, but that they are always about us. They locate us in the very midst of the great story and plot of all time and space, and therefore relate us to the great dramatist and story teller, God himself.[4]

If we are faithfully to play out our role in the drama of God, however, we must understand the direction and character of this drama. We must understand the intentions of the Playwright for His people and His world.

Picture yourself as a member of the audience for this epic production . . . both viewing and participating in all that we are going to experience together. Pay particular attention to God's loving purposes revealed in this drama, because they will inform us as to our role when it is our turn in the footlights.

Prepare for the opening scene.

Watch in hushed silence.

3. Christopher J. H. Wright, "The Use of the Bible in Social Ethics: Paradigms, Type and Eschatology," *Transformation*, January–March 1984, 11.

4. John S. Dunne, *A Search for God in Time and Memory: An Exploration Traced in the Lives of Individuals from Augustine to Sartre* (London: Macmillan, 1969), 7.

act one . . . in the beginning

Act one, scene one, no props, no stage, no earth, no life—nothing. In the darkness, we hear those words ringing through space and time: "In the beginning, God."

"In the beginning God created the heavens and the earth. And the earth was formless and void, and darkness was over the surface of the deep; and the Spirit of God was moving over the surface of the waters. Then God said, 'let there be light'" (Gen. 1:1–3). And the lights come up and the majestic spectacle of creation takes place right before our eyes.

We find ourselves in a lavishly beautiful garden. All around us we see the loving intentions of the Creator. We experience a world of rhythmic night and day, darkness and light—a world of spectacular variety, color, and sound, with birds piercing the heavens and fish filling the sea.

The evidence from Scripture is abundant that "the earth is the Lord's, and the fulness thereof; the world, and they that dwell therein" (Ps. 24:1). Also, "the heavens are telling the glory of God; and the firmament proclaims His handiwork (Ps. 19:1). Throughout both the Old and New Testaments we find hymns affirming the goodness and the glory of God's creation. And we were appointed stewards of this good creation.

act two . . . the fatal choice

Unfortunately, we all know what happens when the curtain rises on the next act. Our forebears, a man and a woman, not content to walk with their Maker in the cool of the Garden, decide to rewrite the script, to try their hand at directing the drama and their own lives. And the consequences are disastrous; everything is disrupted. Unbelievably, not only is the couple alienated from their Creator, but creation itself becomes tragically twisted.

You see, the consequences of the fall are much more far-reaching than many Christians recognize. Humankind does indeed become alienated from God as a direct consequence of the Fall. But the alienation is not just spiritual! Humans become corrupted in every area of our lives. Physically, we become subject to disease, decay, and death. Intellectually, we become driven by the lust to know as God knows and to be powerful as God is powerful. We learn to rationalize our evil, and our minds become darkened.

At every level, human relationships have been fractured and disrupted by the Fall—including family, sexual, parental, societal, and international relationships. The earth itself has fallen under the curse because of human sin and, as a consequence, we human beings find ourselves in a constant life-and-death struggle with the larger environment. And sin and evil become not only personal, but corporate and societal, permeating the entire created order.

So how can this fallen creation be redeemed? Christopher Wright accurately points out that the remedy must match the disease. If the malady of sin has not only corrupted our spiritual lives, but also our personal, relational, international relationships and the earth itself, then we need a cure that is as comprehensive as the sickness.

Obviously, a divine initiative only interested in rescuing people's souls will be totally inadequate for such a task.[5] We need a redemptive remedy that doesn't seek only to reconcile us to God and transform our inner lives. We need a redemptive remedy that restores broken bodies, reconciles broken relationships, and labors for the renewal of this good creation by the power of the living God. That's a tall order.

act three . . . a new initiative

Let's see what the Playwright does to mount a new initiative, to address the comprehensive corruption of humanity and distortion of creation. As the curtain rises on act three, we find ourselves somewhere in the wilderness with what looks to be a nomadic tribe on the move—with their tents, their flocks, their families, all their possessions.

What possible good can God achieve through this small band? It soon becomes a little clearer. For this group is traveling on a promise! They are on the move because God has spoken to their aged leader in words of calling and words of promise, bidding him to leave his home in a thriving city and go into a distant land he has never seen.

God has promised Abraham a new future that has within it the seeds of the promise of a new humanity and a new creation; He has said that all the peoples of the earth will be blessed through this one man and his family (see Gen. 12:3).

---

5. Christopher Wright, 12.

In act three of God's Story, God takes redemptive initiative by establishing a new covenant with Abraham, his wife, Sarah, and their descendants:

> This new history requires a wrenching departure, an abandonment of what is, for that which is not, but which is promised by the One who will do what He says. "And he went!" Sarah was barren! No way to the future. No heir to receive all the riches. Nothing. Future closed off. Everything as good as over and done with. And He spoke and there was newness. The family of Abraham left the history of expulsion and began the pilgrimage of promise.[6]

And we all join the pilgrimage with them.

Unbelievably, God establishes this new covenant with a ninety-year-old couple. The Playwright bets the entire play on their faith and their obedience. But how in the world is He going to make their descendants more numerous than the stars and bless the world when Sarah has never had a child and she is in the declining years of life?

The lights go up on the next scene and there is a woman right in the middle of the stage, laughing uproariously:

> She is an old woman, and, after a lifetime in the desert, her face is cracked and rutted like a six-month drought. She hunches her shoulders around her ears and starts to shake. She squinnies her eyes shut and her laughter is all china teeth and wheeze and tears running down as she rocks back and forth in her kitchen chair. She is laughing because she is pushing ninety-one and has just been told she is going to have a baby. Even though it was an angel who told her, she can't control herself, and her husband can't control himself either. He keeps a straight face a few seconds longer than she does, but he ends by cracking up too. Even the angel is not unaffected. He hides his mouth behind his golden scapular, but you can still see his eyes. They are larkspur blue and brimming with something of which the laughter of the old woman and her husband is at best only a rough translation.
>
> The old woman's name is Sarah, of course, and the old man's name is Abraham, and they are laughing at the idea of a baby being born in the geriatric ward and Medicare's picking up the tab.
>
> She was hiding behind the tent door when the angel spoke, and it was her laughter that got them all going. According to Genesis, God intervened then and asked about Sarah's laughter, and Sarah

---

6. Walter Brueggemann, *The Land* (Philadelphia: Fortress Press, 1977), 18.

scared stiff denied the whole thing. Then God said, "No, but you did laugh," and of course He was right. Maybe the most interesting part of it all is that far from getting angry at them for laughing, God told them that when the baby was born He wanted them to name him Isaac, which in Hebrew means laughter.[7]

Only a playwright with an outrageous sense of humor, or a Creator God committed to redeeming history through the unlikely, would choose a couple on the verge of needing nursing home care to start a new nation! It certainly is not typecasting. How like God, though, to begin redemption with impossibilities and with laughter!

act four . . . a new freedom

After an intermission in which everyone dries their eyes and regains their composure, we return to our seats for the fourth act. The room suddenly grows dark.

In the distance a sun slowly appears, descending in a hot desert sky. Silhouetted in the distance are the shapes of huge temples, sculptured forms, and pyramids. In the foreground, a thousand slaves are dragging massive stones towards a construction site. The noise, the dust, the smells are almost overpowering.

An overseer's rod comes down with ferocity on the back of a crippled slave, driving him to the ground, his own blood running down his arms. A growing number of slaves go down under the whip as the sun sets behind the temple, plunging us into a darkness much darker than before. The groans from the fallen also fade away, and we are plunged into a mysterious silence.

It seems as though we have been in the darkness and the silence forever, when suddenly an anguished scream pierces the night. And then there is silence again.

Finally, one small, dark-skinned child emerges from the shadows before us, and a single spotlight focuses on him. He just stands there looking at us with a quizzical look. "Why is this night different from every other night?" he asks curiously. "Every other night we eat both leavened and unleavened bread."

A voice booms out from the back, "What makes this night different is that this is the night that the angel of the Lord passed

---

7. Frederick Buechner, *Telling the Truth: The Gospel as Tragedy, Comedy and Fairy Tale* (New York: Harper & Row, 1977), 49–53.

over the house of Israel." The voice goes on to describe the miracles that resulted in the liberation of the children of Israel from the bondage of Egypt. Then the lights go up as unleavened bread, bitter herbs, salted water are passed and the celebration of the Passover begins. Folk music starts abruptly in the wings and everyone spontaneously starts dancing the Hora. The air becomes filled with the joy of liberation and festivity and hope as we experience together the deliverance of God's people from bondage.

The Jewish people have long understood the importance of telling one another their story through celebration, dancing, and singing. Every Passover they relive the story of their miraculous deliverance.

God's redemptive intention from the beginning was to create a people for Himself. And even as He selected an unlikely couple to parent a nation, He selected "a people who were no people" to carry out His redemptive purposes in the world. He chose an unlikely, despised group of Semite slaves—the descendants of Abraham—to be His people. And He entered into covenant with them.

In the story of the Exodus, we are forcefully reminded that God's intentions are not just spiritual, but political, economic, and social as well. God ever stands against oppression and is ever on the side of the oppressed, seeking their deliverance.

Of course you know how the story goes. The children of Israel, under Moses' leadership, don't immediately enter the Promised Land once they have left their bondage in Egypt. Instead, they wander for forty years as landless refugees in a wasteland because of their disobedient and recalcitrant behavior.

But God never gives up and never wavers from His redemptive purposes. He gives His children a pillar of fire by night and a cloud by day to lead them. Later He gives them the Ten Commandments to guide their behavior. Always, as Brueggemann reminds us, "He is there with Israel. He subjects Himself to the same circumstances as Israel. He also sojourns without rootage, with His people enroute to the fulfilling land of Promise."[8]

Countless followers in ages since have made this wilderness story their story. Too well we have all known the bitter grief of our sin. Too often we have longed for "the leeks and garlics" of our former life. But like the children of Israel, we are led on patiently by our God, who just doesn't give up on us.

---

8. Brueggemann, 43.

Finally, one bright clear morning, after years of disobedience and compromise, we reach the crest of Mt. Nebo and look down into the Promised Land. As that landscape flowing with milk and honey stretches out before us we are overwhelmed by the goodness of God.

The pure radical grace of God in giving His people a homeland is a foretaste of His loving homecoming for all people. God's promise to Abraham, Isaac, and Jacob is fulfilled:

> For the Lord your God is bringing you into a good land, a land of brooks of water, of fountains and springs, flowing forth in valleys and hills, a land of wheat and barley, of vines and fig trees and pomegranates, a land of olive trees and honey, a land in which you will eat bread without scarcity, in which you will lack nothing, a land whose stones are iron, and out of whose hills you can dig copper. And you shall eat and be full, and you shall bless the Lord your God for the good land he has given you (Deut. 8:7–10, RSV).

And this is our story too. This is a foretaste of all God intends—to bring His redeemed people of all generations home.

Of course, act four of God's Story doesn't end when the children of Israel reach the Promised Land. There are scenes of trumpets blasting and swords clashing as God's people win the land and settle it. There are construction scenes as they build cities and erect a sacred temple. There are scenes of courtly splendor as they form a kingdom (a foreshadowing of the coming of God's transcendent kingdom) and King David leads them to pinnacles of influence and power.

There are also scenes of failure, disappointment, and judgment. God's people repeatedly turn from Him and fall into sin. And repeatedly the powerful voices of the prophets arise over scenes of idolatry, oppression, and immorality with their warnings of God's judgment.

The message of the prophets to the people of Israel is that God's goodness to them isn't automatic; it's provisional, based on their obedience and faithfulness. And when the people fail to heed the prophets, judgment comes. The lights come up on a weary line of Hebrews trudging their way towards captivity in Babylon. All that was foretold by the prophets has come to pass.

God's judgment on His people comes for three major reasons: idolatry, sexual immorality, and oppression of the poor. But many evangelicals only acknowledge the first two. I have heard any number of sermons about God's judgment on His people for

idolatry and sexual immorality. But I can't remember ever hearing
a single sermon that declares God judges those who oppress and
exploit the poor. Most evangelicals I talk with know that Sodom
was judged for its sexual sins, but they are surprised to learn it
was also judged for its treatment of the poor: "Behold, this was
the guilt of your sister Sodom: she and her daughters had arro-
gance, abundant food, and careless ease, but she did not help the
poor and needy" (Ezek. 16:49, NASB).

But the prophets' message is not only one of judgment. While
Isaiah, Jeremiah, and Amos breathe with fury the words of God's
anger, they also speak with compelling hope that His redemptive
purposes will one day be achieved—that the day of the Lord will
come. The prophets speak incessantly of promise—and that
promised future is increasingly identified with One who will come
as a deliverer.

Listen to the powerful words of the prophet Isaiah:

> The people who walked in darkness have seen a great light: light has
> dawned upon them, dwellers in a land as dark as death. Thou hast
> increased their joy and given them great gladness. . . . For thou hast
> shattered the yoke that burdened them, the collar that lay heavily on
> their shoulders, the driver's goad, as on the day of Midian's defeat.
> All the boots of trampling soldiers and the garments fouled with
> blood shall become a burning mass, fuel for fire. For a boy has been
> born to us, a son given to us to bear the symbol of dominion on his
> shoulder; and he shall be called in purpose wonderful, in battle God-
> like, Father for all time, Prince of Peace. Great shall the dominion be,
> and boundless the peace bestowed on David's throne and on his king-
> dom, to establish it and sustain it with justice and righteousness
> from now and for evermore (Isa. 9:2–7, NEB).

act five . . . a new compassion

There is a long silence after the fourth act of God's Story—four
hundred years of silence and anticipation. But finally the footlights come up as we begin the fifth act.

A white-haired figure is signaling to a group of friends, using the
animated gestures of one who cannot speak. Finally, in frustration,
he picks up a slate and begins to write, while his companions look
over his shoulder.

But then the old man abruptly throws down the slate and
shouts, in a voice hoarse from months of disuse, the words he
has just written: "His name is John!"

And then Zacharias goes on to speak these exuberant words of praise to celebrate the birth of his newborn son, foretold to him by an angel:

> Blessed be the Lord God of Israel, for he has visited us and accomplished redemption for His people, and has raised up a horn of salvation for us in the house of David His servant—as He spoke by the mouth of His holy prophets from of old—salvation from our enemies, and from the hand of all who hate us; to show mercy toward our fathers, and to remember His holy covenant, the oath which He swore to Abraham our father, to grant us that we, being delivered from the hand of our enemies, might serve Him without fear, in holiness and righteousness before Him all our days.
>
> And you, child, will be called the prophet of the Most High; for you will go on before the Lord to prepare His ways; to give to His people the knowledge of salvation by the forgiveness of their sins, because of the tender mercy of our God, with which the Sunrise from on high shall visit us, to shine upon those who sit in darkness and the shadow of death, to guide our feet into the way of peace (Luke 1:67–79, NASB).

Then the light dims on Zacharias and comes up on a young woman upstage. She is on her knees, her arms lifted toward heaven and her words, too, ring out with praise:

> My soul exalts the Lord, and my spirit has rejoiced in God my Savior. For He has had regard for the humble state of His bond-slave; for behold, from this time on all generations will count me blessed. For the Mighty One has done great things for me; and holy is His Name, and His mercy is upon generation after generation toward those who fear Him. He has done mighty deeds with His arm; He has scattered those who were proud in the thoughts of their hearts. He has brought down rulers from their thrones, and has exalted those who were humble. He has filled the hungry with good things; and sent away the rich empty-handed. He has given help to Israel His servant, in remembrance of His mercy, as He spoke to our fathers, to Abraham and His offspring forever (vv. 46–55, NASB).

These are words not only announcing the loving intervention of God in history, but restating God's redemptive intentions. Certainly these include forgiveness from sin and mercy for those who serve Him in righteousness, but they don't stop there. God's redemptive initiative will have an impact on every dimension of human experience—not only the spiritual, but the social, political, and economic as well. The One who is coming will turn everything right side up.

Zacharias expects God's new initiative to mean political liberation from those who had oppressed His people. And Mary sees God's redemptive initiative as totally reordering human society—pulling down the powerful and influential from their pinnacles and promoting the nobodies; unburdening the affluent of their wealth and giving good things to the hungry, the powerless and impoverished.

It is clear in both these visions that God's redemptive intent is not just the conversion of sinners but the transformation of *everything*. As David Bosch insists, "When redemption is confined to man's personal relationship to God, when somebody is saved but all his relationships remain unaffected, when structural and institutional sins are not exposed, we are involved with an unbiblical one-sidedness and a spurious Christianity."[9]

But we must return to our play—for the spotlight has shifted once again. And the scene now before us is so familiar that at first we don't even notice how surprising it really is! God's redemptive initiatives come to us in unlikely ways—a senior citizen's giving birth to a son named "Laughter," or a nation of refugee slaves—obstinate in will, rebellious in spirit—being chosen as the people of God. But this is the unlikeliest scene of all—a man and a woman engaged in the struggle to bring life into the world . . . in a cowstall.

It is interesting to note who has shown up at this historic birth. It isn't the religious leaders who have scrupulously studied the Scriptures; they don't seem to have a clue. Instead, it is a band of poor sheepherders (and later, a small group of foreigners) whose hearts apparently were turned towards God.

And now the scenes are shifting quickly. We move to a little town called Nazareth some years later. The infant is now a man. Raised in a small rural Jewish village, trained as a carpenter and not a teacher, He nevertheless stands up on the Sabbath in the synagogue to read. He is handed the Book of the prophet Isaiah:

And He opened the book, and found the place where it was written, "The Spirit of the Lord is upon Me, because He has anointed Me to

---

9. David J. Bosch, *Witness to the World* (Atlanta: John Knox Press, 1980), 209.

preach the Gospel to the poor. He has sent Me to proclaim release
to the captives, and recovery of sight to the blind, to set free those
who are downtrodden, to proclaim the favorable year of the Lord."
And He closed the book, and gave it back to the attendant, and sat
down; and the eyes of all in the synagogue were fixed upon Him.
And He began to say to them, "Today this Scripture has been fulfilled in your hearing" (Luke 4:17–21, NASB).

What does He mean, "Today the Scripture has been fulfilled in
your hearing"? What exactly is the significance of His reading
this portion of Scripture? It is the inauguration of Jesus' ministry,
and He is announcing the new messianic kingdom foretold by the
prophets. He is announcing that the redemptive purposes of God
are breaking into history, bringing grace for the fallen and justice
for the poor and totally reordering society. He is announcing that
the Jubilee of God has come.

And He comes not only proclaiming the kingdom, but also
demonstrating it. As He walks down the back roads of Palestine
healing the blind, feeding the hungry, and raising the dead, we're
given a preview of coming attractions. We are given a glimpse of
the loving intentions of God.

When John sends his followers to ask whether Jesus is the
Messiah, Jesus responds in language very similar to His Nazareth
inaugural: "Tell John . . . [that] the blind receive their sight,
the lame walk, lepers are cleansed, and the deaf hear, the dead are
raised up, the poor have good news preached to them" (Luke 7:22–
23). Clearly while Christ's mission is to bring people back to God,
it doesn't stop there. God is concerned with every dimension of
our lives and every aspect of human society.

One of the first things this itinerant rabbi does is to form a
community—a living foretaste of all that God intends for His
people. Jesus and His followers place the redemptive purposes of
God at the very center of their individual and their common lives.
They celebrate life with the poor and the outcasts. They serve
God with righteousness. They proclaim that His kingdom has
come. They flesh out the values of God's new order. They give
themselves without reservation to working for Christ's kingdom.
And they practice whole-life stewardship of their time and their
resources, making themselves available to those in need and generously giving out of their meager resources to the poor.

The image throughout act five of God's Story is one of restoration. In His life and ministry, Jesus is enacting the redemptive

future of God, when "Things will be restored to their original
state—these images of the garden take us back to the creation in
the first chapter of Genesis."[10] But this movement of restoration
encounters strong resistance. The powers of darkness will not tol-
erate this challenge to their rule.

act six . . . a new sacrifice

When the curtain goes up this time, we are all ushered up on
stage. We find ourselves in what looks like a dusty Palestinian
village. Throngs of people press past us up the narrow winding
walkway; something is in the air.

Soldiers everywhere. Faces watching from windows and door-
ways. The crowd surges past us.

Shouting. Raised fists. Parents carrying children. Someone carrying scaffolding. Centurions push us forcefully back into a doorway, almost knocking us down. Blocking our view.

The parade finally dwindles and passes. We follow. The skies
darken. Huge colonnades of clouds gather on the horizon as the
crowd clusters on a barren knoll just outside the city gates.

It's difficult to see what's happening from back here. It looks
as if they are beginning a construction project on the knoll.
Beams and timbers—workmen and soldiers. A small group of
women, heads covered, quickly press past us, making their way
to the small hill.

As one huge beam is lifted upright, silhouetted against the
blackening sky, the chattering and movement abruptly stop. All
eyes are fixed on the hilltop.

Everything is in frozen frame for what seems like forever. The
only motion is that of the encroaching clouds. The biting wind
whips our legs. We stand as one person, transfixed in uncompre-
hending silence.

Suddenly an anguished voice rises above hilltop and throng:
"My God, my God, why have you forsaken Me?" And then all is
dark and silent.

Godforsakenness, torturous suffering, humiliating death. He
has taken the bitter cup and drunk it down to the dregs. There has
been no holding back. Jesus has tasted it all.

---

10. Donald B. Kraybill, *The Upside Down Kingdom* (Scottsdale, PA: Herald
Press, 1978), 106.

Jesus knows the overwhelming sense of abandonment that a five-year-old child is experiencing on a garbage dump in Manila. He knows the despair of a farmer in Chad who is watching his family slowly die of malnutrition. He knows the hopelessness of a young man in Chicago who learns his malignancy is terminal. Jesus has experienced it all.

And the Creator and Author of this story, through the abandonment, suffering, and death of His Son, has tasted it all, too. Our God is not untouched by our infirmities; He has experienced them. On that humiliating scaffold He has known the pain and despair of human existence.

As we go on to the next scene, everything remains in darkness. All is deadly quiet, stifling. Still echoing in our minds is that last terrible cry: "My God, my God . . ."

And suddenly we realize we are no longer bystanders. We are there—with Jesus' disciples, tasting their hopelessness. We have given up our livelihoods, traveled from village to village. We had thought He was the One. And now He's dead, and it's as though we died with Him. It's over, and we find ourselves entombed in black despair. It's almost as if we are there with Him in the silent, dark crypt.

We sit in the dark, feeling the damp stone walls of the crypt against our backs.

Dear God, why have you forsaken us?

And then, after what seems like days, we hear a sound—a faint sound at first—stone against stone. We almost don't dare to hope. There is a chink of light, and suddenly sunshine floods in, lighting up the damp stone walls around us.

All we can do is blink. But then Someone takes our hand. And as we hit the daylight together we hear the words, "On this side of the resurrection there are no more problems—only opportunities to prove the love and faithfulness of our God."

For our God has not only experienced all Godforsakenness, suffering, pain, and death through Jesus Christ; He has put an end to them. He has defeated the crushing works of darkness and, in so doing, reconciled all things to Himself.

Remember, we said at the beginning of the chapter that everything which was ruptured in the fall must be set right in the kingdom. And that is exactly what God has done through the cross and the resurrection.

Christ's death and resurrection have reconciled us to our God. In that merciful act, as we embrace it as our own, we are made new. Our sins are forgiven, and we are adopted into the family of God.

"Once you were alienated from God and were enemies in your minds because of your evil behavior," Paul wrote to the Colossians. "But now He has reconciled you by Christ's physical body through death to present you holy in his sight" (Col. 1:21–22, NIV).

God acted in Christ to reconcile us not only to Himself, but to one another as well. He is at work in history fashioning a new society of reconciliation in which there will be no distinction based on race, culture, and gender. In this new messianic community, "there is neither Jew nor Greek, slave nor free, male nor female, for you are all one in Christ Jesus" (Gal. 3:28, NIV).

Finally, Christ's loving sacrifice and triumphant resurrection not only reconciles us to God and to one another, but reconciles all things to Him—including the entire created order. "For God was pleased to have all His fullness dwell in him, and through him to reconcile to himself all things, whether things on earth or things in heaven, by making peace through his blood, shed on the cross" (Col. 1:19–20, NIV).

Jurgen Moltmann reminds us that the brutal cross is also our doorway to a future made new. "God suffered in the suffering of Jesus, God died on the cross of Christ, says Christian faith, so that we might live and rise again in His future."[11]

In that moment of awareness as we emerge from the tomb of our despair, we realize that God has already written the last chapter not only for our lives, but also for His world. The bodily resurrection of Jesus Christ is our confidence that God has defeated the principalities and powers of this world, that He has overcome everything that is set against His people.

But the resurrection not only has implications for our personal lives and the community of Jesus in the world today; it is our pledge for tomorrow, as well. The resurrection of Jesus is the pledge that all God promised in the final act of His drama will come to pass—that we, too, will be resurrected to live with Him forever. For as the apostle Paul wrote to the Corinthians:

If there is no resurrection of the dead, not even Christ has been raised; and if Christ has not been raised, then our preaching is vain, your faith is also vain. . . . And if Christ has not been raised, your faith is worthless; you are still in your sins. Then those also who have

---

11. Jurgen Moltmann, *The Crucified God: The Cross of Christ as the Foundation and Criticism of Christian Theology* (San Francisco: Harper & Row, 1974), 216.

fallen asleep in Christ have perished. If we have hoped in Christ in this life only, we are of all men most to be pitied. But now Christ has been raised from the dead, the first fruits of those who are asleep. For since by a man came death, by a man also came the resurrection of the dead. For as in Adam all die, so also in Christ shall all be made alive. But each in his own order: Christ the first fruits, after that those who are Christ's at His coming (1 Cor. 15:13–23, NASB).

After the resurrection of Jesus, His followers enthusiastically regrouped. Dismay, despair, and confusion had passed. Faith and hope had returned. Followers spent a forty-day crash course on the kingdom of God with the risen Lord. And His last word to them was to wait in Jerusalem for the coming of the Spirit. And they did. In the upper room.

act seven . . . a new community

As the lights go up on the next act, we find we are still on stage—in Jerusalem. People everywhere. Color and spectacle. The Jewish feast day of Pentecost. Jerusalem bulging at the seams with travelers from all over the world. We make our way with difficulty through the press of animals and people. We come to a small building. And as we climb the outside stairway, we hear people praying.

Suddenly a tornado fills the house, turning everything upside down. Flames of fire over their heads. They are filled with the Spirit of God, speaking with other tongues.

As we watch, they explode past us into the streets. Amazingly, visitors from many nations hear the message of God in their own language.

Peter raises his booming voice above the din, preaching the death and resurrection of the Messiah, Jesus, and calling his hearers to repent and believe. And they do. Three thousand are baptized that remarkable day.

With the coming of the Spirit a new movement is born. At first, it is really a movement of messianic Judaism. But even on that first day, there are clear signs that the messianic community of Jesus is going to be an international movement. It is only a question of time until Peter learns that even Gentiles can follow the Messiah, Jesus. And the movement begins to change.

From the first act of this drama it has been clear that God intended to create a people for Himself—a new community. And that is what He has given us at the feast of Pentecost, a new community. And as we will see later, this community is radically different from the world around it; it is a living foretaste of God's promised future.

After Pentecost, Jesus' followers set aside all lesser agendas to radically pursue the purposes of that future in their community and their world. And by the power of the Spirit of God, they turn the world upside down.

That brings us almost to the end of The Story as it is told in the Bible. But as I have said, it doesn't end there. Act seven of God's Story continues on through the ages into the present day— and in the next chapter we will look at some compelling scenes that have been enacted in our Western past.

But first, I want to look ahead to acts eight and nine as they are described to us in God's Word. For as we look ahead to the final fulfillment of His promises, we will be able to see how widely God's Story differs from the small stories and dreams to which we have given our lives.

acts eight and nine . . . a new creation

As the curtain goes up, we see a huge mountain stretching out of sight into the clouds. People are streaming to it from all directions. We, too, leave our seats and begin to move towards the mountain of the Lord.

As we approach, we notice that the barren landscape begins to give way to lush olive groves. Pomegranates and citrus line the path. And even as the barrenness around us gives way to exuberant life, the same transformation begins to happen within us. It's almost as though our vision is being radically corrected.

Starting up this gigantic mountain, we find abandoned wheelchairs and crutches discarded along the side of the trail. Singing, dancing, and celebration sweep through the crowd. Arm in arm we go up to the mountain together.

> How lovely on the mountains are the feet of him who brings good news, who announces peace and brings good news of happiness, who announces salvation, and says to Zion, "Your God reigns!" Listen! Your watchmen lift up their voices, they shout joyfully together; for they will see with their own eyes when the Lord restores Zion. Break forth, shout joyfully together, you waste places of Jerusalem;

for the Lord has comforted His people, and He has redeemed Jerusalem. The Lord has bared His holy arm in the sight of all the nations, that all the ends of the earth may see the salvation of our God (Isa. 52:7-10, NASB).

As we continue our ascent, the throng begins to chant in a dozen different languages. "The Bridegroom is coming! The Bridegroom is coming!" The anticipation builds as we serpentine, chanting towards the top.

A huge canopy greets us as we reach the summit. It's festooned with ribbons, flowers, and palm branches. Filipinos, Arabs, Haitians, and a thousand others crowd in from all directions.

And I saw a new heaven and a new earth; for the first heaven and the first earth passed away, and there is no longer any sea. And I saw the holy city, new Jerusalem, coming down out of heaven from God, made ready as a bride adorned for her husband (Rev. 21:1-2).

Listen to the unbridled joy a young Jew experienced on his wedding night and imagine how much more we can anticipate when the Bridegroom comes for His people:

We met under the canopy. . . . The procession broke and crowded round us; all raising their candles high in the air. The Rabbi, his face radiant under the high pointed skull-cap, made us stand with our faces to the east, toward Jerusalem, the holy city, and began the sermon: "This my children, is the most momentous hour of your lives."

Beside me I felt the form of my bride. . . . "And as God's agent on earth, you should know that all your being, all your life is dedicated to the purposes of the Almighty. . . . Remember, O bridegroom and bride, that you are going to be collaborators in the endless story of creation which begins in Genesis." The vows were exchanged. Someone put the bride's arm in mine and the musicians led the way, playing a tumultuous cossack dance. Everything around me danced, the air, the candles, the very stars in the highest heaven . . .[12]

12. Irving Fineman, "The Wedding in Mishinietz" in Philip and Hanna Goodman, *The Jewish Marriage Anthology* (Philadelphia: The Jewish Publication Society, 1965), 137-139.

Of course, the biblical images for acts eight and nine of God's Story are not all ones of hilarity and celebration. As the prophets in act four warned, our God is a God of judgment. And the earth is going to face a time of judgment for our personal and corporate sins. The earth will be purged with fire, and we will be judged by God for serving the false idols of our age, for personal immorality and materialism and our indifference to those in need.

The earth will indeed go through the birth trauma of the judgment of God. But then will come the birth of God's new creation. Howard Snyder assures us,

> Here we face the certainty and the mystery of the judgment. The earth will undergo a change, a refining fire, but it will not be annihilated! The whole creation will be set free (Romans 8:21). As with our bodies so with the earth: "The perishable must clothe itself with the imperishable" (I Corinthians 15:33).[13]

a different dream . . .
the present and coming kingdom

I'm sure we've seen enough by now to realize that God's Story and God's Dream has little to do with the stories and dreams of the people we met in chapter 2.

It certainly bears little resemblance to the mindless accumulation and the frenetic mountaineering of the upwardly mobile. While God's future embraces the material world, it certainly isn't materialistic. God has a better idea, which has to do with finding life by losing it.

Neither does God's vision for the future seem to have much to do with the gradual progress of society that preoccupies many liberal Christians. Biblical material suggests that God's future has a transcendent agenda for change that is more radical than the incremental change of society.

Since God is interested in both our spiritual transformation and our material well-being, His vision certainly has to be more integrated than the dualism that so deeply troubles many evangelicals. His redemptive intention is not to rescue our disembodied souls and destroy the material world, but to redeem us as whole people.

---

13. Howard Snyder, *A Kingdom Manifesto* (Downers Grove, IL: Inter-Varsity Press, 1985) 33.

Nor is God's agenda to erect a super state for Jesus. The agenda of God's kingdom is a transnational agenda that is intended to transform the character of every nation. All nations will come to the mountain of God to face His judgment and accept His reign.

what are God's purposes for the human future?

The entire sweep of the Story of God clearly reveals that God has purposes for His people and His world. He intends through His redemptive initiative in Christ to set right everything that was ruptured in the Fall. He intends to reconcile His people to Himself. But He also intends to reconcile us to one another and to God's good creation.

God's purposes, therefore, are not to rescue our disembodied souls for the clouds. He intends to redeem us as whole persons—mind, body, soul, and spirit—to be a part of a new heaven and a new earth.

Through the death and resurrection of Jesus Christ, God will reconcile all those who trust in Christ to Himself. And He will make us whole. He will complete the good work He began in our spiritual lives. But He will also completely restore us physically and emotionally—healing all that is broken and incomplete. We will, in that day, "know even also as we are known." He will destroy the last enemy, which is Death. And the best that has ever been will be alive again.

But God's intentions aren't just personal; they are corporate as well. From the beginning, our God has longed to create for Himself a community that would reign with Him forever. He plans to bring into being a new international community of reconciliation, peace, and celebration, in which He breaks down all barriers of race, gender, and culture. We will be one in Christ, worshiping our God as one gigantic family.

As we study Scripture, it isn't difficult to understand what God's purposes are for His people and His world:

- *God purposes to create a new realm of righteousness in which there is no more sin—personal or corporate.*
- *God purposes to bring into being a new order of justice in which there is no more oppression of the poor.*
- *God purposes to institute a new era of peace in which the instruments of warfare will be transformed into the implements of peace.*

- God purposes to create a new world of compassion in which the blind see, the deaf hear—and everything partial is made whole.
- God purposes to restore the beauty and harmony of His good creation—even causing the wastelands to bloom.
- God purposes to welcome us to a jubilant wedding feast on His Holy Mountain, in which we will celebrate His reign forever.

Remarkably, the God who promises to make all things new invites us to join Him in this world-changing adventure. For whatever reason, God has chosen to work through His church to manifest something of His Kingdom purposes now—in anticipation of that day when Christ returns and the Kingdom is established in its fullness.

He invites us to set aside our lesser agendas and join Him with our whole lives in working for His purposes to bring righteousness, justice, and peace to the earth. He invites us to join with thousands of others all over the world in linking our lives to His loving purposes and discovering that life at its best is life that is given away.

where does God come in?

And in this drama our God is no impotent deity, passive bystander, or national figurehead. He is the Creator and Lord of history who is alive and well and actively at work reconciling all things to Himself. He is active not only in our private lives, but in every aspect of His fallen world. Our confidence is not in the secular providence of the marketplace, in our can-do technology and military hardware nor in the goodness of the human spirit. Our confidence is in the loving God who promises and the compassionate God who acts. You can be sure He will write the final chapter of this story and we will reign with Him forever.

Furthermore, God's good creation is neither a bag of passive resources nor a pantheistic power to be worshiped. But because it is filled with God's presence and directed by His purposes, it is inherently sacred. And it is to be stewarded reverently and justly for all peoples under the reign of the Creator God.

what does it mean to be human?

Under the reign of God, persons are not reduced to economic beings whose worth is derived from our ability to produce or consume. Neither are we innately good; we are part of a fallen creation. But we bear the image of our God, and as a consequence we have innate worth. And we are being redeemed as we turn in faith to Him.

Though we are of this earth, we are also a part of the transcendent dimension that will live forever. And we find our greatest fulfillment not in individually doing our own thing but in living under the reign of God in community with others . . . seeking to be a living foretaste of His kingdom, and redefining the good life as the life that is given away.

which way is up?

Under the reign of God, we are not dependent on Western know-how, a beneficent nature, or a resurgent nationalism. This drama is being written, directed, produced by God and God alone. Though He invites us to be a part of His Story, His kingdom will come whether we do anything or not. (There's nothing "postmillennial" in this drama; it is being implemented solely by His initiative.) But for whatever reason, God has chosen to work through His people to manifest something of His kingdom within history in anticipation of that day when Christ returns and His kingdom fully comes. In that day every knee will bow and every tongue confess that He is Lord.

Do you want a new way of life? Do you want to be all that God intended you to be? Do you want your life to count? Then turn from half-stories and full fictions and make God's Story your story.

Stanley Haverwas reminds us as we come on stage:

> The church is the lively argument extended over centuries occasioned by the stories of God's calling of Israel and the life and death of Jesus Christ to which we are invited to contribute by learning to live faithfully to those stories. For it is the astounding claim of Christians that through this particular man's story we discover our true selves and thus are made a part of God's very life. We become a part of God's story by finding our lives within that story.[14]

---

14. Stanley Haverwas, "The Gesture of a Truthful Story: The Church and Religious Education," *Encounter,* Spring 1982, 321.

We become a part of God's Story by connecting our dreams to a vision that is bigger than we are—a vision that is big enough for the times and world in which we live. Is there any reason you can't put God's dream at the center of your life and aspirations today? To become more fully connected to the purposes of God that are changing the world? To live in anticipation of the establishment of the reign of God?

In the next chapter we will meet a handful of those who have gone before us and who have placed the dream of God and His purposes at the center of their lives. Then in chapter 5 it will be our turn in the footlights, our opportunity to choose to put His vision first.

Welcome to the drama of God! Welcome to life filled with possibilities, creativity, and celebration! Welcome to a future of significance and hope! Welcome to the wedding feast of God!

for thought and discussion

As you reflect on the story of God, ask yourself:

1. What was ruptured in the Fall?
2. What are God's redemptive purposes to set right His fallen world? How can we work for His purposes now?
3. How does God's dream for human future differ from the dreams we discussed in chapter 2? What are some creative ways we might popularize God's dream through music, drama, and the arts until it captures our imaginations and motivates our lives?

Vision of God

life linked to the purposes of God

life direction ▸	linkages ▸	consequences
God's Story makes it clear that He has a dream for His people and His world—and it's not to be found in the clouds! He intends to create a new heaven and new earth in which we will be redeemed as whole persons to participate in His celebrative future of righteousness, justice, and peace. Remarkably, He invites us to make His purposes our purposes.	The first believers—those described in the biblical Story—chose to link their lives not to the aspirations of the culture around them, but to the purposes of God. They chose to seek God's kingdom purposes before anything else in their communities of faith, laboring to see God's righteousness, justice, and peace manifest in this world.	As a direct consequence of linking their lives with the purposes of God, the first Christians discovered the meaning of life. They were involved with the Lord of History in seeing the world changed. And God by His Spirit used this small company to turn the world upside down. They had the satisfaction of seeing God use their lives to make a difference for His kingdom.

chapter four

remembering stories of hope

Remembering! One of the marvelous gifts of human experience is remembering. When we look backwards, we remember who we are and who we are becoming. We recall those tender moments with those we love, and we relish those outrageous carnival moments when we become children again. Even painful memories of loss somehow instruct us and become a part of who we are.

This is true of our personal lives—and also of our collective past. For the road to more significant living begins not only by becoming more fully connected to God's Story, but also by remembering those who have gone before who have sought to live out that Story. For as we saw in the last chapter, the vast drama of God didn't end in the Book of Acts. Each succeeding generation has had its moment in the footlights as the church age marches towards consummation.

By looking backwards and seeing God's drama acted out in history, we are reminded of who we are and who we are called to be. As we remember our Christian past, we are strengthened in our resolve to live out the Story of God with courage and compassion today. We are given heroes we can look up to.

Author Jamie Buckingham recently said that he had asked a group of Christian youth who their favorite heroes were. And they had responded, "Mr. T, Rambo, Spiderman, and Jesus." Jamie expressed relief that Jesus had made the list. But the fact is that the majority of heroes the young look up to these days use violence to accomplish their ends. It's time we help both young and old alike discover a whole new set of heroes out of our Christian past— heroes who use self-giving love instead of violence to accomplish the purposes of God.

85

There are thousands of such heroes. In this chapter, we will meet a small handful.

You will note they are extremely ordinary people . . . possessed by an extraordinary commitment to put God's purposes first in their lives. We will take a remembering journey into some compelling moments from our common past. *The purpose in this chapter is to help us find in the stories of those who have gone before the courage and commitment to follow Christ today, to place His Story and Vision at the very center of our lives so that we can find a way of life that truly counts.*

remembering who we are

When we rummage through the attics of our memories we often come up with some very strange items. For example, I can remember traveling for World Concern to visit some development projects in Bangladesh. Bud and Patti Bylsma, who were directing the work from Dacca, were kind enough to put me up for the night. I had heard that the area had recently experienced the immigration of an awesome population of mosquitoes, some of which carried malaria. So, explaining that mosquitoes adored my body, I asked Bud and Patti if I could borrow some mosquito repellent.

Bud searched around and came up with a tiny dark-green bottle. He said it was the most effective mosquito repellent he had ever found, and he assured me the mosquitoes wouldn't even come into the same room with me if I used the stuff.

He instructed me to rub it thoroughly over all the exposed areas of my body and wished me a good night's rest. I followed his instructions explicitly. As I rubbed it over my arms, I noticed that it developed an interesting white frothy appearance. No matter. I used the whole bottle on my face, neck, arms, and legs.

After a very exhausting day visiting fish ponds, agricultural projects, and rice paddies, I crashed in my hot, muggy room, looking forward to a good night's sleep. But no sooner had I turned out the light than I sensed I was not alone in the bed. A pricking pain in my leg convinced me I was right.

I dispatched the mosquito with one hand and turned the light on with the other. Must have missed a spot! After sighting a couple more mosquitoes flying near the curtains, I did them in, turned out the light, and rolled over to go to sleep again.

Just as I was dozing off I was dive-bombed, submarined, and

blitzkrieged all at the same time. I couldn't believe it. And I didn't seem to be able to stop the attack.

I spent the rest of the night in armed combat—attacking and being attacked. When morning came, the room was a disaster. Bedding everywhere. Blood spots all over the walls and ceiling where I had terminated my unwelcome intruders. My body was a mass of mosquito welts.

Bleary-eyed, alternately slapping and scratching my swollen body, I got dressed for breakfast. When Bud and Patti saw me dragging myself to the breakfast table, they immediately sensed it had been an unusual evening. To their astonishment, I told them of my night-long foray and showed them some of my battle scars.

I handed Bud back his little green bottle and made some unkind remark about reporting the company to the Better Business Bureau. They were completely puzzled. So we went on with breakfast, trying to forget my troubled night and swollen body.

Suddenly a broad smile broke across Bud's face. "I know what happened! Doggone, I completely forgot we used up all the mosquito repellent and I filled that little bottle with shampoo. You made yourself into a gigantic mosquito dessert!" He and Patti almost fell off their chairs, they were laughing so hard.

I was rude. I didn't join in. But as the years have passed I have been able to appreciate the humor in the situation a little more.

Sometimes things appear funnier when you look back on them than they did at the time. A little distance gives us a sharpened perspective, and for this we are all more dependent on the past than we realize.

The Jews were uniquely a people of remembrance and a people of anticipation. They lived in remembrance of God's acts in their past and in anticipation of God's promises for the future. In fact, their entire sense of identity as a people was linked to remembering and looking forward.

Listen to the plaintive cry of Jewish exiles from Psalm 137:

By the rivers of Babylon we sat down; there we wept when we remembered Zion. On the willows nearby we hung up our harps. Those who captured us told us to sing; they told us to entertain them: "Sing us a song about Zion." But how can we sing a song to the Lord in a foreign land? May I never be able to play the harp again if I forget you, Jerusalem!

Of course they didn't forget Jerusalem. And they did eventually
return home to Jerusalem and Zion with incredible joy, dancing,
and feasting. Their strength was in their memory because they
never forgot who they were. And as a consequence they were able
to return home.

If you and I are to come home to all God intends for our lives
and His world, then it is essential that we remember who we are,
too. We must remember not only the stories of Jerusalem and
Zion, but also the other exhilarating, life-directing stories of our
Christian past. There are thousands of such stories whose remembrance would renew our lives and set right our rudders. Here we
have time for only a few.

To help us remember, we are going to take some imaginative
journeys backward in time. The places we will visit are real, as
are the people living there. The stories in which we will participate are based on true accounts of actual happenings in those
people's lives.

If our remembering journeys work as I hope they will, we will
have a small glimpse into the lives of Christians of other days. In
the process, I hope we will be reminded who we are and who we
are called to be. And we will have a fresh awareness of the secret
that lives deep inside of us: We are destined to a better way of
life—better not only for us, but also for all those with whom we
share this world. We are following in the lineage of a great, proud
company of servants and saints who have collaborated with their
God in seeing the world changed.

a remembering journey to a roman tribunal

To get underway, simply set your imagination free, buckle your
seat belt, and prepare to move rapidly backwards in time to the
third century A.D. Our remembering journey has begun. In fact,
look around. We have already arrived. (Sorry. We seem to have
landed in a huge convoy right behind a camel, and he is very
aromatic.)

It's hard to see where we are going, but the rolling countryside
around us is parched, the heat intense. There are children everywhere.

Look over that rise. The front of the caravan seems to be enter-
ing that walled city in the distance. Faint wisps of cloud streak the
bright blue sky, the sun is reflecting off domed roofs, and the walls

give off a soft, golden glow. A narrow column of smoke is rising from a clearing inside the walls. Look at the red poppies by the wall. The camel in front of us is absolutely loaded down with leeks, onions, grapes—and I think those must be olives. (I must be getting used to this place; I can hardly smell that camel at all anymore.)

As we make our way through the gates, the crowd seems to be headed for a large structure at the end of the road. My best guess is that we have landed in a town somewhere in Palestine. On the veranda of the building stands a group of people in chains, waiting.

"In the name of the Emperor Maximinus let the trials begin!" announces a Roman soldier. A portly, toga-clad gentleman seats himself at the table of judgment, and we hear someone behind us whisper that he is Severus, the governor of the province.

As a young man in chains is brought forward, Severus asks him, "What is your name?"

He replies, "My family name is Balsam, but I received the name of Peter in baptism."

Severus: "Of what family and country are you?"

Peter: "I am a Christian."

Severus: "What is your employment?"

Peter: "What employment can I have more honorable, or what better thing can I do in the world, than to live as a Christian?"

Severus: "Do you know the imperial edicts?"

Peter: "I know the laws of God, the sovereign of the universe."

Severus: "You shall quickly know that there is an edict of the most clement of emperors, commanding all to sacrifice to the gods or be put to death."

Peter: "You will also know one day that there is a law of the eternal King, proclaiming that everyone shall perish who offers sacrifice to devils. Which do you counsel me to obey, and which, think you, ought I to choose—to die by your sword, or to be condemned to everlasting misery by the sentence of the great King, the true God?"

Severus: "Since you ask my advice, it is that you obey the edict and sacrifice to the gods."

Peter: "I can never be prevailed upon to sacrifice to gods of wood and stone, as are those which you worship."

Severus: "I would have you know that it is in my power to avenge these affronts by putting you to death."

Peter: "I had no intention of affronting you. I only expressed what is written in the divine law."

During this exchange, the governor grows visibly frustrated. His voice rises a little as he continues: "Have compassion on yourself, and sacrifice."

But Peter answers, "If I am truly compassionate to myself, I ought not to sacrifice."

The governor tries a different tack: "I want to be lenient; I therefore shall allow you time to reflect, that you may save your life."

But once again the young man replies, "This delay will be to no purpose, for I shall not alter my mind; do now what you will be obliged to do soon, and complete the work which the devil, your father, has begun; for I will never do what Jesus Christ forbids me."

Severus, on hearing these words, grows angry and orders Peter to be stretched upon the rack. The crowd murmurs as soldiers suspend the young Christian on a wooden instrument nearby. Then the governor says scoffingly to him, "What say you now, Peter; do you begin to know what the rack is? Are you yet willing to sacrifice?"

And Peter answers, "Tear me with hooks, and talk not of my sacrificing to your devils; I have already told you that I will sacrifice only to that God for whom I suffer."

Hereupon the governor commands Peter's torture to be intensified. But the young man, instead of crying out, sings out some verses from the Scriptures: "One thing I have asked of the Lord; this will I seek after: that I may dwell in the house of the Lord all the days of my life. I will take the chalice of salvation, and will call upon the name of the Lord."

The spectators, seeing Peter's blood run down in streams, cry out to him, "Obey the emperors! Sacrifice, and rescue yourself from these torments!"

But Peter replies, "Do you call these torments? I feel no pain; but this I know, that if I be not faithful to my God, I must expect real pain, such as cannot be conceived."

The judge threatens, "Sacrifice, Peter Balsam, or you will be sorry."

Peter: "Neither will I sacrifice, nor shall I be sorry."

Severus: "I am on the point of pronouncing sentence."

Peter: "It is what I most earnestly desire."

And so Severus dictates Peter's sentence in this manner: "It is our order that Peter Balsam, for having refused to obey the edict of the invincible emperors, and obstinately defending the law of a crucified man, be himself nailed to a cross."

They lead Peter away, his head uplifted, to face the same death his Lord had known. . . . [1]

Peter Balsam is just one of thousands of Christians in those early years who was asked to lay down his life for his Lord. He was crucified over two hundred years after the crucifixion of the One he so faithfully followed, whose story he fully embraced.

a remembering journey to the family of hy

Ready for another trip? We're going to about 565 A.D. this time, and I recommend you bring a coat; our remembering journey will take us north.

Well, here we are. Don't be alarmed. This cowhide and wicker boat is completely safe, and it sure beats following a camel!

I think those guys in the back of the boat want us to row, too; they are handing us round wooden paddles. Behind us is a rugged coastline banked with large cumulus clouds. We are surrounded by rough choppy seas. And we seem to be heading for that small island over there, though the irregular course of our boat makes it unclear where we are headed. (I'm sure our rowing has something to do with that.)

My best guess is that we are off the coast of Scotland somewhere. Notice it's considerably cooler than Palestine. The island we are slowly approaching couldn't be much more than three miles long. It's relatively flat except for that huge rock outcropping at the north end shaped like a loaf of bread. The entire island, including the sides of the outcropping, appear to be upholstered in a luxurious shamrock-green velvet.

Remarkably the clouds have been left behind us. And this isle is framed in singular beauty against the expansive cloudless blue sky. One can sense something special about the place.

Look out! We almost hit those rocks. Now you can see a small collection of stick-and-stone wattle huts just to the right of the primitive harbor where we appear to be heading. Looks like they have a welcoming party to greet us. They look friendly. And they appear to be wearing some type of coarse, brown, woven robes.

The welcome couldn't be warmer. Several of them have run into

---

1. Based on Herbert Thurston and Donald Attwater, eds., *Butler's Lives of Saints,* vol. 1 (New York: P. J. Kenedy & Sons, 1956), 26–27.

the cold surf and almost capsized the boats getting us ashore. We find ourselves being embraced by these friendly, rough-clad greeters. (We almost seem to get a little whiff of camels again.)

We are ushered to their largest dwelling, a very basic round structure of mud and thatch. But marvelous aromas greet us as we enter. As our eyes become accustomed to the seal-oil light, we see a rough wooden table laden with food—joints of mutton, roasted fish, wild berries, pitchers of milk, barley loaves, and fresh butter. They have been expecting us, though they don't understand who we are. They treat us like royalty. And I think they call themselves the family of Hy.

After dinner we are invited to worship. To our amazement, we don't go to a chapel or some type of a crude sanctuary; we climb the huge rock outcropping we had seen from the boat. At the top we have a spectacular view of the Scottish coastline on one side and the Atlantic Ocean on the other. In this outdoor setting, one can sense that these people's spirituality is inseparably related to creation itself.

A man named Columba, whom we have learned is the head of this unusual family, gestures for us to form a large circle. He then leads us in a simple liturgy of chanting, reading, and song. The songs are particularly moving; the family sings with such evident joy they almost break into dancing. Then, as the sun begins to set over the isle of Iona, Columba raises his large hands and all heads bow. As he prays passionately in his rhythmic Gaelic dialect, one can sense that this is a special place of God's favor.

Morning comes early, and after a brief breakfast of barley cakes and milk, Columba and two other brothers escort us back to the harbor and join us in the cowhide boat. We cross the choppy water to the mainland, then trudge over the rough terrain until we come to a village of Picts.

With one of the brothers translating for him, Columba preaches the gospel to the villagers. Immediately an entire family believes, and he baptizes them in a stream nearby. Shortly afterward, we say goodbye, and our small party journeys on.

Several days later, while staying in a village miles up the coast, we receive a report that the son of the household which had been converted had been seized by a severe illness and died suddenly. When the boy became ill, magicians in the community began to taunt the boy's parents and belittle the Christian God as too weak to intervene.

When Columba hears what has happened, he says that we must return.

We arrive just as the parents are performing the funeral rites. Columba interrupts the funeral service and asks to be taken to the boy's dead body. He enters the dwelling alone, tears streaming down his face. From where we are standing outside, we can hear him say, "In the name of the Lord Jesus Christ, be restored to life and stand up." And a few minutes later he reappears, leading the child by the hand. The boy's parents cry out and run to embrace their son, and then a shout arises from the people.

Mourning is turned into rejoicing—the God of the Christians is glorified. Unfortunately, we aren't able to stay around to watch Columba deal with the magician. . . . [2]

Columba and his followers not only carried the good news of the sacred story from Iona to Scotland but to England and much of Europe. This aggressive Celtic Christianity brought the joy and vitality of God's Story wherever they went.

a remembering journey
to the bishop's palace in arezzo

Our next remembering journey takes us south and some six hundred years into the future. The year is 1289, and the climate is definitely warmer.

We find ourselves seated in the splendor of a palace somewhere in Italy. Above us soar high vaulted ceilings. Around us, elegant furnishings announce that we are in a place of wealth and power.

Look, that man coming in that large door—he's dressed like a bishop. As he settles his frame in a large chair, a visitor is announced: Margaret of Cortona. As she enters the chamber, the contrast between the two people is striking; her clothing is as simple as the bishop's costume is extravagant. But it is clear that this Bishop William of Arezzo takes this Margaret of Cortona very seriously.

She explains to him that she comes as an emissary from God. She has received a warning from Him that the bishop should cease strife with other powerful men in his diocese and thus avert war.

The bishop listens respectfully as Margaret delivers her message, but he shakes his head heavily as she is escorted out. What she had to say was not what he wanted to hear.

---

2. Based on Adoman, *Life of Columba* (London: Thomas Nelson, 1961).

But just who is this Margaret of Cortona who speaks so confidently to a bishop? We walk around the palace until we find a clerk painstakingly transcribing a document. He tells us that three years ago the bishop granted Margaret a charter enabling her to work for the sick and the poor on a permanent basis. And he doesn't need much encouragement to lay down his pen and tell us what he has heard about this remarkable woman's background.

It seems that Margaret was not always a woman who walked closely with God and cared for others. She was the attractive daughter of a farmer in Tuscany. A dashing young man from Montepulciano induced Margaret to run away with him, promising to marry her. And I am sure you can guess what happened—he never kept his promise.

Margaret lived with him as his mistress and bore one son. Then one day the young man failed to return from touring his estates, and his dog led Margaret to the shallow grave where his murdered master had been buried.

The tragic event totally upset Margaret's world and confronted her with the judgment of God. She turned her life back to the Creator, and two Franciscan priests became her fathers in Christ. But that was only the beginning of the struggle.

For the next three years, Margaret went through turbulent battles with temptations and depression. On one of these occasions, she said, "Father, do not ask me to come to terms with this body of mine, for I cannot afford it. Between me and my body there must needs be a struggle till death."

Initially Margaret earned her living by nursing the affluent women in the city. But eventually she gave up this work to have more time for prayer and the care of the poor. She began to subsist on alms and handouts. Any unbroken food she got she gave to the poor.

After her son was sent to school in Arezzo, one of Margaret's deepest prayers was answered; she was invited to become a member of the third order Franciscans. And from that time her prayer life soared. From time to time she even received prophetic insights from God such as the one she just delivered to Bishop William. At this point, however, the clerk shakes his head—just as the bishop did. Margaret has gained respect for her good works, he tells us, but perhaps she is going too far. She is becoming controversial, and some have even begun to question her conversion.

We thank the clerk and take our leave of the palace, but we linger awhile in the town. We talk to many who are convinced

Margaret of Cortona is a woman of God—others who are skeptical. And we learn that the town is astir because the bishop is preparing for war. . . .

If we had stayed a little longer, we would have heard the news that the bishop had been killed in battle—ten days after Margaret delivered her message. And we would have seen Margaret's ministry continue to grow. For God led Margaret into a public ministry of evangelism, reconciliation, and healing that not only confirmed what God had done in her life, but demonstrated how God can use an ordinary person in extraordinary ways. Through the ministry of this single mother, God called wrongdoers to repentance, reconciled those who were alienated from one another, attacked public vice, healed the sick, and preached good news to the poor.

Hardened sinners flocked to Cortona from Spain, France, and other parts of Italy to hear Margaret preach. Not only did countless numbers come to faith in Christ, but even the character of the town of Cortona changed as they began to acknowledge the reign of God in their midst.

As Margaret of Cortona placed the purposes of God at the center of her life, I think you will agree she found her role in His Story and it did make a difference.[3]

a remembering journey to a bible study in belgium

We are headed north again about three hundred years into the future. You can almost sense the landscape changing as we travel into the night.

I'm not sure where we've landed this time; it's too dark to see. But it's quite warm; it feels like springtime. And there are some flickering lights over to the right. Let's go over there. Our eyes gradually adjust to the darkness as we approach an old mill. Then the door opens. People are leaving, extinguishing their lamps to walk through the night. Let's follow that family that's headed for town from this clandestine Bible study.

Birds begin to call to one another from darkly sculptured oak trees as Maeyken Wens and her husband, Matthews, both of whom were leading Bible studies, hurry home with their children. No sooner do they get to their tiny home in an ancient building

---

3. Based on *Butler's Lives of the Saints,* vol. 1, 397–398.

in Antwerp than Matthews has to go to work. He hides his Bible under the bed, grabs a crust of bread and his mason's tools, kisses Maeyken warmly, and leaves.

Maeyken plays with her three-year-old, Hans—chasing him, catching him, hugging him, and making him laugh uproariously. Fifteen-year-old Adriean and his sister fix themselves and us some breakfast of bread and cheese. Maeyken finally calms her chunky three-year-old, gives him some milk and bread, and puts him to bed in an old basket.

She picks up her Bible and hides it under her cloak, hugs her two older children, and heads for the door. She stops as she gets out into the street, looks cautiously both ways, and proceeds north up the narrow, cobblestoned roadway. We follow a short distance behind her.

Look. There's another woman joining her with a bulge under her stole. I can't believe it. Apparently, it's Bible study time again—but they've been up all night studying the Bible. I don't know how Maeyken does it; she has remarkable energy.

Two more people join the parade, and they seem to be headed for that shop at the next corner. A group gathers in front, welcoming Maeyken and the others as they arrive.

Oh, my God! Soldiers. They swoop down from nowhere and surround the entire group. Where are they taking them? Let's try to keep them in sight.

They seem to be heading for that huge castle. They are dragging the women inside and taking away their Bibles.

Anabaptists. That's who these people are. They have the unique distinction of being persecuted by both Protestants and Catholics.

Let's wait here out of sight. The word must have reached the community; here comes Maeyken's family. Matthews is holding Betteken's hand, and Adriean is carrying Hans. They are obviously troubled, and Matthews looks ill. He must be risking his own life to visit his wife.

After a long delay, the family is finally given permission to visit Maeyken in the Steen prison. We follow them in. She is elated to see her small family. She reaches her slender fingers through the lattice of the cell door to touch each of her three children. Little Hans sticks his arm through the lattice for his mother to kiss.

There seems to be no fear in Maeyken's voice, and she is obviously encouraging her husband and other children to maintain their faith whatever happens. We are ushered out of that dark,

smelly hole as the prison suddenly becomes alive with the powerful music of women's voices singing a hymn of praise.

Now we jump ahead just a little bit in time. Maeyken's family
has kept hoping and praying for the release of their mother and
her friends, but nothing has happened. And now they learn that
Maeyken has been sentenced to death because she will not recant
her personal faith in Jesus Christ.

Matthews is overcome by grief; he cannot bring himself to attend his wife's execution. But young Adriean feels he must go.
Leaving his sister and father behind, he takes little Hans by the
hand, and they slowly make their way to the central square in
Antwerp.

Look. They are already putting the stakes in the ground, and a
huge throng is forming. Adriean and Hans have no sooner found
a place to sit than the jailers bring in five prisoners, including
Maeyken. She walks resolutely toward the stake, her face beaming,
but she says nothing. The jailers have put a tongue screw through
her tongue so that she cannot speak nor witness her faith to the
crowd. As she is tied to the stake and wood is heaped up around,
Adriean is overwhelmed by the horror of what is happening. He
crumples to the ground and blacks out.

Some time later, Adriean regains consciousness and looks
around. The square is almost completely empty now. Hans stands
there quietly watching him. He looks at the stake and sees nothing
but a pile of smoldering ashes. His mother is gone. He sits and
weeps uncontrollably while Hans tries to console him. Finally, he
picks up a stick and digs through the ashes. All he can find is the
iron tongue screw, which he wraps in a handkerchief to remember
his mother's courage.

When Adriean gets back home, he finds a letter his mother had
written to him:

O my son, though I am taken from you here, strive from your
youth to fear God, and you shall have your mother again up yonder
in the New Jerusalem, where parting will be no more. My dear son,
I hope to go before you; follow me in this way as much as you value
your soul, for besides this there can be no other way to salvation.
So I will now commend you to the Lord; may he keep you. I trust
the Lord that he will do it, if you seek Him. Love one another all
the days of your life; take Hansken on your arm now and then for
me. And if your father should be taken from you, care for one another. The Lord keep you one and all. My dear children, kiss one

another once for me, for remembrance. Adieu, my dear children, all of you. . . . [4]

Anabaptists such as the Wenses were just one example of Christians who suffered for their beliefs during the turbulent period called the Reformation (1517–1648). By the end of this time, the Christian world had been turned upside down, and Europe had been split in half between Catholics and Protestants—not to mention dissenting groups of Protestants.

On a recent trip to Europe, I found the church in which my grandfather's grandfather was married in 1780. The church, constructed in 1730, is actually two churches—one Catholic and one Protestant, with a common roof and a common bell tower. In my mind, this church symbolizes what happened to Christendom as a result of the Reformation. The church was no longer monolithic and unified, but divided into many different expressions of faith. And yet, the Story of God remains one Story.

Although the Reformation did bring turmoil and suffering and division to the church, it also brought renewal and reform. And of course, the spirit of reform and renewal didn't end in the seventeenth century. Over the years, groups such as Moravians, Methodists, and many others attempted to give fresh expression to the faith of their fathers and mothers. And although their efforts often alienated them from traditional expressions of Christianity, they also brought renewal and reform to God's people.

a remembering journey to newgate prison

Now we will take still another journey forward in time. This has to be the industrial age! All around us is noise and bustle, and that building over there looks like a foundry.

Where are we? From the architecture and the clothes people are wearing, I would guess in England—London, probably—in the early 1800s.

It *is* London—that forbidding compound over there has a sign that identifies it as the infamous Newgate Prison. And look. There's a solitary young woman walking up to the massive prison

---

4. Myron Augsburger, *Faithful Unto Death: Fifteen Young People Who Were Not Afraid to Die for Their Faith* (Waco, TX: Word Books, 1975), 85–91.

gates. She doesn't look as if she belongs here; she's well-dressed and carrying a Bible. And she's asking for an audience with the prison governor. What could she have to say to him?

When the governor appears, the woman introduces herself as Elizabeth Fry. And then she asks in gentle Quaker accents: "Sir, if thee kindly allows me to pray with the women, I will go inside." (To tell the truth, after our last adventure, I am more than a little inclined to avoid prisons. But let's follow her, anyway.)

The smell hits us even before our eyes become accustomed to the dark. And then we see them—three hundred women prisoners and their children, blinking back at us. They are dressed in rags, thin and sickly-looking from trying to exist in four basement rooms with no beds or adequate sanitation. A filthy old woman with crazed eyes yells and snatches at our clothing as we pass.

Elizabeth Fry stands before us absolutely overcome at what she has discovered hidden away in the brutal bowels of Newgate. She says a feeble prayer as the women and children stare at their unlikely visitor. And then she escapes back into the streets.

Back out in the bright light and fresh air, Elizabeth hurries briskly away, dabbing a handkerchief at her eyes. But then she walks more slowly and even turns her head for another look at the forbidding walls. It is clear that something—or Someone—is calling her back. . . .

Elizabeth Fry accepted God's challenge to go back to Newgate Prison. Though a busy wife and mother, she joined with other Quakers in 1816 to found the Association for the Improvement of Female Prisoners in Newgate. And of course she undertook personal risk to work directly with the women prisoners.

The initial goals were modest: to try to clean up the abominable living conditions and provide the women with clothing, employment, and instruction. Elizabeth herself personally instituted a Bible study program to help these women understand that God's love is extended to everyone regardless of class or station. Many women prisoners were powerfully moved as she read the Scriptures, and many came to faith in Jesus Christ. And Elizabeth Fry's faithfulness to God's call spawned a sweeping movement of prison reform that would touch lives in institutions in Europe, Australia, and America.

As Elizabeth's ministry of prison reform blossomed, her husband's business failed, and they had to learn to live much more modestly. But she found she was more comfortable with a simpler way of life, because she believed luxurious living was a serious threat to the spirit.

On her deathbed, Elizabeth Fry reflected on the drama of God in which she had played a part: "I can say one thing—since my heart was touched . . . I believe I never have awakened from sleep, in sickness or in health, by day or night, without my first waking thought being how best I might serve my Lord."[5]

a remembering journey to wheaton college

Our final journey takes us a little further into the future and across the Atlantic Ocean. The same winds of the Spirit that have stirred Elizabeth Fry, William Wilberforce, and John Wesley in England have stirred up a Great Awakening on this continent, stirred by the preaching of Charles Finney. People are coming to radical faith in Jesus Christ and are committing themselves to change the world of which they are a part. Slavery, alcohol, and war are all under attack by this generation of born-again Christians.

Let's take one last trip to an American city in the 1800s. It is a cold, blustery October day. From the layout of this city I would guess we have landed in Chicago. But I must be wrong; this looks like a war zone. Scarcely a building is left standing. Smoldering ruins everywhere. People huddling together trying to keep warm. Families cooking over campfires on the sidewalks.

And the street scene looks like a reenactment of the Exodus. Wagons bulging with belongings. Children perched perilously on top. Masses of people with bundles on their backs.

All the wagons, donkey carts, and people are going in one direction—out of town, away from this chaos. But wait! There's a solitary wagon with a lanky driver doing his best to come *into* town. People seem oblivious to his efforts, but somehow his persistence is paying off. He's getting through.

Some of the families cooking over the campfires spot him and start running toward the wagon. The driver pulls up his wagon into a clearing and immediately starts passing out food and milk to the homeless. They almost turn his wagon upside down as he passes out the last parcel.

---

5. Elliot Wright, *Holy Company: Christian Heroes and Heroines* (New York: Macmillan Press, 1980), 120–123.

The year is 1871. The tragedy is the great Chicago fire. The determined driver is Jonathan Blanchard, president of Wheaton College—a man whose entire life has been committed to God's kingdom purposes and a driving determination to make a difference. . . .

This is a man who once declared, "Every true minister of Christ is a universal reformer, whose business it is, so far as is possible, to reform all evils which press on human concerns." Blanchard fully realizes that one "cannot construct a perfect society out of imperfect men," but he has argued that "every reformer needs a perfect state of society ever in his eye, as a pattern to work by, so as far as the nature of his materials will admit."[6] Little did Jonathan Blanchard realize, when he said this, how his vision for the kingdom of God would impact the direction of his own life, let alone the lives of countless others.

Again and again, Blanchard found his life as a Christian propelled him into a life of reform. He became active in the abolitionist movement, eloquent in advocacy of the poor, firm in opposition to intemperance and war "and whatever else shall clearly appear to contravene the kingdom and the coming of our Lord Jesus Christ."[7]

In 1860 Jonathan Blanchard accepted the invitation to be president of Wheaton College. He later said, "I came to Wheaton in 1860, still seeking 'a perfect state of society' and a college 'for Christ and His kingdom.'"[8]

Blanchard understood that we are called to be a part of God's work in establishing His reign in history. In fact, he once defined the kingdom of God as "Christ ruling in and over rational creatures who are obeying Him freely and from choice, under no constraint but love."[9]

back to the present—and the future

Welcome back to the present. We have at least as many needs, challenges, and opportunities in our world as anything Peter

---

6. Ibid., 9.
7. Donald W. Dayton, *Discovering An Evangelical Heritage* (New York: Harper & Row, 1976), 12.
8. Ibid., 12.
9. Ibid., 10.

78237

Balsam, Columba, Margaret of Cortona, Maeyken Wens,
Elizabeth Fry, or Jonathan Blanchard faced in theirs. But do
we have their vision for the kingdom of God? Are we taking God's
Story and agenda for action as seriously as they did? Have we
placed the transforming purposes of God's kingdom at the center
of our lives and congregations?

As we return from our remembering journey, our minds are
flooded with images and memories of those who had the courage
to place God's vision first in their lives. Obviously, there is much
that can nurture and challenge us as we remember the stories of
our Christian past. For in these stories and thousands of others
we have our legacy: We locate our lives in relationship not only
to the Story of God, but to the history of a people. And we are
members not only of an international community, but of a historical movement that has its origin in the redemptive initiative
of God.

for thought and discussion

*Bottom line. What does it all mean for us today? What have these
stories to do with our stories? Well, before we can really go on to the
next chapters, which help you to discover your role in the Story of
God, we need to answer some questions:*

1. What are some specific choices the people in this chapter
    made to place God and His Story first in their lives?
2. How did placing the Story of God at the center of their lives
    alter their life direction and impact the world around them?
3. In what ways have these stories challenged you to link your life
    to the purposes of God? Give specific examples.

life links

chapter 4

life direction ▶	**linkages** ▶	**consequences**
God's Story is an ongoing story, and His vision has captured the imaginations and commitment of people in all generations. As Christians through the centuries have sought to put His purposes first, they have become a part of the unfolding vision of God's restoring all things to Himself.	Our Christian past is filled with the stories of tens of thousands who have chosen to link their lives to the purposes of God. Their stories challenge us to follow their example—and invite us to join them in placing God's purposes first.	Our forebears not only discovered life with meaning; by God's Spirit, their lives also made a difference! They dramatically changed the landscape of our common past as a foretaste of all God plans to do in our promised future. And as we follow their example, our lives, too, can make a difference.

choosing a life
that counts

Choosing! One of the exciting and risky gifts of our humanity is choice. God gave that gift to our first parents. And they chose to turn their backs on their Creator and all He intended for their lives.

The history of the children of Israel is a history of a rebellious people who chronically struggled with the choice as to whether to serve God and receive His promised future or go their own way.

Christ came inviting people to choose to set aside their lesser dreams and join Him in embracing the dream of the Father, who promised to make all things new. And over the centuries, as we have seen, many made the choice to follow Christ, welcoming the inbreaking of the future of God.

Every day you and I are confronted by countless choices. But none is more important than the decision to follow this Christ and wholeheartedly embrace His world-changing vision.

Remarkably, there are many who have accepted Christ into their hearts but have never embraced Christ's vision for a world made new. But can we really be satisfied with the American dream and church on Sundays once we have understood something of God's loving purposes? We are called to a better dream and a better way of life.

The purpose of this chapter is to persuade you to choose to set aside lesser dreams and place the vision of God at the very center of your life, discovering how through whole-life discipleship you can live out the joyous presence of God's Story in the world.

There are three major steps we must take if we are to become something of the presence of God's Story in the world: (1) We need to choose to become whole-life disciples; (2) We need to choose to invest in a life of spirituality and prayer; and (3) We need to choose to become a part of a loving community of God's people. These choices will be the format of this chapter.

You see, we are not only invited to accept Christ into our hearts. We are challenged, like those who have come before us, to accept His Story and Vision into the core of our lives. And that will probably mean choosing to relinquish some of the false visions, values, and stories with which we have been raised.

a word from tony

When I think of stories, I always think of Tony Campolo—he's full of them. One of the things I dread worse than walking barefoot on broken bottle-glass is having to follow Tony Campolo in a speaking situation. The major reason is that he is absolutely bursting at the seams with stories, humorous anecdotes, and one-liners.

Once, while working with Tony at a church conference in the Midwest, I confessed my dread to him. I told him I thought he was the evangelical answer to Don Rickles—with substance, minus the insults. He's even got a delivery like Rickles's. I explained that I hated following him because I don't have all the marvelous humorous material he does.

His sympathetic response was immediate, "I will give you a story."

I asked hesitatingly, "Is it true?"

"Of course it's true," he replied.

Tony explained that he was flying from his home in Philadelphia to be the keynote speaker at a youth conference. Busily working on his notes on the plane, he suddenly found he was having difficulty breathing. A horrendous smell filled the cabin. It smelled as if the plane were on fire.

Tony immediately stood up and looked around to see what was happening. There on the other side of the aisle in the non-smoking section was a very large man with an even larger cigar putting out clouds of putrid blue cigar smoke.

Tony said, "Being the brave guy that I am, I immediately called the flight attendant and asked her to talk to this joker."

The attendant gave the man the standard spiel, requesting that he go to the back of the plane if he wanted to smoke and reminding him that cigar smoking is not allowed anywhere on the plane.

The portly man didn't respond; he just rudely blew cigar smoke in the attendant's face. She walked off in a miff.

Tony decided not to make an issue of it. He simply took a deep breath, tried to hold it until they landed, and went back to preparing his address. Fifteen minutes later, there came another flight attendant rushing down the aisle with a trayful of hot drinks. She had not talked to the first attendant and had no idea what had happened.

Just as she reached the point in the plane at which the confrontation had taken place, the plane hit an air pocket and dropped fifty feet. The tray of hot drinks went up in the air and came right down on the rude man, dousing his cigar. He jumped up screaming.

The stewardess fell backwards and landed right in Tony Campolo's lap, who was instantly ready with a one-liner. He exclaimed, "And people say there's no God."

The point of this chapter—and this book—is that there *is* a God—and that God has a plan not only for our lives, but for His world. If we want to discover how to live significant, satisfying lives that make a difference, it isn't enough simply to live out the stories and aspirations with which we were raised. It isn't enough simply to try to live up to the expectations of family, community, and church with a little faith worked in around the edges. We must make the conscious choice to embrace God's dream as our dream . . . God's purposes as our purposes.

a retrospective look at the future

Let's briefly recap the ground we've covered together thus far. We were reminded in chapter 1 of how busy and frenetic our lives have become, lacking a clear sense of direction and purpose. And deep down we all long to have our lives count for something.

But we live in a world, as we discussed in chapter 2, that is filled with dreams and stories that would claim our lives and energy. We have been raised with notions of the better future that have much more to do with "catching the escalator to the Land of Evermore" than with any biblical vision. And too many have misunderstood the biblical vision as "soul rescue" for a disembodied existence in the clouds.

That's why in chapter 3 we reviewed the panoramic drama of the Story of God as told in the Bible. We were reminded that God is not interested in rescuing our disembodied souls for the clouds. His loving intention is to redeem us as whole persons to be a part of His new heaven and new earth. And God's purpose is to create a new society of righteousness, justice, and peace in which He reigns with His people forever.

In the last chapter we met a handful of ordinary people who in their own time and season not only accepted Christ into their hearts, but devoted their lives to working for His loving purposes in their world. Without exception, their lives made a difference as they became living representatives of God's kingdom in their own society.

a whole-life discipleship

So now it's our turn in the footlights. What does it mean to follow this visionary Jesus today? What will happen if we accept Jesus into our hearts and accept His vision of the present and coming kingdom into our lives?

For one thing, our understanding of what it means to be a disciple is likely to be radically altered.

A surprisingly large number of American Christians have succumbed to a compartmentalized discipleship and a privatized piety. We have compartments in our lives for work, family, recreation, leisure time, vacations, and shopping. And, of course, we have one little compartment for church, discipleship, and spiritual life. But in all honesty, the so-called "secular" compartments tend to dominate our lives, and we Christians are virtually indistinguishable from our non-Christian neighbors.

Those of us who have narrowed God's redemptive activity to that of rescuing our disembodied souls have particularly tended to trivialize what it means to be a disciple and minimize the scope of what God is doing in our world.

You see, in the popular understanding of what it means to be a Christian, Christ comes in and transforms our hearts—the spiritual compartment of our lives. And, of course, He heals our psychological hang-ups and even gives us a little hand with our dispositions and relationships. But our fundamental life direction and life values are set by the visions and values of our secular American culture.

For example, what is our life direction before we become Christian? Upward mobility! What is our life direction after we become Christians? Upward mobility—except God is there to help us become more successful in our high-altitude scrambling!

And what were our values before we became Christians? Materialism, individualism, and looking out for number one! What were our values after we became Christians? Exactly the same. In fact, we have found an amazing array of ways to sanctify and rationalize our greed, autonomy, and self-interest by embracing the gospel of success and prosperity. (Ben Franklin, inventor of the success gospel, once wrote, "Reason is a wonderful thing because one can always find a reason for whatever it is that one wants to do.")

In fact, a disappointingly large number of Christian books, broadcasts, and sermons seem to encourage this limited view of discipleship by accepting the visions and values of American culture as an unquestioned given. By default we allow the secular culture to set the agenda for all the "non-spiritual" compartments of our lives. And then we try to work our faith in around the edges of already overcrowded lives.

You can be sure that in the first century the disciples of Jesus Christ weren't doing Roman culture nine-to-five with church on Sundays! They understood that following Christ is a whole-life proposition that transforms life direction, values—everything.

Whatever commands our time, energy, and resources commands us. And if we are honest, we will admit that our lives really aren't that different from those of our secular counterparts. I suspect that one of the reasons we are so ineffective in evangelism is that we are so much like the people around us that we have very little to which we can call them. We hang around church buildings a little more. We abstain from a few things. But we simply aren't that different. We don't even do hedonism as well as the folks around us . . . but we keep on trying.

As a result of this unfortunate accommodation, Christianity is reduced to little more than a spiritual crutch to help us through the minefields of the upwardly mobile life. God is there to help us get our promotions, our house in the suburbs, and our bills paid. Somehow God has become a co-conspirator in our agendas instead of our becoming a co-conspirator in His. Something is seriously amiss.

Listen again to the invitation of the Master:

Anyone who wishes to be a follower of mine must leave self behind; he must take up his cross, and come with me. Whoever cares for his own safety is lost; but if a man will let himself be lost for my sake and for the Gospel, that man is safe. What does a man gain by winning the whole world at the cost of his true self? (Mark 8:34–36, NEB).

The message is clear. Either we put His agenda first or we miss it entirely! But we have trouble hearing that. As John Alexander explains,

> Christians spend a lot of time and energy explaining why Jesus couldn't possibly have meant what He said. This is understandable; Jesus is an extremist and we are all moderates. What is worse, He was an extremist in His whole life—not just in the narrowly spiritual areas—but in everything, so we have to find ways to dilute His teaching.[1]

Tragically, in contemporary Christianity we keep finding ways to soften Jesus' radical teaching and ignore His compassionate vision. As a consequence, His vision has very little impact on either our lives or God's world. But thankfully, Christ never gives up. He keeps urging us to set aside our lesser agendas and seek His kingdom first.

The Scripture makes it pretty clear that this business of following Jesus is a whole-life proposition. Listen to Paul's challenge to the Roman Christians:

> Therefore, I urge you, brothers, in view of God's mercy, to offer your bodies as living sacrifices, holy and pleasing to God—which is your spiritual worship. Do not conform any longer to the pattern of this world, but be transformed by the renewing of your mind. Then you will be able to test and approve what God's will is—his good, pleasing and perfect will (Rom. 12:1–2, NIV).

Urging us to give our "bodies to Christ" is simply another way of challenging us to give ourselves totally to God, inviting Christ to renew our minds and transform our values.

Therefore, if we want to discover our role in the drama of God, we won't find it simply by making church on Sundays one compartment in our upwardly mobile scramble. Christ reminds us not to worry about our lives by asking, "'What shall we eat?' or 'What shall we drink?' or 'What shall we wear?' For the pagans run after all these things, and your heavenly Father knows that you need them. But seek first his kingdom and his righteousness, and all these things will be given to you as well" (Matt. 6:33, NIV).

---

1. John Alexander, "Why We Must Ignore Jesus," *The Other Side,* October 1977, 8.

a captivating vision

So all right. We decide to give in and follow Jesus with our total lives and seek His kingdom first. How do we become whole-life disciples?

I believe that in our culturally convenient Christianity we have seriously misunderstood what it means to be a Christ follower. You see, we cannot accept Christ into our hearts without accepting Christ's vision for the future into the very center of our lives. To follow this Jesus, we are called not only to repent of our sins, but to relinquish the illusory dreams with which we have been raised and embrace a new dream.

But how do we discover God's purposes for the human future and our own lives?

First, I believe we need to go back to the Bible. Begin with the prophets. Open Isaiah. Underline every portion that reveals God's loving intentions for His people and His world. Meditate on the passages you underline. Imagine Isaiah's vision becoming a reality today. Pay particular attention to portions such as Isaiah 2:1–4, 65:17–19, 25:6–9, 35:1–10, 61:1–3. Allow yourself to savor the compelling beauty and power of the promised future of God. Ask, "What impact will His compelling future have on the urgent challenges that fill our world today and tomorrow?"

Now, turn to the Gospels. Begin with Luke. Against the rich tapestry of Isaiah's prophetic vision, listen to Jesus as He speaks to us of His Father's kingdom. Watch Him act out its loving intentions—healing the sick, feeding the hungry, and setting free the possessed.

It may help to reread chapter 3 of this book, particularly the portions in which I sketch my sense of the biblical vision. Allow the biblical images to take root deeply in your soul and begin replacing the other dreams and aspirations. Only to the extent that we are captured by the compelling imagery of God's vision will we be able to live out that vision in the culture that surrounds us.

You see, the first call of the kingdom of God is not to action; it's to being. The first call is not to proclamation or to social action, but to incarnation. Christ calls us—in spite of our brokenness—to become quite literally the living presence of His body in the world today. We're to be the living good news that the future of God has broken into human history. Unless we do that, we have no basis on which to speak or act.

The Charismatics are right in that we must be filled with the Spirit of the living God. There's no way we can be whole-life disciples, bearing the fruits of the Spirit, without the Spirit's Christ dwelling in us. But I believe we must also be filled with the vision of the loving God. For it is only as people see the compelling vision of God and the counterculture values of God fleshed out in our lives that they will believe Christ's remarkable claim—that the kingdom of God has broken into our world!

discovering the good life of God

After we begin to allow the vision of God's kingdom to capture our imaginations, we need to encourage it to filter down into our daily lives. How do we do that? The journey towards whole-life discipleship begins when we struggle to translate the vision of God's better future into a whole new understanding of what the good life is all about.

Let's be candid. The rat race is a fraud! It isn't the good life at all. It isn't good for us. It isn't good for our kids. And it certainly isn't good for the poor with whom we share this planet.

Consumerism is not synonymous with happiness. Life is more than bread. Our identity, security, and happiness will never be derived from our possessions and our heroic mountaineering.

As John Alexander points out,

> What appears to be in our self-interest isn't always. In fact, it rarely is. That's a lot of Jesus' message to us. . . . The question Jesus raises is about ultimate concern. We're concerned about things like pleasure, happiness, food and clothing, wealth and power. But Jesus tells us that these things are not of ultimate concern. It's when we do find the things of ultimate concern that other things find their rightful place and life becomes worth living.[2]

And it's in finding the things that *are* of ultimate concern that we discover the doorway into the good life of God. It's a doorway into a lavish garden of serenity and beauty. And we go through that door by reconciling with the God who created us and by learning to delight in our Creator. Through prayer, worship,

---

2. John Alexander, *Your Money or Your Life: A New Look at Jesus' View of Wealth & Power* (New York: Harper & Row, 1986).

communion, and retreat, we reach the point where our lives are no longer centered on self-aspiration. Instead, we choose to center our lives in love, celebration, and intimacy with the sovereign God who has called us.

When we do that, His vision for a world made new and the values of His kingdom slowly become ours. Instead of being obsessed by "making it," we long most of all to see His kingdom blossom and flower in our lives and His world. Instead of struggling to find security in our things, we are moved to trust the Father who makes His verdant garden grow. Instead of living a life of frantic, acquisitive materialism, we are encouraged to slow down, take time for people, enjoy friends and loved ones, and celebrate the splendor of God's creation. Instead of "doing our thing" in splendid American autonomy, we are called into the loving community of God's people. And Jesus tells us that paradoxically, instead of finding life by seeking it, we find it only by losing it.

Even as Jesus was a man for others, we are called to be a people for others. And we will only discover the good life of God when we, like the One we follow, become servants and give our lives away. In fact, we will never find God's better way of life by scaling the heights of society. It is only when we descend into the depths of submission before God and servanthood towards others that we have any hope of really discovering how to have the time of our lives.

For some, this will mean struggling to flesh out the presence of God and His kingdom in suffering and impossible circumstances. God's beauty is often perfected most fully in the lives of those who submit to their God in situations they cannot change.

Mark is a beautiful example of someone who did just that. Before he was dramatically converted to Jesus Christ five years ago, Mark was part of the large gay community in San Francisco. But when he became a Christian, he reoriented his life, married a young woman in the Covenant Church they attended, and became a spiritual leader in the church.

Then, a year and a half ago, Mark discovered he had contracted AIDS in his former life. But he accepted the reality of his situation by God's grace, and went on to carry out an amazing ministry from his hospital bed—bringing others to Christ and encouraging fellow Christians who were struggling with their faith.

Through his sickness and death, Mark was able to be the living presence of Christ's kingdom. Not all of us are called to flesh out the kingdom in tragic circumstances; many of us have a broader

range of choices than he had. But we are all called to represent the
kingdom through our own circumstances—even if that means suffering. But the good news is that our Lord has promised, whatever
the circumstances, that He will give beauty for ashes, and that He
will bring us safely home. And so Mary's prayer must become
ours: "Do to me even as you said" (Luke 1:38).

Graham Kerr (the former Galloping Gourmet) and his wife,
Treena, once had everything this world calls the good life. They
owned a seventy-five-foot yacht, an enormous mansion, a Rolls
Royce, millions of dollars—the whole nine yards. And they were
miserable. They discovered that even opulent wealth does not
bring happiness.

For the Kerrs, accepting Christ was a real comedown in the
material sense. For instance, it meant choosing to give up a highly
successful career, because Graham understood that following
Christ meant a radical change in his values; he could no longer
be the foremost proponent of American hedonism and still follow
Jesus. And so Graham left his career, and Graham and Treena
gave away their riches.

Graham and Treena Kerr invited Christ to transform not only
their hearts, but their values and their life direction too. And
He's doing it. Today they live in a modest home in Tacoma,
Washington, and spend their lives teaching others how to simplify
their lifestyles to advance the gospel of Jesus Christ. They are
many times happier than they ever were in their days of extravagant wealth, because they have discovered that the good life of
God is the life given away.

You see, this business of whole-life discipleship means more
than a little Jesus veneer over the top of our self-involved lives.
We simply can't accept Jesus into our hearts without accepting
His values into the core of our lives.

Jesus really expects us to live out the right-side-up values of
the kingdom in an upside-down world! He really expects us to
go the second mile, turn the other cheek, put others first, forgive
our friends, love our enemies, trust God for everything. He really
expects us to place His cause before everything else. But He also
promises us a new life that is far more satisfying than anything
upscale living can offer us.

an exercise in kingdom values

Inviting Christ to transform our values is so foreign to most of
us that we don't even know where to start. To help you, let me

suggest an exercise you might try in a small group in conjunction with a study of the Gospel of Luke. (You could also try it on your own, but a group study will help you come up with more ideas and help you be more objective about your values.)

(1)   First, before the study begins, have everyone in the group cooperatively list the values of our dominant culture—consumerism, individualism, egocentrism, etc. (You don't have to list them as "isms." Try listing common assumptions such as "I've got to take care of myself first" or "If the TV commercial says I need it, then I need it!")

(2)   Second, have each person privately list, as honestly as possible, to what extent the values of the dominant culture are also his or her values. (You may highly value privacy, for example.)

(3)   Then, as you begin to study the Book of Luke, keep a running list of the values that are reflected in Christ's servant life and expressed in His kingdom teachings—losing life instead of seeking it, going the second mile, putting others first, turning the other cheek, loving our enemies, forgiving our friends, etc.

(4)   As the study concludes, have each person honestly identify which of the values of Christ and His kingdom actually are a part of his or her life, too.

What happens, of course, is that we all wind up on two lists. Then we can begin the difficult and challenging work of inviting God to work with us to transform those values that are antagonistic to His kingdom. To the extent that God changes our values, we become the joyful presence of His new society to those with whom we share community.

Another helpful resource in this process of discovering how to let God transform our values is Donald Kraybills's fine book, *The Upside Down Kingdom.*[3] He asks what our lives would look like if we lived out the Beatitudes. I would strongly recommend finding this book and reading it for a better understanding of how we can make kingdom values our values.

As our lives are captured by God's compelling vision and transformed by His right-side-up values, everything else will begin to change, too—our priorities, our schedules, our politics, our lifestyles. We will move from a compartmentalized discipleship to

---

3. Scottsdale: PA: Herald Press, 1978.

a whole-life discipleship under the reign of God. We will begin to understand that God calls us to a way of life more significant and satisfying than anything the rat race can offer.

adding some celebration to your life

When I conclude a presentation on whole-life discipleship in a church, people frequently ask how they can begin changing their values and their lifestyles. They are expecting me to tell them what they should give up. And they are surprised when first of all I tell them to *add* something to their lives.

I encourage them to begin by adding a little celebration!

One of the reasons the world isn't knocking our door down to find out about Jesus is that, frankly, many of us are a little boring. Tragically, many cults often have more vitality and enthusiasm for their illusory messages than we do for the gospel.

We ought to live lives exploding with joy—as though we actually believe that Jesus Christ rose from the dead! We need to be Christmas, Easter, and the kingdom of God all at the same time to the people around us.

Remember, the Bible describes the kingdom again and again with pictures of hilarity, festivity, and celebration. It describes the sumptuous banquet feast of God, the discovery and sharing of lost treasure, the festivity of harvest, the jubilation of the prodigal's party—and, of course, the unspeakable joy of the wedding celebration of our reigning King.

We're headed for a party to end all parties, so let's start living like it now! We really can do better than James Bond and Trivial Pursuit. We can do better than letting our culture call the tune to which we dance. We can create our own celebrations.

For example, some students at Goshen College recently threw a manna party—everyone had to bring his or her idea of manna. Wouldn't it be interesting to see what they brought?

Another time, students at Trevecca Nazarene College came up with the idea of a biblical masquerade party where people came dressed as their favorite saints as a way of celebrating our Christian past.

We can celebrate the marvelous Jewish festivals in our community. And we also create our own celebrations around biblical themes, from jubilee to the wedding feast of God. Ethnic and religious holidays provide yet other opportunities. Or we can celebrate one another for absolutely no good reason.

The point is: if we are going to be the joyful presence of God's future in our world, then we must give ourselves much more energetically to celebrating the good news that the future of God has broken in among us.

Recently, friends and I created a celebration around the theme of Advent; we called "Advent II: Homecoming." (Advent I, of course, was Christ coming to us. Advent II will be when we go home to be with Christ.) We invited thirty to forty people who didn't really know each other. And we started the evening by asking people to share some of their most vivid memories of homecoming. One brother shared what it was like to come back alive from Vietnam. A young woman shared the welcoming expression she saw in her mother's eyes every time she came home. The stories were wonderful.

Then we read passages from Isaiah that referred to the Jews' coming home from Babylon. We tried to picture ourselves in that long march home, breathing heavily in anticipation of that first glimpse of the city of David. Once we began to picture in our minds that weary but eager crowd of refugees coming home to Jerusalem after so many years, we joined in singing the songs of Zion that we have sung dozens of times before. This time we sang them as captives coming home.

Finally I announced, "Now we are going to dance into the streets of the Holy City." You could see instant terror register in the eyes of these Presbyterians. People who had never moved their bodies in their entire lives began edging towards the exits, but it was too late. The Jewish folk music began, and our instructor led us in dancing into the city of David.

At first you could almost hear peoples' bodies creak, and you could see pained expressions on their faces. But after a few moments they got caught up in the spirit and excitement of coming home—and even got caught up in expressing the joy of the Lord with their bodies.

In the final act of the Story of God, we are taught that the nations will come home to the mountain of the Lord for a wedding celebration to end all celebrations. Therefore, after we were done dancing, we had an international buffet with foods from a host of different countries. Finally, we concluded the evening together by sharing the bread and the wine together—not only to remember the sacrifice of Christ, but to anticipate that wedding feast in which we will eat with our Lord, His kingdom fully come on earth and in heaven. What better cause for some celebration?

the journey within

We don't make this journey into whole-life discipleship by ourselves; our God goes with us. This adventure begins as we encounter Him in prayer, the Eucharist, and the Word. It begins as we encounter Him in the mystery of the bread and the wine and in the quiet place of listening and praying. Only as we hear our God and personally receive His grace is there any possibility of reflecting anything of His joyous Story to the world around us.

Most of us are so incredibly busy we have very little time for prayer or study; it simply isn't a priority among most Christians these days. But if we are to be the presence of God's new future, we must be filled with His loving Spirit. And that is an event and a process that can happen only as we draw close to God in prayer. Only as we realize our own barrenness and turn to Him for life is there any possibility of His kingdom seed's growing within us.

Whole-life discipleship begins by giving priority to prayer, study, and retreat. It begins by finding our confident center in the living God.

The inner journey and the life of prayer has come to mean so many different things to Christians today. For some, it means five minutes of rushed devotions before work. For others, it's simply a table grace shared at meals or an occasional plea for help shot up out of a problem situation.

For many families, the major time of praying together comes at bedtime, when children "say their prayers" and parents listen. You might enjoy this little humorous piece written by my sister-in-law, Karen Sine, about children's night prayers, in a Catholic family:

> Children pray "Matthew, Mark, Luke, and John, bless this bed that I lie on," and the evangelists, abruptly summoned from rapture, dash wildly to earth for bed blessing. On the way they dodge flights of angels and assorted saints. Between the hours of eight and nine at night, when the children say their prayers, Christianity is an extremely hectic religion.
>
> The Medieval philosophers have suffered considerable snide criticism for wasting their time estimating how many angels could dance on the head of a pin. The climate of modern thought does not support the spectacle of any angels whatever, let alone merry ones dancing. Yet there they are on a hot night, roosting on bedposts in a cluttered room with a gang of saints, taking notes:
>
> "Please find my walrus, Boomer. I can't go to sleep without him." That's an easy one. Get St. Anthony for the walrus.

"Bless the whales." Whales? Who's got whales? Oh, good ole Jonah, he hates whales. Give the whales to Jonah.

". . . all the ships at sea and the planes in the air." Elmo, Christopher, Raphael. That should do it.

"And bless our country." Where are we? Oh, anybody here got the United States? Yes, all of it. (Powers, thrones, dominions take the U. S.) Good luck.

"Bless the bad people and get their heads chopped off." Hmm. Sounds like Simon Peter. He likes whacking people.

"Bless our house." Cuthman? No, you have churches. Joseph, you take the house like a good fellow, and do something about that porch. Somebody is going to get killed.

"And bless Mommy and Daddy." Silence. The archangels shrink from parenthood. They stare appraisingly at the saints who shuffle, sneeze, cough, rattle, blush, shrug and check one another for lint. Hilary? Charles? Cosmas or Damien?

Pass.

How about you, Francis? You always liked martyrdom. I've got sharks this week. You take them. But it's only two people this time, a man and a woman. Happily married, too. Fear not.

Ha. That's what they all say.

Now, who had Mommy and Daddy last time? Nobody since Christopher, and he's been defrocked; lost his feast day over it. I'm not going to take them. Something always happens. Every night the same old thing? How about God the Father? (Wild applause). Well done, Aquinas! That settles it. Mothers and fathers to God Almighty. Lights flick out. A child sighs to sleep, clutching a wet walrus St. Anthony found in the vaporizer.[4]

However one feels about saints, angels, or parenthood, children's bedtime prayers can be valuable as the beginning of a lifetime prayer habit. And they can remind us that we are encouraged to come to God about every need in our lives, as well as the needs of others.

But, of course, there is much more to prayer than just petitioning—asking God for things for ourselves or someone else. It is also a matter of contemplation, meditation, and solitude.

In my opinion we have a lot to learn in this regard from our Catholic friends, who have a long history of emphasizing these things. But as I travel around the United States, I find that Protestants, too, are experiencing a growing hunger for a much

---

4. Karen Sine, "Night Prayers," an unpublished manuscript, 1–4.

deeper spirituality. Books by Henri Nouwen, Thomas Merton, and
Richard Foster—all advocates of contemplation and spiritual discipline—are becoming increasingly common on Protestant book-
shelves. Courses on spirituality in Presbyterian churches on the
West Coast are packed. I am convinced this reflects a growing
longing by both Protestants and Catholics to be much more pro-
foundly linked to their God and His Story for their lives.

Thomas Merton writes,

> The union of the Christian with Christ is a mystical union in which
> Christ Himself becomes the source and principle of life in me. Christ
> Himself . . . "breathes" in me divinely in giving me His Spirit.[5]

And Henri Nouwen explains,

> There is probably no image that expresses so well the intimacy with
> God in prayer as the image of God's breath. . . . We receive a new
> breath of freedom, a new life. This new life is the divine life of God
> Himself. Prayer, therefore, is God breathing in us, by which we be-
> come part of the intimacy of God's inner life and by which we are
> born anew.
>   So the paradox of prayer is that it asks for serious effort while
> it can only be received as a gift. We cannot plan, organize or manip-
> ulate God, but without a careful discipline we cannot receive Him
> either.[6]

A growing number of Christians are realizing that if their lives
are to genuinely become a part of God's Story, they must first
become a part of God's life. And the receiving of the gift of God's
life requires a lot more discipline than most of us know anything
about. It means more than quickly praying, "God bless Mom and
Dad" and off to bed or work. We must develop a life of prayer
centered in God.

a modest proposal for a life of prayer

If we are serious about becoming whole-life disciples—the living presence of God's kingdom—we must take significant time for
prayer. Right now I am in a nine-month program in spirituality

---

5. Quoted in Henri Nouwen, *Reaching Out* (New York: Doubleday, 1975), 89.
6. Nouwen, *Reaching Out,* 89.

that is really helping me get some movement in my spiritual life again. Out of that experience, let me outline some beginning suggestions for a discipline for your life:

(1) Find a regular time and place for your spiritual disciplines and protect it. Try to spend at least thirty minutes a day in prayer and study, and then try to work towards an hour a day.

(2) Learn to center your attention on God—not on your problems. Quiet your spirit before Him. Release to Him all the things that fill your mind. I am having to learn to do this. My prayer life used to be totally wrapped up in my problems, and I was getting nowhere. But now I am learning to focus on God, and it is changing my prayer life.

(3) Try to use the format of the Lord's Prayer for your own praying. Begin by praising God, and then pray for the accomplishment of His kingdom purposes. Pray in response to the needs of others before you pray for your own needs. Pray that God will bind the powers of darkness and release His renewing Spirit in the world. (Prayer, after all, is spiritual warfare.) And remember to forgive any towards whom you feel resentment.

(4) Use Richard Foster's book, *The Celebration of Discipline,* as an aid in learning how to meditate, contemplate, and focus on God in your prayer life. Learn to use your imagination in study, meditation, and prayer. Actually picture yourself present during events in Scripture and invite God to minister to you. Make this a major part of your life of prayer—a time of private worship.

(5) If possible, find someone whose life is given to prayer to teach you more about the spiritual disciplines—to be a "soul friend." Spend time with that person, learning about spirituality and the life of prayer at least once every two weeks.

(6) Develop a systematic program of reading through the Bible. Also, try studying your way more carefully through a single Book. For example, try going through the Book of Isaiah, underlining every portion that refers to the loving purposes of God for the human future and meditating on the imagery. There is also benefit to memorizing Scripture passages that are important to your life.

(7) Finally, one thing I find helpful is to go on retreats at least twice a year, taking nothing but a Bible and a journal. As I

read the Word and wait in silence before the Lord, I always gain new direction for my life. I also find it helpful to spend time every Sunday journaling and evaluating how consistently I live out God's call on my life. This process might also help you as you try to focus your life and alter your values and priorities to bring them in line with the kingdom.

recovering community

There's absolutely no way we can follow Christ in whole-life discipleship or become the joyful presence of God's kingdom by ourselves. We can only begin to flesh out His right-side-up values in community. And spilling coffee on one another Sunday morning isn't community.

We must challenge our religious bureaucracies to give birth to genuine community again. We need to create extended families where we can be known, loved, and nurtured in our discipleship. Only in community can we, the people of God, be a festive foretaste of all that God has promised.

Listen to Michael Green's description of the earliest Christian community, which can be a model for us:

> They made the grace of God credible by a society of love and mutual care which astonished pagans and was recognized as something entirely new. It lent persuasiveness to their claim that the new age had dawned in Christ. The Word was not only announced but seen in the community of those who were giving it flesh.
>
> The message of the kingdom became more than an idea. A new human community had sprung up and looked very much like the new order to which the evangelist had pointed. Here love was given daily expression; reconciliation was actually occurring; people were no longer divided into Jew and Gentile, slave and free, male and female. In this community the weak were protected, the stranger welcomed. People were healed, the poor and dispossessed were cared for and found justice. Everything was shared. Joy abounded and ordinary lives were filled with praise.[7]

We can only become the living, joyful presence of Christ's new order in community. We need to find other sisters and brothers

---

7. Quoted in Jim Wallis, *The Call to Conversion: Recovering the Gospel for These Times* (San Francisco: Harper & Row, 1981), 15.

who are committed to putting His kingdom first and join together to form communities of life and service.

What I mean by community is simply creating extended family groupings of Christians to nurture one another, celebrate together, and equip one another for service. Let me give you some examples of different forms of Christian communities I have discovered in my travels.

a church of small groups

West Hills Covenant church in Portland has broken their entire membership down into small face-to-face groups where people are known, loved, and held accountable. These groups are centered in worship. They are comprised of couples, seniors, and single parents. They are family to each other, and they help each other discover God's call on their lives so they can make a difference outside of their church. Over sixty percent of the people in these groups are actively involved in ministering to others outside the church.

Unlike many congregations with small groups, these groups don't randomly do their own thing. All the groups are trained to be nurturing extended families to each member and to help the members discover and use their gifts to advance God's kingdom. To facilitate the groups, the pastoral team has trained a "servant staff" who meet with the pastoral team once a week to coordinate the care of the congregation. They have a sense of the pulse of the entire congregation, and they are equipping their people for mission.

sharing life in a house church

At five o'clock on Sunday afternoon, a house church begins gathering at a home in North Seattle. This house church represents another model of community. The house is filled with the inviting aromas of savory lasagna, fried chicken, and tangy Italian salad loaded with avocados and olives.

If you didn't know better, you would think that this was the gathering of a huge farm family. But as they begin to share, you realize that these twenty-two people are not biologically related, though they are indeed family to each other.

Over the chicken and salad and lasagna they begin to get in touch with one another and the week past. Good-natured humor and gentle teasing sets the tone. These are people who have learned to love and trust each other. During these weekly times of sharing they have helped one another through times of unemployment and marital crises—just like family. They even share some of their possessions with one another . . . cars, tools, and so on.

After dinner, this house church takes some time to plan their common ministry and worship. Last Saturday, they mounted an assault on an old peeling house in their neighborhood. The elderly gentleman who lived there said he was "real worried" when he saw a crowd of men, women, and children descending on his house with ladders and brushes. But after they painted the entire house in two days, his apprehension was replaced with pride: "It looks great."

After their evening planning time, this American Baptist house church shares in corporate worship. Tom Nielson, one of the leaders, explains that children and adults actually plan the worship time together. In fact, last week the worship time was planned and conducted entirely by the children.

Since the house church doesn't have to support a building and the leaders are trained volunteers, overhead costs are minimal. Sometimes they hire an educational specialist to work with the kids.

This church helps its members financially when they are unemployed. Even so, they are able to contribute over sixty percent of their income to mission outside their congregation. And perhaps more importantly, they are becoming a fragrant sample of the Story of God. Thank God for those who are discovering they can be the church without spending millions on buildings.

mustard seed house

Residential community—actually sharing living quarters—isn't for everyone. But God bless those at communities such as Reba Place in Illinois, Bruderhoff in New York, and Community of the Servant King in California who do live together residentially. Nowhere have I discovered the joyful presence of God's kingdom more evident than among those who have risked becoming the people of God together in their total lives.

Recently I had the privilege of visiting some people who were inspired to try residential community.

These four couples—students at the University of Washington medical school and their spouses—had been meeting together weekly as an ecumenical study and sharing group. But after studying *Mustard Seed* together, they wanted to take some action towards freeing up their resources for kingdom living. And so they found a large, beautiful, four-bedroom house with a full basement in the Ravenna district of Seattle and decided to share housekeeping. Each couple had one large bedroom to themselves, with huge walk-in closets. The rest of the house they shared in common.

One evening this group invited me over to their "Mustard Seed" house and told me their story. Over a lovely meal, they reported that their experiment in cooperative living had significantly reduced their costs, enabling one couple to stay in school who otherwise would have dropped out. They also said they ate much better; each couple took turns cooking, and everyone always came home to a good meal.

Community is never without its adjustments—the women complained about the guys' leaving the toilet seat up. But they said on balance they were glad they took the risk because they had really come to know one another in a way they never would in their weekly meeting.

These eight people, through their cooperative living venture, have discovered something of what it means to be the community of God. And for many of us who know them and enjoy their hospitality, they are indeed a delightful foretaste of that celebrative community that God is bringing into being.

And there's more! These people aren't just saving money. I had dinner with them right after Christmas. They had saved enough money through their cooperative living to totally finance a Christmas celebration through the Salvation Army—including gifts, tree, and food—for a needy family living in Seattle.

finding community

I am not advocating that everyone attempt residential community. But I am insisting that in the first century, community of some kind was normative. It wasn't optional, for those who chose to follow Christ with their whole life. It is in community that we most fully become the living presence of the Story of God.

If you are going to choose to follow God's call into whole-life discipleship, then I would urge you to consider becoming a member of a community in which you are known, loved, and held accountable.

But how do you find such community—if you haven't already? I suggest you start with your church. If they don't already have a small group program, then ask your pastor to help you find some other serious Christians to start a small group in your congregation. If all else fails, find some Christians in other congregations who are determined to seek God's kingdom first and form an ecumenical community.

Make sure that your small group has a clear purpose: to be an extended family to one another, committed to reflecting the presence of God's kingdom and enabling each member to grow in his or her whole-life discipleship and active service.

encountering God in community

Have you ever seen the 1985 film, *Places in the Heart?* It is the story of a young wife in Texas in the 1920s whose husband, a law officer, is accidentally shot by a young black man—who is subsequently lynched. The young widow struggles to support her children by farming. She takes in a blind boarder to make ends meet and hires an unemployed black man who shows her how to grow cotton. The family endures a tornado and other setbacks as they struggle to get the crop in. Eventually the black farmhand is threatened by the Ku Klux Klan and forced to leave town.

When I first saw this film, I watched it the same way I'm afraid most of us watch most of life—as a secular drama in which there is no God present. But then came the last scene, which takes place in a church on a Sunday morning. The pastor routinely begins a communion service, and the bread and the wine pass from hand to hand—to the young widow, her children, her sister, the blind boarder. Everything seems routine. But then the elements are handed on to people we aren't expecting to see—first the black farmhand who had helped the widow, then the dead husband, then one or two others. And finally the camera zeroes in on the last person to be handed the bread and wine—the young black man who had been lynched.

As the camera lingered on that young man's face, it was as though scales fell from my eyes. Suddenly, I discovered God had been there all the time and I hadn't seen Him. God had been there in the struggling determination of a young widow to keep her family together. God had been there in the compassion of a black man and the courage of a blind man. God had been there all the time and I hadn't seen Him—until the bread and wine were passed. As I saw the dead husband and the young man who had accidentally killed him share the elements in reconciliation, I was completely overcome. I was overcome in worship—in a movie theater.

God is like that. He comes to us in some very unlikely places. But it is as we share the bread and wine together in community that we most fully remember our story and rediscover that we are not alone—that ours is not an exclusively private faith, but that God sacramentally permeates our common life, our society, and His created order. We the people of God are called into community to be the celebrative, reconciling presence of His new order.

If we are to sacramentally be the presence of the living God in the world, we must not only commit our lives to Christ; we must also choose to be filled with the presence of the living God and His vision for a world made new. And if we are filled with His presence and vision, we will discover a discipleship that changes every dimension of our lives and values. We will discover in community a way of life that is more festive and jubilant than anything the American dream can offer—the life of Christ given away for others.

And we will discover a new direction for our lives that fills them with meaning and purpose. In the next chapter we will help you find the pathway from vision to vocation—your specific role in the Story of God.

one more look back—and forward

This chapter has suggested that God's first call on the lives of those who have embraced His Story is to become, with others, the presence of God and His new order. But we must remember:

(1) *We can't do it with compartmentalized discipleship.* We must move towards whole-life discipleship in which we invite God to transform all our values, dreams, and priorities.

(2) *We can't do it on our own.* We must be filled with the presence of the living God. And we will increasingly be filled with His presence as we invest our lives more seriously in prayer, study, and worship.

(3) *We can't do it alone.* We must be part of His community. Only as our lives are in committed relationships with others can

we hope to be the celebrative presence of His kingdom in a world that needs a little good news.

And remember that the Great Commission to which Christ calls us is a call to be disciple makers: "Teaching them to obey everything I have commanded you." And if we do indeed teach them to obey the radical teachings of Jesus, they will become whole-life disciples who become the living presence and the active agents of God's kingdom on earth.

for thought and discussion

In preparation for discovering vocational direction in the next chapter, let's review the following questions:

1. Who are some of the Christians and groups you know of who really reflect the unique loving, festive presence of God and His Story in our world today?
2. How are you going to begin allowing God to change your values to bring them into conformity with the values of His kingdom? What specific values are you going to begin with?
3. What are some specific ways you are considering moving more seriously into whole-life discipleship, a life of prayer, and a life joined with others to become a community that reflects the joyful presence of God? Write down some specific ideas for ways of adding more celebration to your life, intensity to your prayers, intentionality to your community.

life links

chapter 5

life direction ▶	linkages ▶	consequences
God's future is both present and coming. He invites us to join those who have gone before us to place His vision first in our lives, embodying the presence of His kingdom and working with Him to bring righteousness, justice, and peace on earth.	We can choose to continue connecting our lives to the false dreams that fill our society and our congregations. Or we can choose to link our lives to the purposes of God . . . and learn to orchestrate our entire lives around His purposes in community with other brothers and sisters.	If we choose to place God's purposes first, we will discover our lives are filled with meaning. And by His Spirit we will, in community with others, become something of the presence of His new order, participating in His world-changing agenda. We will discover that we are called to be a joyful foretaste of God's new future.

discovering your role in the Story of God

Discovering! With hands outstretched we reach out as infants to discover. And there is no more fundamental discovery than learning how we can be more fully a part of the Story of God. God wants each of us to discover how we can orchestrate our lives around His purposes and join Him in seeing the world changed.

In the last chapter we were confronted with the choice of taking God's vision seriously enough to place it in the very center of our lives. We learned that God's first call on the life of every believer is to reflect the presence of His kingdom in the world—to abandon the rat race and flesh out the values of His new order in our lives and communities.

But there's more. God not only expects us to flesh out His kingdom in our lives; He wants us to become His agents actively advancing His purposes on earth.

Do you have any idea of the unique role God wants you to play in His world-changing saga? Do you know how God wants to use your life and gifts to advance His kingdom? *The purpose of this chapter is to help you find out. It is designed to enable each of us to begin to discover more fully his or her specific role in acting out God's Story and advancing His purposes on earth. We will do this by: (1) exploring some of the myths regarding Christian vocation and defining a biblical basis for discovering God's purposes for our lives and His world; (2) looking at some creative new ways we can steward our entire lives around the purposes of God; and (3) introducing a process for active listening that can help us discover God's kingdom purposes for our lives.*

This is the time of your life. God has called you on stage for such an hour as this. And He has a specific role for you to play. Do you want to find a clearer sense of direction in your life? Do

you want to understand God's call to you? Then prayerfully join
us as we search together.

the struggle to find direction

As I travel around the United States, I run into so many Christians of all ages who couldn't be busier, but who have absolutely
no idea where they are going—or where God wants them to go.
Many of them, ironically, are terribly busy in their churches, while
lacking any overarching sense of call or purpose in their lives.

My experience is that the majority of people seem neither to
understand God's Story nor have any idea how they are supposed
to participate. And so it should not be surprising that many inside
the church as well as those outside it live life with no clear sense of
direction.

Lily Tomlin, playing a middle-aged woman in her stage routine,
says, "It was always my goal to be something when I grew up. Now
I realize I should have been more specific." I think many folks can
probably relate to that sentiment.

Frankly, this business of living without direction isn't much
fun. I know. At times it seems I spent the better part of my early
life disoriented, misdirected, and chronically lost.

I can still remember a very traumatic night I spent as a boy of
ten at Camp McCoy near Yosemite. It was the Fourth of July, my
first week at camp. We watched fireworks that night until our
pupils were dilated large as saucers, then made our way back to
the cabin. It was fortunate we all had flashlights to help us find
our way. There was no moon, and the combination of dilated
pupils and looming blackness would have made the journey
impossible without them.

It was an unusually hot night. And I, like most of the guys in
our cabin, opted to sleep in next to nothing—on top of my sleeping
bag instead of inside.

Sometime about two-thirty in the morning, the gallons of soda
pop I had consumed that evening caught up with me. Still in my
underwear, I stumbled sleepily out of the cabin, but in the darkness I was unable to find the latrine. So I finally did my part to
lessen the fire danger for those gigantic Sequoias.

Semi-conscious and not really able to see anything, I cautiously
made my way back to my cabin. I repeatedly ran into trees. Finally,

after some twenty minutes, I ran into a cabin. Thank God!

I felt my way around the perimeter until I rather violently discovered the stairs with my shins. Not wanting to wake my compatriots, I kept my screams as muffled as possible. Then, since I couldn't see what I was doing, I crawled into the cabin on my hands and knees and made my way over to my bunk. With a tremendous sense of relief, I jumped back in bed.

Dismay and unbelief! Someone was playing a practical joke. Someone was sleeping in my bunk. As I hung suspended between the bunk and the floor it suddenly dawned on me. I was in the wrong cabin.

As I crawled back out, it occurred to me that this could be a very long night. Camp McCoy had almost fifty cabins scattered over three rolling hills.

The rest of the story is almost too painful to relate even at this late date. Through the random encounter method I think I found almost every one of the fifty cabins at least once—plus an interesting assortment of trees, stumps, and ditches. After two hours of alternately bumping and crawling into cabins and finding the place where my bunk was located filled with someone else's body, I got seriously frustrated. My skinny body was bruised, skinned, and scraped. And I was getting cold. I felt someone had exiled me on the dark side of the moon without benefit of clothes, compass, or good sense. And I became almost paralyzed with fear that this aimless wandering would never end. It was terrifying.

Well, thank God, my fears as usual were false counselors. Sometime just before dawn I fell over the stairs of a cabin and found the empty bunk I never thought I would see again.

Believe me, I know firsthand what it's like to lose direction. I've done it all over the world. I have wandered for hours lost in cowfields in the south of France. I searched futilely for my guest house in the wee small hours of the morning in Bangkok and wound up sleeping at the airport. I lost the address of my host at a Christian mission in Bangladesh, and Muslims graciously took care of me until my friends found me.

So I come at this business of finding direction for one's life very sympathetically. I know firsthand about feelings of confusion and uncertainty and frustration. But I am making progress. Over the years I have learned a few things about finding direction. I hope my experience can help you as you search to understand God's purpose for your own life.

a kingdom vocation

In this chapter I will be talking a lot about *call* and *vocation*. But these words can have many different connotations, so I probably should start by clarifying what I mean.

I am defining vocation not as a job or a career, but *the way God wants to use your life to make a difference in His world*. Christian vocation is something that belongs not just to the clergy or other "professional Christians," but to every one of us who has accepted Christ into our hearts and lives. Similarly, we are all called in one way or another to play an active role in God's story.

I am convinced that one of the reasons people don't discover God's call in their lives is that there is so much confusion in the church regarding Christian calling and vocation. Myths and misunderstandings abound, and people don't know how to sort them out. What makes it even more difficult is that all these viewpoints have elements of truth.

Let's look at a few of the most common myths concerning call and vocation.

the myth of split-level vocational calling

Just as a number of Christians have a schizophrenic view of their faith—waiting for soul rescue while continuing to work for fat city—many have a dualistic view of Christian vocation. They draw a very hard line between those called into clearly "spiritual" vocations and everyone else. In this "split level" model, the highest level of calling is assigned, of course, to missionaries, pastors, and Christian "pros" of all sorts. The rest of us are on the lower level.

One of the most troubling features of this nonbiblical dualism is the sense of split level expectations. We expect those called as missionaries to Africa to place God's purposes absolutely first in their lives, to give 150 percent, and, if necessary, to lay down their lives for the gospel.

For the rest of us who aren't, thank God, "called" to Africa, there is a very different set of expectations. Somehow we have embraced the notion that for us our jobs, bills, recreation, schedules, and so forth come first. We try to make it to worship when we can, give out of our leftovers, and serve on a committee once in a while. But it really seems unreasonable to expect most of us to participate regularly in active ministry or to put God's purposes first.

The consequence of this tragic dualism is that we wind up with a few full-time folks and a core of committed laity who are knocking themselves out while the rest of us are apathetically sitting on our hands in the bleachers. Of the churches I work with, fully 75 percent of the folks are passively watching from the bleachers with no regular ministry involvement with anyone outside the building. In fact, you can be considered a spiritual leader in virtually any church in America today and never in your entire life be involved in a caring ministry to anyone outside the church building.

Strategically, there is absolutely no way we can see the Great Commission or the Great Commandment go forward unless there is a major lay awakening—unless we empty the bleachers and everyone makes time to serve. We simply can't get the job done with a professional class of paid specialists alone. It's time we in the church abandon our schizophrenic faith and our dualistic view of vocation and tell people the truth. For the Bible teaches that there aren't any Christian elites. We are *all* called to be actively involved in the ministry of God's kingdom. We are *all* called to get out of the bleachers and down onto the field of play.

the myth of circumstantial witness

Another view of vocation that has high currency in some sectors of the church is what I call the "circumstantial witness." These folks simply rely on circumstances to set up their ministry opportunities for them.

Of course, God does from time to time providentially bring us into situations in which we have opportunities to share our faith with others. And we must be ready for such opportunities.

But there are two major problems with defining this kind of circumstantial vocation as the *primary* Christian vocation.

First, most of us tend to hang around folks like ourselves. And most of us live in closed middle- and upper-middle-class white enclaves. There is no way, with this approach, that we can begin to touch the vast number of unreached people in our own society with whom we have no contact—let alone people in other countries—if we simply rely on circumstantial opportunities.

Perhaps the most troubling aspect of this approach is that, for many, the circumstantial witness becomes a copout from any real involvement of our time or resources in witness or service. We get by with a little word for Jesus on the job, or once in a while we may invite someone to church—and we are off the hook.

Again, if we are serious about carrying out Christ's mandate, then we each need to find *regular* time every week for planned ministry involvement, while at the same time being prepared to give reason for the hope that is within us if the circumstances present us with the opportunity.

the myth of penetrationist thinking

Certainly the most popular view of Christian vocation on Christian college campuses is the "penetrationist mythology." In its simplest form, it reasons that if we simply enable Christian young people to get their heads together (integrating faith and learning), then they will automatically go out and penetrate the world for Jesus. In this model there's no dualism. It's assumed every Christian is a "penetrationist."

Now, ideally it would be great if all Christian young people upon graduation automatically became an influence for Christ and His kingdom. But as a former alumni director in a Christian college, I have to tell you that most of the time the penetrationist approach doesn't work. Sure, a few young graduates have an influence on the culture around them. But in a number of cases I have seen, young Christians were more influenced by the expedient ethics of a large corporation where they went to work than the other way around.

The only way I can see that the penetrationist approach has a prayer of working is if Christian colleges actually teach Christian young people: (1) to place God's purposes first in their lives before career or success; (2) to intentionally use their lives to have a strategic influence for God's kingdom in their profession, their workplace, and the larger society; and (3) to develop a small-group support structure to support their efforts to have a strategic influence in their workplace and profession.

But I am not optimistic that our Christian colleges will move beyond a naïve hope that somehow their graduates will penetrate society for the gospel. The reason I am not optimistic is that our colleges really seem to be increasingly more interested in preparing the young to fit into the world than to change it. Christian colleges seem to be more interested in preparing graduates to fit into upwardly mobile lifestyles and successful professions than seriously to prepare them to challenge or change the institutions in which they work.

As a consequence, I believe more and more of our graduates are moving away from serious mission and towards life in the Land of Evermore. Often they graduate with huge college debts that make it impossible to go into mission even if they wanted to. Christian mission is in decline on many of our campuses, while professional programs are booming. The naïve penetrationist approach simply won't get the job done.

the myth of "anything you do is your vocation"

In my view, this vocational model is long on title but short on substance. It attempts to challenge vocational dualism with an inclusive view of vocation that I believe is broader than Scripture.

I have been to any number of churches in which I've heard ministers teach, "whatever job you work at is automatically your Christian vocation." And of course, I agree with Luther that "all we do we should do to the glory of God." But where does one find biblical support for the view that one's job automatically becomes one's Christian vocation? Where is the scriptural support for the view that every job is as good as every other job?

Does a job doing advertising for the tobacco industry or producing compounds for our chemical warfare stockpiles rank as a Christian vocation? Isn't it true that some jobs are actually counter-kingdom? And aren't there jobs in which employees spend large amounts of time and energy creating products or services that are essentially useless or unnecessary?

Certainly, there are a number of jobs that have to do with the supply of essential human services and products. And while the provision of these products and services is unquestionably a part of the creation mandate, are they really linked to the inbreaking of Christ's new kingdom?

To read most Christian literature on vocations you would think so. Most of the books chronically confuse vocation, jobs, careers, and professions as though they are all one and the same. We seem rather unconsciously to accept and endorse the economic world view of the Land of Evermore as though it's the same as the biblical world view. We have come to believe that occupations which advance the dream of Evermore also advance the purposes of God.

Are they really the same vision? I think not. Remember, Christ's earliest followers quit jobs that provided fish for the homes of Galilee in order to invest their working hours more intentionally in the advance of God's kingdom, which was radically challenging the existing society.

The consequence of the "anything you do is your vocation" model is that we wind up with a lot of Christians doing more to maintain the status quo in a fallen world than they are doing to advance the cause of God's kingdom. In my opinion, that is not what God has in mind when He calls us to take part in His Story.

a biblical alternative—putting God's purposes first

We have looked at several models for Christian vocation that have proved unbiblical and inadequate. In their place, I would like to suggest another—a vocational model that I believe is based in Scripture and clearly connected to the larger drama of God and His purposes in the world.

First, I would like to point out that in the Book of Acts it appears that everyone was actively involved in the advance of God's kingdom. One doesn't find a distinction in the New Testament between full-time and part-time laity and clergy. The bleachers were empty. The field of combat was overrun with Christians. These folks did not see themselves called to simply maintain the status quo; they believed they were called to turn the world upside down. And they did. They quite simply put God's purposes first in their lives—before career, security, or good times.

Read again Christ's invitation to those who would follow:

> If anyone comes to me and does not hate his father and mother, his wife and children, his brothers and sisters—yes, even his own life—he cannot be my disciple. And anyone who does not carry his cross and follow me cannot be my disciple. Suppose one of you wants to build a tower. Will he not first sit down and estimate the cost to see if he has enough money to complete it? For if he lays the foundation and is not able to finish it, everyone who sees it will ridicule him, saying, "This fellow began to build and was not able to finish." Or suppose a king is about to go to war against another king. Will he not first sit down and consider whether he is able with ten thousand men to oppose the one coming against him with twenty thousand? If he is not able, he will send a delegation while the other is still a long way off and will ask for terms of peace. In the same way, any of you who does not give up everything he has cannot be my disciple (Luke 14:26–33, NIV).

You see, God's Story is a very radical story. Essentially, as we discussed in chapter 3, our God is actively at work in history—not in maintaining the present order, but in changing everything.

This doesn't mean He has set aside the creation mandate; of course, we still have a responsibility to provide for our loved ones and for the larger society. But God's kingdom purposes aren't designed to *preserve* our present society. They are designed to transform it into what He intends it to become.

God intends to create a new kingdom of righteousness in which there is no personal or corporate sin; a new kingdom of justice in which there is no more oppression of the poor; a new kingdom of reconciliation in which there is no longer any discrimination based on race, culture, or gender; a new kingdom of peace in which the instruments of warfare are transformed into the implements of peace; a new kingdom of wholeness in which the blind see, the deaf hear, and the lame run; a new community of the redeemed people of God in which God reigns in the midst of His people and His creation forever.

That's what we are headed for. That's God's vocation, and it must become our vocation too.

In the last chapter I asserted we couldn't receive Christ into our hearts without accepting the values of His kingdom into our lives. Now I would like to add with strong emphasis that *we can't receive Jesus Christ into our hearts without also receiving His kingdom vocation into our lives.* And Christ's vocation was announcing and demonstrating that God's kingdom had broken into human history and would transform absolutely everything.

In light of this discussion, Walter Brueggemann provides a compelling new definition of Christian vocation. "Vocation," he says, "is finding a purpose for being in the world that is related to the purposes of God."[1]

I believe Brueggemann is right on target. That's why we have taken so much time in this book to talk about God's Story and His redemptive purposes. Our first step towards finding our vocational calling is realizing that His purposes must become our purposes. We are called to work for righteousness, justice, peace, reconciliation, wholeness, and love. We are called to labor for the establishment of God's reign not only in the hearts of men and women, but in homes,

---

1. James W. Fowler, *Becoming Adult, Becoming Christian: Adult Development and Christian Faith* (New York: Harper & Row, 1984), 93.

neighborhoods, corporations, nations, and creation itself. And we
want to help you find a purpose for being in the world that is directly derived from the redemptive purposes of God.

Now some *will* find ways to pursue the purposes of God through
their jobs. Others will find ways to do it through their leisure time.
But we all need to find ways to be regularly involved in advancing
the redemptive purposes of God.

James Fowler defines vocation as

> the response a person makes with his or her total self to the address
> of God and the calling to partnership. The shaping of vocation as
> total response of the self to the address of God involves the orches-
> tration of our leisure, our relationships, our work, our private life,
> our public life, and of the resources we steward, so as to put all at
> the disposal of God's purposes in the services of God and neighbor.[2]

This definition begins to move us forcefully away from all the
compartmentalized, dualistic, circumstantial, "I gave at work"
approaches to vocation. We have the incredible opportunity of
orchestrating every aspect of our lives to maximize our availability
to participate in the adventure of God.

What does all this mean for someone who is trying to discover
God's call on his or her life? Quite simply that the moment we
accept Christ into our hearts, God's purposes become our pur-
poses. We enter into a covenant with the Lord of history to join
Him in the partnership of seeing His reign established on earth.
That should provide a compelling vocation for every Christian.

the face of Christian vocation

As we seek to find God's direction in our lives, what does Christian vocation look like today?

While our Christian vocations aren't automatically synonymous
with our various occupations, the two can work together.

For example, Al, a friend of mine, got his undergraduate degree
in engineering and was determined to use his training for the
kingdom of God. Fresh out of college, he turned down a very high-
paying position helping design cruise missiles for an aeronautics
firm; for him, that job would have been counter-kingdom.

---

2. Fowler, 95.

After searching for some time, he took a job redesigning hospital equipment; that was closer.

Then one day he met some children who had cerebral palsy; they were trapped in bodies that didn't move and communicate very well. And in that encounter Al discovered his role in the Story of God.

Al is now at the University of Chicago, learning to use advanced engineering design and computer science to help kids with cerebral palsy move and communicate. And he's doing it for the kingdom of God! Do you see how he found a direction for his occupation that aligned itself with God's purpose for wholeness and restoration?

Virtually any education, training, or professional preparation can with a little imagination find a kingdom application.

But when we talk about Christian vocation, we aren't limited to our working hours. We have the opportunity to creatively steward our leisure hours for the kingdom, too. I know Christians who spend an evening a week working with alienated young people. Others donate their Saturday mornings to working in a Christian feeding program. Attorneys donate their spare time on a regular basis to minister through Christian mediation, working for reconciliation in broken homes and ruptured businesses.

And then there is always the vocational option of actually cutting down on the hours we spend supporting ourselves so we have more time to deliberately devote ourselves to ministry. I know quite a few Christians who have found this a viable and fulfilling way to answer God's call.

For example, six young people recently graduated from Westmont College and felt God's call to work among the poor in an inner-city area. They discovered that by living together cooperatively they could support themselves on a half-time salary. As a consequence, they were each able to free between twenty to thirty hours a week to invest in their vocation.

These young people visited a huge downtown Baptist Church in the neighborhood and asked if they could open a gym that had been closed up for years. When the church board responded affirmatively, they immediately had forty to sixty young people in off the streets. And in addition to this program of recreational evangelism, these six young people are now operating half a dozen ministries made possible through the creative whole-life stewardship of their time and money.

A Christian doctor in Denver found another imaginative way

to put God's kingdom intentions first in His life. He sold half his practice and chose to support his family on a twenty-hour-a-week income.

He has taken the extra twenty hours a week and money he freed up through that action and started an inner-city health clinic in Denver. Reportedly, he and his family live very comfortably on half an income. And he has found a much greater significance in his life by going into partnership with God to help those in need.

Let me be very clear here. There is nothing wrong with earning quantities of money; we should be thankful that some are gifted that way. And there is nothing wrong with being employed full time in productive work that benefits society. But our question must always be: What are we productive *for*—ourselves or the kingdom? And we must always realize that our employment and our kingdom vocation are not necessarily the same thing.

Affluent, employed Christians clearly have the opportunity in some ways to advance the kingdom in their work—and certainly through their monetary generosity. But I believe that even those who are employed full time could find one evening a week to work in more direct ministries—caring for abused kids or starting a job training program. God's kingdom purposes have to come first for everyone, even those who are gifted in making money and lead very busy lives.

called to whole-life stewardship

You see, kingdom vocation is really a matter of stewardship. For we are not only called to be whole-life disciples. We are called to be whole-life stewards as well.

One has only to reflect back to the first century to realize that following Jesus Christ has always been a whole-life proposition. It has always meant a change of heart, a change of values, a change of life direction, a change of priorities. And it almost always means a change in how we use our time and material resources.

When we place God's Story and purposes at the center of our lives, a host of creative new possibilities open up. For we hold our very lives in our hands. We don't have to be constrained by convention or beguiled by familiar tales. We can imagine and create new ways to steward our entire lives to advance some small part of the world-changing purposes of God. With a little imagination, we can find all kinds of possibilities for stewarding our time and resources differently.

first things first

But again—what must happen first is a transformation of our values and life direction. Before we can begin to practice whole-life stewardship, we must become captured by God's Story. His purposes must become our purposes. And then we will discover that our lives and resources must become His in the bargain.

Have you ever wondered what became of the Christian lifestyle discussions of the 1970s? It seems like only yesterday that Ron Sider was leaning on the side of his old Volkswagen on the cover of *Eternity* magazine and we were all reading *Rich Christians in an Age of Hunger.* Hundreds of churches started small groups and adult studies to discuss ways we could "live more simply that others could simply live."

Whatever happened to this compassionate concern for the poor and for lifestyle change? A few years ago I ran into a handful of young Christians in Berkeley who had been so effective in their program of lifestyle change and downward mobility that they had eroded their economic base to almost nothing. They were burned out, bombed out, and broke. They were disillusioned not only about lifestyle change, but about life in general and their faith in particular.

It seems to me that where we went wrong in our advocacy of lifestyle change was the tendency to characterize that change principally in economic terms. It felt as if we were all being encouraged to join the young people at Berkeley in their self-induced spiral into downward economic mobility—and that terrified folks.

But what seems to have happened in the Book of Acts was not just a change in economic status, but a fundamental transformation of peoples' values and priorities. Listen to a description of that community:

> All the believers were one in heart and mind. No one claimed that any of his possessions was his own, but they shared everything they had. With great power the apostles continued to testify to the resurrection of the Lord Jesus, and much grace was with them all. There were no needy persons among them. For from time to time those who owned lands or houses sold them, brought the money from the sales and put it at the apostles' feet, and it was distributed to anyone as he had need (Acts 4:32–35, NIV).

The early Christians did use their time and money differently—but it happened as a consequence of their change in values. The reason they were able to have all things in common in the Jerusalem church was they had come to value their relationship to God and others above their need for things—and apparently it became easy for them to share. We see countless examples of radical lifestyle change in the early church as the purposes of God became their purposes. Clearly, they orchestrated their entire lives around a new set of purposes.

God does not call us to a life of self-imposed misery and asceticism, any more than He calls us to a life of more successful scrambling. We are called to a way of life that is much more festive, celebrative, and satisfying than anything the rat race can offer. God calls us to a good life that elevates relationships, celebration, worship, family, community, and service above the values of acquisition, individualism, and materialism. To really begin living, then, we need to begin by going back to the Bible, as we suggested in the last chapter, and discover and embrace the values that are a part of the good life of God.

Jesus' call to whole-life stewardship

And *then* comes the question of stewardship. Because Jesus reigns not only in our hearts, but in every dimension of our lives, we begin looking for creative ways to steward our lives differently. If we are to be whole-life disciples, then of course it must be reflected in the ways we use our time and our money.

In fact Jesus talked about stewardship of resources more than any other topic except the kingdom of God. Listen to His challenge to those who would follow Him:

> You must not set your heart on what you eat or drink, nor must you live in a state of anxiety. The whole heathen world is busy about getting food and drink, and your Father knows well enough that you need such things. No, set your heart on his kingdom, and your food and drink will come as a matter of course. Don't be afraid, you tiny flock! Your Father plans to give you the kingdom. Sell your possessions and give the money away (Luke 12:29-33, PHILLIPS).

Listen to Christ's teaching about wealth and poverty in the Beatitudes:

Blessed are you who are poor, for yours is the kingdom of God. Blessed are you who hunger now, for you will be satisfied. Blessed are you who weep now, for you will laugh. Blessed are you when men hate you, when they exclude you and insult you and reject your name as evil, because of the Son of Man. Rejoice in that day and leap for joy, because great is your reward in heaven. For that is how their fathers treated the prophets. But woe to you who are rich, for you have already received your comfort. Woe to you who are well fed now, for you will go hungry. Woe to you who laugh now, for you will mourn and weep. Woe to you when all men speak well of you, for that is how their fathers treated the false prophets (Luke 6:20–26, NIV).

Christ's radical teachings on stewardship always surprise and upset us a bit because they are so different from what we teach in our churches. What has happened is that our compartmentalized view of discipleship has been complemented by a fragmented view of stewardship. Our popular understanding is that we are to give up to 10 percent of our resources to the church (actually, the church in America receives 2.4 percent) and that what we do with the rest is essentially our own business.

But my problem is that, while I understand the Old Testament origins of the tithe, I can't find a single place in the New Testament which indicates that the tithe view of stewardship is normative for Christians. And I am finding a growing list of biblical scholars who insist that the tithe view of stewardship isn't to be found in the New Testament. For example, John Howard Yoder states that what is being modeled in the New Testament is "jubilary" or whole-life stewardship. Of course, Christians should give at least 10 percent—but most of us can do much better than that.

Following Christ in the first century was always a whole-life proposition. Peter and Andrew left their fishing business and never returned. Zaccheus gave half of his substance to the poor and four times to any one he cheated. The rich young ruler was told to give everything away and follow Jesus, and the messianic community of Jesus clearly practiced whole-life stewardship.

This whole-life stewardship was founded on the biblical premise that "the earth is the Lord's." If the earth is indeed the Lord's, then it is no longer a question of how much of mine do I have to relinquish. The question becomes how much of God's do I want to keep in a world of escalating hunger . . . in a world in which

the Great Commission is going backwards not forwards . . . in a
world in which millions of Christians are having difficulty keeping
their kids alive.

We need to remember that our lives and resources are not ours,
but God's. And they are entrusted to us to be generously and actively shared in the life and mission of the international church of
Jesus Christ.

You see, we are a part of an international movement. God has
entrusted to His movement a certain given amount of time,
money, education, and so on. To the extent that we use those resources exclusively for our personal or institutional desires—to
that extent they are not available for the advance of God's kingdom in the world.

whole-life stewardship . . . beginning at home

Let me tell you about one couple who are finding a creative,
responsible way to steward their whole lives to advance the kingdom of God. John and Pam began their journey in whole-life
stewardship by asking the question, "How much floor space do
we really need for ourselves and our two little boys?"

They decided they didn't need a house large enough to have
roller skating parties in on the weekends. They concluded, in a
world in which millions of Christians can't adequately feed or
shelter their families, all they needed was a two-bedroom house.

They have just completed construction of a lovely split-level
suburban home with a spacious living/dining area. The house is
super insulated. They used only the highest grade materials
throughout, and it beautifully meets the needs of their family.

Total cost? Excluding land, the house cost them a total of
$24,000. Because they built their own home, they are going to be
able to live without mortgage payments. That means they will
have significantly more time or money to invest in the work of
God's kingdom.

In fact, one of the first consequences of this creative approach
to whole-life stewardship is that John has been able to take two
weeks off from work to go overseas for a Christian mission and
development organization. He is training staff in the use of video
equipment in Nepal.

Now what does constructing a house have to do with your discovering your role in the Story of God? Everything! As we move

from a compartmentalized view of our Christianity towards whole-life stewardship, there's no decision more important than the shelter decision.

The reason it's so important is that not only is shelter the most expensive investment for most families; it also tends to dictate how a family stewards all other areas of life—including relationships, time, and money. For example, for most couples, the decision to buy a house is also a decision for both husband and wife to work full time. As a consequence, they have less time for family and probably no time for ministry for others. For most, it is also probably a decision not to take off extra time for more intensive ministry at home or overseas.

What do houses cost where you live? The most common figure I hear is $100,000. Do you know what a $100,000 house really costs over thirty years? Approximately a half-million dollars. So what is the difference between paying $24,000 front-end cash and $500,000 over thirty years? The difference is obviously a major savings of money or the equivalent time—not to mention the tremendous reduction of pressure on a family and the extra time for relationships. And think of the time and money that could be freed for the advance of God's kingdom.

One Mennonite pastor told me that his church is seriously exploring providing young married people in their congregation with short-term, no-interest loans to construct modest homes (in the $25,000–$35,000 range). In exchange, the couple would be expected to invest time or money in local ministry after the loan is paid off.

Whole-life stewardship begins with the question, "How much is enough?" How much house, wardrobe, transportation, and recreation do I really need in a world in which many go hungry? (There is growing evidence that if we don't cut back voluntarily, changes in the American economy will force us to cut back coercively.)

Whatever we are able to free in terms of our time or money could be invested in our sense of God's kingdom vocation for our lives. I realize that not everyone can build their own house, live together cooperatively, or work half-time. But we all have more opportunities than we are aware of to creatively steward *all* of our lives for the purposes of God.

We can all begin by trimming our expenses down to the essentials. Pay off your high-interest credit card bills, then work to pay off all debt. If you are already buying a house, consider paying an additional down payment to reduce interest. Some might consider

moving to a less expensive home or apartment.[3] Or that extra
space in the home you have could be used for a handicapped child
or an international student. And almost all of us could, with a
little creativity, find one evening a week to invest in ministry to
someone else.

I have been troubled to find virtually no guidance programs
in our Christian colleges or in those Christian groups that work
on secular campuses that help young people look at a broader
array of stewardship options. They don't introduce them to the
nontraditional vocational or lifestyle options. As a consequence,
the Christian young are limited to those traditional options for
ministry that often demand very little and aren't getting the job
done.

whole-life stewardship . . . changing your timestyle

When I speak in churches about the possibility of everyone's
being involved in active weekly ministry, I can actually see people
starting to get overwhelmed.

Folks are working day and night to make ends meet. Between
making the mortgage payments, serving on church committees,
and looking after their kids, they simply don't have any time left.
Most people I meet are overbooked, overcommitted, and nearing
burnout. When they hear me challenging them to be involved in
regular weekly ministry, all they hear is "systems overload."

We middle-class people book every night of the week. If somehow we get a free evening, we immediately book something else in
that space. And then we chronically complain about how busy we
are—as though someone else did it to us.

I know what it's like to feel overbooked and overcommitted. In
an earlier life I used to be a classic "type A." I was absolutely
driven and I made life pretty difficult for the people around me.

A pastor once told me, "This business of dying for the
cause . . . it isn't necessary. It's been done once already and it
doesn't have to be done again." He was right. Much of our driven-
ness is almost messianic. We really believe that we have to kill
ourselves if God's kingdom is going to come.

One day, when my youngest son was a preschooler, he asked in
all seriousness, "Dad, do you think if they put you in a slower

---

3. "Living Well on Less," *Changing Times*, March 1987, 26–28.

group you could get your work caught up?" Actually that's what I did. I joined a slower group. My Haitian friends helped me to discover that the good life is to be found in taking time for life, relationships, and things that are important. I came back from Haiti several years ago determined to free one night a week. It was so easy that I freed two and then three. Now I have five evenings a week free. It's a little bit like being out of debt—you can get used to it.

If you are serious about finding and following God's call on your life, I urge you to consider taking some radical action on your timestyle. I am not talking about becoming a more efficient "time manager," as some seminars and books propose, so that we can try to squeeze everything in. No! I am talking freeing major chunks of time, reordering your life to put first things first.

How do you do this? I suggest you begin by clearing the decks. "As much as lieth in you," try to cancel every time commitment you can reasonably let go of, even if it only means initially freeing up one evening a week. Then continue to whittle away on committee responsibilities and other obligations until you can see some real blue sky in your schedule.

Don't add anything new at this point. Instead, savor the freedom. Begin to assess in prayer how other peoples' stories and expectations have unnecessarily pressured your life. Particularly, look at the lifestyle commitments you have made that require maintaining a certain income level, and consider how those commitments in turn put serious pressure on your timestyle. Ask yourself how you might ease pressure on your timestyle by simplifying your lifestyle—reducing costs for shelter, transportation, recreation, and so forth.

After you have made as much room in your schedule as possible, I encourage you to get away by yourself on retreat and try to discern how God would have you steward your time in relationship to His call on your life. Consider:

(1) How much time should you set aside for daily prayer, contemplation, and Bible study?

(2) How much time should you allow for weekly participation in a small community group as well as going to church?

(3) How much time should be invested in God's vocational call on your life? If you aren't able to advance God's kingdom intentionally through your job, can you find at least one evening a week to care and minister with others?

(4)   And, of course, how much time do you need for family,
      friends, and celebration of God's creation? God doesn't want
      you to cram everything in or to burn out. He wants you to
      discover your purpose and catch your rhythm and live the
      good life He intended for you.

Now, I realize that there are some in nursing homes and others
raising small children whose vocation is fully expressed in being
the loving presence of God's Story where they are. But most of us,
with a little effort and imagination, could alter our timestyles to
become much more directly involved in promoting the purposes of
God. I think we would discover, as millions of others have, that the
good life of God is indeed the life given away. We would start
having the time of our lives.

finding our vocation— a guide for listening

Once we have unmasked the many myths regarding Christian
vocation, examined a more biblical model, and begun to participate in whole-life stewardship, we are still left with a very difficult question: "How can we discover the role God wants us to play
in His redemptive drama?" How can we decide what the ministry
focus in our lives should be—whether we do it for four hours a
week, twenty hours a week, or through our forty-hour-a-week
jobs? How can we link our lives to the purposes of God?

asking the right question

This brings us to the issue of "finding God's will for our lives."
There are so many different methodologies Christians use in their
attempt to find God's will—from "putting out a fleece" to moni-
toring circumstances to listening to our feelings. I won't take time
to discuss the merits of each. Rather, I would suggest that as these
methodologies are commonly used, they all suffer from a common
flaw. They all start with the wrong question.
   Let me illustrate it with an example. When speaking at a Christian campus recently, I said that the most popular extracurricular
activity of Christian colleges is a little game entitled "Finding the
ideal, perfect, private, desirable will of God for my life."

Typically this little game begins with the question, "What do I want and what will God let me have?"

For example, the game typically goes something like this as a young male senior—we will call him John—begins to play. He enters into this negotiation process with God that is euphemistically called prayer: "Dear God, if you could help me get that high paying job when I graduate, I would have enough money to get my BMW and the apartment. And, Lord, that woman in my senior class is incredible. If we could work out something there, too, it would be unreal. I would have the job, the car, the apartment, and her."

After he gets all his ducks in a row, the last question that is asked, if it is asked at all, is the question of ministry vocation. Picture John out of school and settled in a church, and the pastor asks, "John, now that you are out of school, could you usher for us once in awhile?" "Pastor, no problem. If the slopes aren't good you can count on me. I will be there." In this approach to finding God's will, ministry comes in dead last if it is even mentioned at all.

The point quite simply is that you can't get there from here. We can't find God's will for our lives by starting with the self-preoccupied question from the Land of Evermore, "What do I want and what will God let me have?"

The only way we can find God's call on our life is to begin with the kingdom question, "What does God want? What is God doing in history, and how does He want me to be a part of what He is doing?

It simply isn't possible to find God's will for your life if you begin with the wrong question. We will only find God's will when we ask how we can be a part of God's purposes.

Once we begin with the right question, we can discover through studying Scripture what God's purposes are for His people and His world. And through prayer, retreat, and active listening, we can learn how to link our lives to the purposes of God.

a prescription for active listening

How do we go about discovering how God wants us to be a part of what He is doing in history? I come across so many talented, committed people who have no idea of God's call on their lives. I have to assume it's either because God isn't speaking or they aren't listening. I suspect it's the latter.

If we can assume that God is speaking—inviting and welcoming us to be a part of His loving initiative, the question then becomes: How can we become better listeners? Let me suggest the following process in active listening.

Even though it has been helpful to a number of people who have tried it, it may not work for everyone. The important thing is that whatever process we follow, we all need to spend more time in Scripture, in prayer and in active listening, if we are going to hear from God. And we need to remember that God is sovereign and the working of His providence is mysterious. We can neither control nor manipulate His will.

It is important at the onset to affirm that at the moment we became Christians we received our marching orders. We are all called into kingdom service. So the question is not *whether* God wants us to serve, it's only a question of where.

We also need to remember that His call is dynamic. As we grow in our gifts and ministry, our sense of vocation may change as well.

To set the stage for a period of active listening, I suggest you take a Bible and a journal to a retreat center or someplace where you can be alone for at least a day. The Catholics have a number of excellent facilities for this purpose that others can use. (I suggest you call your local archdiocese for a list.) I suggest you begin this process of active listening with your journal open, taking notes as you listen.

(1) *Begin with the right question.* Inscribe the right question across the first page of your journal: "Dear God, what are you doing in history? What are your loving purposes, and how do you want to use my life and gifts to advance Your kingdom in the world?" Take ample time to quiet yourself before the Lord so you can be receptive—simply wait on Him.

(2) Now, consider: *What is your earliest memory of the call of God on your life?* Journey backwards in your story to the time of your earliest Christian experience. Remember those moments when you seemed to sense God calling and challenging your life. Write down in your journal everything you remember of that earliest sense of the call of God on your life.

(3) *What has God been saying to you through His Word?* God is constantly nurturing, calling, and chastening us through Scripture. What has God been saying to you through the Bible in recent months? Write those impressions down in your journal. If you have time, I would also encourage you to do a study of Isaiah and Luke/

Acts on the kingdom of God to get a more compelling sense of God's loving initiative. Or read through chapter three of this book to get a good overview of God's loving purposes for the world. The more we embrace these purposes as our own, the more effectively they can speak into our lives.

(4) *What has God been saying to you through the needs and suffering of others?* Mother Teresa said it best: "Jesus Christ is thinly disguised in the poor and the suffering of the world." When various human needs—from the plight of children in the *barrios* of Brazil to the trashed lives of teenagers in a suburban strip—grip your heart, that very grip may be God's call on your life, as it was for Elizabeth Fry in chapter four. Write down in your journal all those human conditions, situations, and needs that tug at your life and your heart.

(5) *What is God saying to you through your gifts?* You have been gifted for a reason, and it isn't simply to increase the profits for IBM or advance the agenda of a professional organization or club. You have been gifted for the kingdom of God. What are your natural gifts in relational, intellectual, mechanical, creative areas? How have you had an opportunity through education and employment to develop those gifts? Write them down in your journal and estimate their stage of development.

Now, write down your spiritual gifts. Read 1 Corinthians 12. What are some of the spiritual gifts that God has placed in your life? What opportunities have you had to use these gifts in your church? Write them down in your journal.

(6) *What is God saying to you through the broken places in your life?* What are some of your areas of weakness and failure? What are some problem areas in your life God has been changing? Remarkably, in the economy of God's kingdom He can often do more through our weaknesses than through our strengths. Look at Chuck Colson. God has created a marvelous ministry for His kingdom out of Chuck's conviction and prison experience. Write down those areas of your life that are the broken places and ask God to show you how He can transform your weakness into the tools of the kingdom.

(7) *What is God saying to you through your imagination?* Invite the Spirit of God to flow through your imagination and help you to discover all kinds of creative ways that everything you have listed thus far can come together. Allow yourself to imagine how that earliest sense of calling and what you hear God saying through Scripture, the needs of others, and your own giftedness

and brokenness could converge in whole new possibilities. Use your journal as a dream book. Jot down ideas. Make outlines. Try sketching different clusters of possibilities, trying to visualize them on paper.

When you are done writing and drawing, spend an extended period waiting in silence on the Lord to discern if He has anything else you need to hear directly from Him. At the end of your period of silence, jot down any additional impressions God has given you.

You may be surprised what God has to say. He may lead you into a more intentional way to use your professional training for His kingdom. Or you may feel called into a part-time ministry with internationals in your community. God may challenge you to build a fourplex for Christian families, or to go overseas on a short-term mission, or to begin a whole new mission in your area. Only God knows what He has in mind for you.

At this point your initial work is done, and you can return home from your retreat center or motel or wherever you went to be alone. But your listening isn't over yet; there are more steps to be taken. Over the next few weeks, consider:

(8) *What is God saying to you through your active research?* Upon returning from retreat, begin researching the different possibilities you have come up with. If at all possible, visit those who have already engaged in ministry or vocational activities similar to what you are interested in. If you can't visit, develop a systematic process to write or call those you can identify who are already underway. Keep a file of all your correspondence, and also write down in your journal what you are learning from your research.

(9) *What is God saying to you through community?* Bring everything that you are hearing from God and collecting in research to your small community group. If you haven't found one by this time, try to find two or three mature Christians who are committed to making a difference in God's kingdom. Share with them the possible new direction you are hearing from God. And ask them for more than a "common sense" response; ask them actually to listen with you in prayer for God's confirmation or guidance. Write down what they have to say in your journal, too.

The autonomous individualism that is so much a part of the secular society is also very much a part of our Christian culture—even when it comes to seeking the Lord's guidance. We tend to seek His will for all occasions autonomously and privately. Seldom do we listen to God's voice through community.

But remember, Paul and Barnabas were called out by community. And once God's vocational call comes into focus in your life and you actually start your partnership in ministry with Him, you will still need the community to nurture, support, and encourage you in your new venture.

(10) *When is the time to get moving?* Eventually, it will be the time to take the risk, with the support of those who have been praying with you, to begin moving on your sense of God's call on your life. Begin orchestrating your whole life around your emerging sense of vocation. Reorganize your use of time and resources around your new sense of life purpose. Enjoy the adventure of whole-life stewardship.

(11) *What is God saying as you continue to listen?* This isn't the conclusion of the listening process; it is only the beginning. You may find it beneficial to go on several retreats to sharpen the listening process. But whatever you do, it is absolutely essential that you develop an ongoing listening process. Even after you find a creative way to express God's vocation through your occupation or your leisure time, you will need to keep listening. Periodically you will need to retreat and listen for any new direction God has for your life.

(12) *How should you make decisions in other areas of your life?* As your sense of kingdom vocation comes into focus, it will become your criterion for making decisions in every other area of life. If God is calling you to be a missionary in Africa, for instance, it makes no sense to marry someone who is firmly committed to staying in the United States. And if God's call is to work in the inner city, then you probably don't buy a house in the suburbs. All other life decisions need to be made in light of your sense of God's call on your life. Issues such as career, singleness or marriage, and utilization of time and resources are secondary to the number-one issue—how to link your life to the purposes of God.

your role in His Story

I've said it before: It is no accident you are alive in the twilight years of the twentieth century. You are here for a reason. This is the time of your life.

God has loving purposes not only for His world, but for our lives as well. To the extent that we understand His purposes, we also discover His role for us in His world-changing initiative. And to the extent that we discover His role for our lives, we also find creative new ways to orchestrate our entire lives around His purposes.

Jesus Christ stands at the threshold of history. He invites us to set aside all lesser agendas and join Him in the adventure of seeing the world changed. I promise you that as you place His kingdom purposes first in your life, you will discover a way of life that is overflowing with meaning and significance.

for thought and discussion

1. Which of the four "vocational myths" described in this chapter have you heard most often? How do these viewpoints square with Scripture?
2. On a piece of paper, write down a single line describing what you do professionally—writer, accountant, homemaker, or so forth. Then jot down what occupational training, practical experience, or professional education you have received that makes it possible to do your job. Now, try to think of some ways your training or experience could be more directly aligned with the redemptive purposes of God in your work or leisure time. (Use the questions in the active listening section to prompt you.)
3. On a blank calendar, in pencil, jot down how you use your time in an average week. Then use your pencil and eraser to reschedule that average week to free more time for working in partnership with God to advance His purposes. Get radical—clear the deck. Try to dream up creative ways you could reprioritize your schedule to make time for the essentials: prayer, community, ministry, celebration, and relationships.

compartmentalized discipleship

In the conventional view, Christian discipleship is compartmentalized. God comes in and transforms our hearts and sometimes even heals our psychological hangups, but leaves our life direction and life values untouched. What was our life direction before we became Christians? Upward mobility. What was our life direction after we became Christians? Upward mobility. The only difference is that now we have God to help us. What were our life values before we became Christians? Materialism, individualism, and looking out for #1. After conversion? Exactly the same. Since the core of our lives is devoted to the culture around us, the things of faith tend to be shoved into little compartments at the periphery of our lives. This view obviously trivializes what it means to be a follower of Jesus in our present world.

whole-life discipleship

Those first Christians weren't doing Roman culture nine to five with a house church on weekends! *They understood that it is absolutely impossible to accept Jesus into our hearts without accepting His mission purposes into our lives.* Jesus Christ doesn't come just to change our hearts and heal our psychological hangups. He also wants to transform our life direction from upward mobility to outward ministry and our values from those of American culture to those of the kingdom of God. When the core of our life is thus transformed by the power of God, then everything begins to change . . . the way we house ourselves, the way we celebrate—everything! We begin orchestrating our whole lives around the kingdom purposes of God. This is whole-life discipleship, which takes seriously Jesus' call to follow Him and really make Him Lord of *all* of life.

chapter seven

sharing life beyond the doors of home and church

Sharing! As children, we show we are growing up when we begin to be able to look beyond ourselves and share with others. As members of families, we learn to share life with those we love. And as we are grafted into the family of God, we learn to share ourselves and our resources beyond anything we believed possible. We even learn to share in response to urgent needs of people beyond our families and churches—as an extension of God's love in our world.

The purpose of this chapter is to look at some of these needs — both present and future—and to explore some creative ways that we as the Body of Christ can reach out in compassionate sharing as an extension of God's love.

Of course, we know that we are supposed to share ourselves with friends and family. But listen to Jesus' challenge to us to move beyond just sharing with family and friends to caring for everyone—even our enemies:

If you love those who love you, what credit is that to you? Even "sinners" love those who love them. And if you do good to those who are good to you, what credit is that to you? Even "sinners" do that. And if you lend to those from whom you expect repayment, what credit is that to you? Even "sinners" lend to "sinners," expecting to be repaid in full. But love your enemies, do good to them and lend to them without expecting to get anything back. Then your reward will be great . . . because he is kind to the ungrateful and wicked. Be merciful, just as your Father is merciful (Luke 6:32–36, NIV).

159

And in the Gospels we see Jesus doing just as He told us to do in caring for all kinds of people—a servant of the occupation army, a prostitute, a leper, a person who is possessed. Every time we turn around, we see Jesus restoring sight to the blind, feeding the hungry, and preaching good news to the poor. From Genesis to Revelation we are shown a God who demonstrates preferential care for the poor, the strangers—those at the fringes of society.

Above all else, then, the Story of God is a story of sharing. The God we serve is a God who cares for everyone, particularly the powerless ones. And because He cares, He shares His life through the servant life of His Son, Jesus Christ. On the cross He even shared our suffering and pain. And in the resurrection He gave birth to a new community of compassion that He instituted as His agency for sharing His loving kingdom with the world. It is that kind of sharing that is at the heart of what we call "missions."

the joy of sharing

I am a Christmas person. I absolutely love Christmas and all it represents. And the older I get, the more deeply I appreciate this season in which we celebrate God's extending His remarkable love into our troubled world.

But the year I was sixteen, Christmastime was the pits. The season that most fully symbolizes sharing and caring for others was on the skids for me. Try as I might, for the first time in my life I couldn't get into the spirit of the season.

I had gotten a job at a Christmas tree lot near my home in San Mateo so I would have some money to buy gifts for my family. And that Christmas tree lot was a laboratory study on greed and corruption.

Because my employer, Anthony, had been a little less than forthright in paying all his taxes in years past, the Internal Revenue Service had stationed a full-time agent at the lot to monitor total receipts. But whenever the agent's back was turned, Anthony would sell a tree and pocket the cash.

The other sales staff saw what was going on and followed Anthony's example. When the boss wasn't looking, they would pocket the cash. Virtually everyone was stealing everyone else blind. I was depressed. I didn't even want to be around these people, but it was too late to get another job.

The only small consolation in this dreary situation was that Anthony gave each of his employees a Christmas tree for their families on our last day of work. But even that incentive did little to elevate my sagging spirits—that is, until I ran into my friend Lou Janakos.

Lou saw me moping down the hall at San Mateo High and asked, "What's happening?" So I told him my morbid tale. Lou responded that he knew a new student named Chick Gomes who was really facing the all-time bleakest Christmas of his life. His family had just come from Chicago, and his dad hadn't been able to find work in San Mateo yet. The family had used all their money in the move and had nothing left for gifts, tree, food—nothing.

I guess I had known that some people go without Christmas, but I had never before personally known anyone who was in that spot. My attention shifted from my own depression to the situation facing Chick's family. I wanted to do something, but I didn't know what.

Then, as I was riding my Schwinn® to my final day's employment at the Christmas tree lot, I remembered that I would get a free tree—and I knew exactly what to do with it!

I picked out the biggest, best-shaped tree I could find on the lot. And at the end of the day I picked up my pay, wished Anthony Merry Christmas, and somehow tied that huge bushy fir on my bike. Then I struggled down the street looking like a forest on parade. It was ridiculous; I should have taken a smaller tree.

It took me about an hour and a half to pedal with full foliage to Chick's house in Shoreview—about ten miles from the lot. No one was at home, so I put the tree up on the porch and rode off. I felt much lighter biking home, and I had a pretty good Christmas in spite of everything.

The next week I ran into Lou again in the hall. "Guess what?" he said. "Somebody gave Chick and his family a Christmas tree, and that was all they needed to get their spirits up. They tied ribbons and strung popcorn over it. They didn't have any gifts, but they still had Christmas."

Of course, that completely took care of any lingering depression I was feeling. I hadn't had much experience before with sharing outside of my family. But now I had discovered how gratifying it is to know that something I shared had made a little difference for someone else.

I am sure you can remember similar experiences in your past

when you had the opportunity to brighten someone else's life.
Didn't you find it gratifying?

God has built us for sharing, and we are most fully ourselves
when we are sharing life with someone else. Sharing is really at the
heart of significant living.

More recently—in 1977—I stood in a circle in a small rural
village in Haiti. At the end of a three-day planning session for
development in the area, we were singing in Creole and English,
"We are one in the Spirit. We are one in the Lord."

And we *were* one in the Spirit and in the Lord. As I stood there
holding hands with Chavannes Jeune and another Haitian brother,
I was almost overcome with emotion. I realized that all we had
planned in those three days could influence the lives of ten thousand people for the kingdom of God. Though I was only a liaison
from World Concern, a Christian development organization, and
had little to do with either planning or implementation, I was
deeply grateful to God for the opportunity of sharing the beginnings of that work for His kingdom.

That project in Haiti's Plaisance Valley is now complete. There
is a rural health care system in place where there was none before.
People have learned how to increase agricultural production, dig
wells, and generally better the quality of life in the valley. Since
World Concern pulled out, the community has started a cooperative economic development effort using its own resources. And the
witness of the church has been significantly strengthened
by these programs.

There are so many examples where members of the Body of
Christ have found similar ways to share life and make a difference
in their world. For whatever reason, God has chosen to carry out
His loving purposes not only through the Messiah, Jesus, but
through that community of people who choose to follow Him. God
instituted the church as His instrument to continue sharing His
love with the world.

And God intends that His people not only reflect the counter-
cultural presence of His new order, but work for His compassionate purposes, too. In the Great Commandment Jesus instructed
us not only to love God with our whole hearts, but also to love
our neighbors as ourselves. And in the Great Commission He
commanded us to go into all the world and make disciples of all
nations. Those two statements of Jesus summarize the mission of
sharing to which our Lord calls us. We are commanded to share
life with one another as the people of God and then reach out in

sharing to help meet the spiritual and physical needs of a hurting world.

But unfortunately, as you will see in this chapter, while the needs and challenges of the larger society are escalating, American churches have tended to become more ingrown, more self-serving, more committed to simply maintaining the status quo. As a consequence, compassion, sharing, and mission have all too often been shoved to the back burner.

If we are to have any hope of authentically being the people of God in this generation, I believe we need to radically reevaluate our priorities and to move the mission purposes of God back to the center of our life together. We must set aside all lesser agendas in order to make God's purposes our purposes—and that will mean a commitment to sharing our lives both with each other and with those in the world around us.

In this chapter, then, we will be exploring some of the reasons compassion, caring, sharing, and mission have been pushed to the edges of our congregational lives. And we will also explore some practical ways we can work together with others in our churches to: (1) anticipate more effectively the growing challenges that face our world, (2) recover a biblical vision for mission, and (3) create imaginative new ways to act out God's loving purposes in response to anticipated challenges.

looking into the fields

anticipating global and national challenges

If we seriously intend to move mission back to the center of the life of the church, then we need to begin by getting in touch with the world around us. We must make an effort to understand our neighborhoods, communities, and the larger society more fully, particularly identifying those compelling new areas of human need.[1]

---

1. Ray Bakke, a Christian urbanologist who works for the Lausanne Commission, does the best job of anyone I know in helping people to understand their cities. He has helped Christian leaders from Manila to Chicago learn what makes their community tick and how to identify arenas for Christian mission response. His videotape entitled "The City for God's Sake" is available from World Vision, 919 W. Huntington Drive, Monrovia, CA 91016.

And we must also try to understand what are likely to be the emerging challenges of the future. Quite frankly, most Christians I know have very little sense of what the needs are today, let alone what they might be tomorrow!

Virtually all of the denominations, Christian organizations, and local churches I work with tend to plan as though the future will simply be an extension of the present—with the same needs and challenges we're facing today. Anyone who has survived the 1960s and 1970s should know better, and the rate of change seems to be increasing. But unlike the corporate sector, which spends a great deal of time and money anticipating where the new needs and challenges are likely to surface, it's the unusual Christian organization that makes any effort at all to take the future seriously.

In an age of dramatic change, it is absolutely essential that we in the church learn to anticipate tomorrow's challenges. If we can do this with even a few of the challenges coming down the tracks at us, then we will have lead time to create compassionate new responses. We will have an opportunity to be *proactive* instead of *reactive*.

One way this can work at the local church level is to anticipate who is moving into the community and what needs these newcomers bring with them.

For example, Brentwood Presbyterian Church in Los Angeles expects to see a rapid increase in the number of single-parent families in their community. What are the special needs of such a population? Child care, emotional and economic support, and so forth. As a result of anticipating this growing population and its special needs, the members of Brentwood Presbyterian are exploring innovative ways to minister more effectively to single moms and dads and their families.

But we need to plan ahead at national and international levels, too—to anticipate the emerging challenges our nation and our world are facing as we approach the twenty-first century so that we can develop new creative Christian responses. Anticipatory planning must become an integral part of strategic missions planning at all levels. If we are going to be effective in carrying out the mission of God in a rapidly changing world, then it is essential that we learn to take the future seriously.

Futurist Alvin Toffler has predicted that we will experience as much change in the next ten years as in the past three decades. I forecasted a number of changes in my previous book, *The Mustard*

Seed Conspiracy[2]—burgeoning population growth, a widening gap between the planetary rich and poor, and increasing famine and hunger. Unfortunately, most of these predictions have been on target—as the recent African disasters illustrate.

As we approach the year 2000, we will share planet earth with some 6.2 billion people. And as the gap between rich and poor continues to widen, it is important that we understand who the poor are. Some 800 million people live in what's called "absolute poverty"; they make less than $90 per person per year, and half their children die before they reach their fifth birthday.

David Barrett, who edited the *World Christian Encyclopedia*, informs us that 195 million of those 800 million are our brothers and sisters in Jesus Christ. There are 195 million Christians who aren't making it—half of whose kids will die if someone doesn't respond.[3] This reality must have an impact on our view of responsible Christian stewardship.

And we are going backward, not forward, in the task of global evangelization. Even while more short-term missionaries are being sent, more Third-World missionaries are being mobilized, and the gospel extended to more unreached groups, the percentages continue to work against us. Present trends indicate that in the year 2000 there will be a smaller percentage of Christians in the world than there are today.

There's simply not space to discuss the future of the nuclear arms race, escalating Third-World debt crisis, and the growing instability of the global economic environment. But all indications are these threats will loom even larger in the coming decades.

Frankly, the situation in the United States isn't much brighter as we enter the final decade of the twentieth century. Unfortunately, my forecasts regarding America have been on target, too. We see cities filled with thousands of homeless. Seniors are having to choose between "heating and eating." And we are creating a huge underclass of young people who will live and die without jobs because they can't read and write.

Only one Western country—South Africa—has a greater disparity between rich and poor than the United States. And given present trends and widespread indifference, the gap between the

---

2. Waco, TX: Word Books, 1981.
3. David B. Barrett, "Annual Statistical Tables on Mission 1986," *International Bulletin on Missionary Research*, January 1986.

rich and poor in America is likely to widen. The mythology of the 1980s was that when the government cut social programs the church would step in, but that simply hasn't happened.

As we enter the 1990s, America is faced with an AIDS epidemic that threatens to deplete public health resources and seriously challenge the compassion of the church. We are confronted with growing dishonesty in government and on Wall Street, as well as ever-more-frequent environmental accidents.

We are facing a host of new ethical issues—from cross-species genetic research to sperm-bank fatherhood. And I am convinced there is white water ahead for all of us in the economic arena as a result of the American debt crisis, global economic instability, and an anticipated dramatic increase in oil prices after 1995. Abortion will continue to be a major issue. Child abuse is clearly on the rise, as is the distribution of pornographic materials. Alcoholism and drug addiction among the young are contributing to a national crisis that shows little sign of being resolved soon.

Further, we are witnessing increasing pluralization of American society. Ethnic populations are growing rapidly. Youth cultures (who have their own music, costumes, and customs) are proliferating. And adult culture is taking new forms—hence the differentiation of various groups such as "Yuppies." (Someone even told me about a new cultural group called "Dinks"—double income and no kids!)

This means that if we are really serious about bringing the good news of God's love to all who live in America, we will need some new cross-cultural evangelistic methods. We aren't going to get anywhere relying on our suburban middle-class cultural approaches to church planting and evangelism. We need to prepare youth and adults alike to live and minister in a world that is increasingly going to be transnational and cross-cultural. And we need to enable our churches to anticipate the new needs and challenges in our own neighborhoods so we can have lead time to create new ministry responses.

assessing our response

How effectively are Christians mobilizing resources to respond to these anticipated challenges? What is the likelihood of our making any significant headway with the Great Commission or the Great Commandment now or in the future, given our present level of commitment to God's purposes?

While the church is experiencing remarkable renewal and growth in Argentina, Brazil, China, Kenya, and a number of other Third-World countries, these churches simply do not have the physical resources to meet the mounting challenges or singlehandedly carry out God's mission in their region. They can't do it alone, even though many of their churches are experiencing much more of the renewal of the Spirit than most churches in the United States.

Looking at the church in America gives me little more cause for encouragement. For example, mainline Protestant churches are generally graying and declining. These days very few mainline denominations send substantial numbers of personnel overseas, with the exception of the Southern Baptists and a few others. And for many mainline denominations the resource base for supporting domestic and international mission is likely to decline even further because they are decreasing in numbers.

While the Roman Catholic Church continues to have an impact on America's social conscience through Bishops' Pastoral Letters and their historic concerns for peace and justice, Catholics aren't likely to be able to do a great deal more than they're doing right now. There is a steady decline in those joining the priesthood and the religious orders. And while Catholic giving to mission is level and holding its own, there is little indication that they will have the resources to begin to respond to the escalating human challenges of the nineties and beyond.

Evangelical churches are experiencing a moderate growth in numbers, and in some cases, a growth in giving. Yet, even though evangelicals and fundamentalists have had a historic commitment to mission and they still talk missions, *giving* to missions is generally down. An increasing share of evangelical income is being spent on buildings, staff expansions, and bulging bureaucracies.

For example, a large evangelical church in California was packed out for three hours on Sunday morning. And so, instead of creatively exploring other options, they decided to build a six-million-dollar education facility to resolve the crowding. Had they moved one of their three Sunday worship services to a weeknight and included a complete adult and children's educational program, they could have solved their space problem with the existing facilities. And then they could have raised money for church buildings in the Third World—the same six million dollars could have provided worship space for 250,000 believers!

But what about the so-called "religious right"—fundamentalist groups who have developed a very strong right-wing political agenda? There is growing evidence that this movement, which experienced phenomenal growth in the early 1980s, is now in disarray and its influence is declining. Furthermore, while they are still experiencing growth in numbers and giving, many of their resources are not being invested in Christian mission. Large amounts of their income are being used to finance special interests such as political campaigns in the United States and supporting the Contras in Central America.

Mission efforts by conservative Protestants (evangelicals and fundamentalists) are also being hindered by the current atmosphere of bickering and infighting. Of course, there's nothing wrong with Christians' disagreeing when it's done with mutual respect. But a growing number of evangelicals and fundamentalists are attacking and intentionally discrediting others. And I see little effort being made to follow the biblical injunction to go to each other in love and seek to work out misunderstandings in private.

The electronic leaders, especially, have gone beyond simply discrediting their colleagues to vitriolic attacks and counterattacks. Apparently they don't realize their public "holy war" threatens not only to undermine everything they have built but to seriously tarnish the witness of the entire church of Jesus Christ.

It has become a very "mean spirited" time in conservative Protestantism. If we don't have the witness of our unity in Jesus Christ, we have no witness whatever. "By this all men will know that you are my disciples, if you have love for one another" (John 13:35, RSV). We all need to influence our leaders to be reconciled to one another in a spirit of humility and love.

Against this troubling backdrop, let's look at giving patterns among Christians. David Barrett tells us that while Christians (Catholic, Protestant, and Orthodox) comprise only 32 percent of the global population, they receive 62 percent of global income—certainly not a powerless minority. Further, he reports that we spend 97 percent of what we earn on ourselves. Of the 3 percent world Christians give to the church, only 5 percent is invested in any kind of international mission.[4]

In the American church, our giving is even lower; we give 2.4 percent to the church. And as already mentioned, a growing share

---

4. Tom Sine, "Shifting Christian Mission into the Present Tense," *Missiology: An International Review,* vol. XV, no. 1, January 1987, 19.

of that is spent not on missions, but on expensive buildings and swelling bureaucracies.

One of the most disturbing statistics is that the giving of American Christians under thirty-five to any type of Christian organization is significantly lower than the giving of those over thirty-five. As this younger population approaches middle age, the economic base of all kinds of Christian enterprises will be in trouble if we don't teach our young people to look beyond themselves.[5]

looking beyond ourselves

As we race towards the twenty-first century, we are on the one hand facing a world exploding with mounting challenges. On the other hand, we are witnessing a church in the United States that is doing less, not more, to respond to those challenges—a church that appears largely indifferent to God's redemptive purposes in His world and is spending a growing share of its resources on itself.

Frankly, given our present level of commitment and investment, I can see no way for us to complete either the Great Commission of the Great Commandment—or even make much serious headway. We will not even keep pace with tomorrow's challenges unless we radically alter our priorities and the ways we use resources in our individual and institutional lives. And this brings us back to the importance of whole-life stewardship and the importance of sharing. We need entire congregations committed to whole-life stewardship—congregations which place God's loving purposes at the center of their common life.

Someone has facetiously developed a flyer for something called The American Foster Parent Plan. The brochure reads:

POOR NATIONS: ADOPT AN AMERICAN! For only $26,000 per year you can adopt an American child and provide the basic necessities of life—television, roller skates, and Twinkies®. For years you Third World countries have subsidized American gluttony. Now you can be specific and choose your individual American child and know him by name!

---

5. *The Charitable Behavior of Americans: A National Survey* (Washington, D.C.: Yankelovich, Skelly and White Inc. Independent Sector, 1985), 17.

And then we are shown a cartoon of a cute little overfed American child on roller skates, with a caption reading:

> Little Brad, above, is nine years old. He has a cheap stereo and only one good leisure suit and is forced to live in a tri-level. There are many others like him. Write today.

The parody would be hilarious if it weren't so tragic. We desperately need a new recognition that we live in an interdependent, interconnected world—a world in which the lifestyle choices I make in Seattle have consequences for my brothers and sisters in Christ in Haiti. A world in which there are plenty of resources for everyone to live decently, but not enough for everyone to live like Americans—not even Americans. A world in which responsible stewardship by Christians could go a long way towards bringing God's message of salvation and justice to the poor and the unreached.

We need to realize that God has entrusted to the international Body of Jesus Christ a certain given amount of money, time, and education. To the extent that we use more than a fair share of those resources on ourselves and our churches, to that same extent those resources will not be available to the loving purposes of God in the world. Christians will suffer, and mission won't go forward.

There's something desperately wrong in the Body of Christ when some Christians and congregations are living palatially and others are barely managing to survive.

Dietrich Bonhoeffer, in the concluding days of his life, wrote, "The church is only the church when it exists for others. The church must share in the secular problems of ordinary human life—not dominating, but helping and serving. It must tell men of every calling what it means to *live in Christ,* to exist for others."[6]

Pray God that He will create within His people that willingness to reach beyond ourselves and share—out of a compelling love for His world and a total commitment to His mission.

---

6. Dietrich Bonhoeffer, *The Cost of Discipleship* (New York: Macmillan, 1963), 225.

recovering a biblical vision

a crisis of vision

Why has the American church apparently lost its interest in mission at a time when the challenges are escalating so dramatically? Why do we appear to be so indifferent to the world where God has placed us and His mandate to world mission?

In my opinion, one of the major reasons mission gets shoved to the back burner is that our churches are experiencing a crisis of vision. I find very few congregations who are captured by a vision of what God is doing in their world or discovering how they are to be a part of it. People don't seem to comprehend the Story of God or understand the scope of His redemptive purposes.

The Bible is right: "Without a vision the people perish"—and we are perishing. Unfortunately, so are those we are called to serve.

It is this absence of vision that has caused us to embrace the half-truths and full fictions of our age. As earlier chapters have shown, Christians of all persuasions increasingly are buying into the most extravagant preoccupations to be found in the Land of Evermore. Often Christian leaders are the ones leading the charge up the slopes of affluence and status.

In the absence of vision, many of our local congregations seem to be afflicted by what I call "chronic randomness." The men's group is going one direction, the women's in another and the young people in a third—and then we have a potluck once a year to congratulate one another that we are still doing some of the things we did the year before. But nobody knows how it all fits together, because there is no integrating vision.

The closest thing we have to overarching purpose in most congregations is the unstated goal of "cultural maintenance." Many of our churches seem to see themselves primarily as cultural maintenance stations where we can maintain certain cultures to raise our kids as Presbyterian, Baptist, Assembly of God, or so forth. Our primary commitment isn't to radical kingdom change in our society, but to maintaining the cultural status quo at all costs. And the last thing we expect is that the neighborhoods in which our churches are located will be changed because we are there. We don't expect it, we don't work for it, and if anything actually happened it would knock our socks off.

Frankly, I have discovered that even major Christian organizations lack a clearly defined biblical vision. While most Christian groups have some kind of credal statement that affirms they are biblically orthodox, it is the rare organization that has worked out an operational statement to articulate their vision of mission. Instead, most Christian organizations work from a set of unexamined assumptions about what the mission of the church is. I call these "immaculate assumptions" . . . we haven't discussed them. We don't write them down. And if we ever did discuss or write them, we might discover many of our unstated assumptions about mission aren't biblical.

Too many of us, for example, have made God's Story an exclusively private story about our relationship with God on earth and our disembodied rescue into the clouds. Not surprisingly, as a direct consequence of this schizophrenic view of God's future and our preoccupation with private piety, many have wound up with a dualistic view of mission.

They have planted churches in the United States and throughout the world in which they viewed mission as "proclamation only." In their view, it's OK to help those in need, but that has nothing to do with mission. As a result, it isn't unusual in the Third World for Christian development agencies to have to move in alongside such churches in order to help people meet their nutritional, economic, and health-care needs. All over the world you can see examples of this two-track approach to mission that reflects our schizophrenic view of God's purposes.

Recently, a church leader working for a church planting organization asked if I thought his agency should seek to respond to physical needs as my agency, World Concern, does. I answered, "No, your agency shouldn't respond to physical needs, but you need to plant churches that do. If you plant churches that compassionately respond to the needs for nutrition, sanitation, health care, and economic development, as well as evangelization, World Concern won't have to come to that region."

a vision for whole-life mission

If we are to discover God's vision for mission, we must go back to the Story of God and try to understand afresh how He responded to the human condition. In the Old Testament narrative, it seems clear that God was concerned about every aspect of the lives of the children of Israel—not just their piety. Of course,

He wanted His people to turn from idols and serve and worship the living God. But He also laid down codes for diet. He mandated economic programs to promote justice for the poor. He ordered His people to care for widows and orphans and welcome strangers into their midst.

And in the life and ministry of Jesus Christ, it was impossible to draw a line between the life lived in love, the words spoken in love, and the deeds acted out in love. His life was a seamless garment of God's love. And we are called to be the living Body of Christ in society with the same agenda He had—a whole-life mission for the kingdom of God.

Historically, the church in its many traditions has understood that we are called both to proclaim *and* to demonstrate the good news of the inbreaking of God's kingdom. But in the last hundred years, unfortunately, many conservative Protestants have chosen to understand the mission of the church almost entirely in terms of evangelism, church planting, and discipling:

> In the past, especially perhaps in nineteenth-century Britain, evangelical Christians had an outstanding record of social action. In this century, however, partly because of our reaction against the "social gospel" of liberal optimism, we tended to divorce evangelism from social concern, and to concentrate almost exclusively on the former.[7]

Over the past three decades, Christians from many different traditions have been holding conferences on the nature and mission of the church. International conferences such as Lausanne 74 and CRESR 82 have attempted to clarify a biblical view of mission and help us reach a balanced understanding of our Christian responsibility to those in need. Under John Stott's leadership, evangelical theologians concluded at CRESR 82 that "evangelism and social responsibility are like two wings of a bird or two halves of scissors"[8]—neither is fully operational without the other.

When the Wheaton 83 conference was convened at Wheaton College by World Evangelical Fellowship, a group of participants was assigned to study an evangelical understanding of Christian responsibility to a world in need. Over a hundred participants,

---

7. Lausanne Committee for World Evangelization, *The Lausanne Covenant,* Lausanne Occasional Papers No. 3, (Minneapolis: World Wide Publications, 1975), 15.

8. *Consultation on the Relationship between Evangelism and Social Responsibility,* a report from CRESR 82 (Grand Rapids, MI: Reformed Bible School, 1982), 15.

half of whom were from the Third World, hammered out a statement, which says in part:

> Some who are inspired by a utopian vision seem to suggest that God's kingdom, in all its fullness, can be built on earth. We do not subscribe to this view since Scripture informs us of the reality and pervasiveness of both personal and societal sin. . . .
>
> Other Christians are tempted to turn their eyes away from this world and fix them so exclusively on the return of Christ that their involvement in the here and now is paralyzed. We do not endorse this view either, since it denies the biblical injunctions to defend the cause of the weak, maintain the rights of the poor and oppressed (Psalm 82:3), and practice justice and love (Micah 6:8). . . .
>
> We affirm that the kingdom of God is both present and future, both societal and individual, both physical and spiritual.[9]

The Wheaton 83 statement worked hard at avoiding the pitfalls of either left or right. Unlike many liberal viewpoints, it recognized that salvation is not the same thing as humanization—that simply helping people become "more fully human" is not saving them. But it also reached for a more comprehensive statement of mission than some conservatives might endorse, stating that the mission of the church is to speak to the totality of human experience, not just the private spiritual dimension.

The exciting thing is that evangelicals aren't the only Christians coming around to such a biblical understanding of Christian mission. Recent reports on world evangelization from the World Council of Churches, usually seen as a relatively "liberal" organization, contain many of the same points of biblical emphasis as the Wheaton statement. Arthur Glasser of Fuller Theological Seminary points out that there is an important convergence in reformed, Anabaptist, and Catholic theology around a kingdom-of-God theology which offers a compelling alternative to the highly politicized theologies of the religious right and left.

the purposes of God and the mission of the church

Against this backdrop, I would like to propose a definition of Christian mission that reflects the growing understanding of

---

9. "Social Transformation: The Church in Response to Human Need," statement issued from the Wheaton 83 conference, sponsored by World Evangelical Fellowship, Wheaton, IL, 1983.

Christians all over the world and avoids confusing salvation with humanization, on the one hand, or limiting God's agenda to the spiritual dimension, on the other. Simply stated, Christian mission is *our working in partnership with God to see His comprehensive purposes realized in our lives and in His church—and, in response to the urgent human challenges throughout the world, anticipating that day when Christ returns and the reign of God is established in its fullness.*

In other words, mission means laboring to see God's reign established in the lives of individuals, families, neighborhoods, corporations, and nations—but realizing that only at the return of Christ will "every knee bow and tongue confess" His reigning lordship. You see, God cares about every dimension of our lives and His world—not just the spiritual.

Doesn't this way of looking at mission bring it all together in an integrated biblical vision? When we think in terms of laboring with God to see His reign established in the lives of individuals, in the church, in the fabric of communities, and in all aspects of our world, doesn't the whole concept of Christian mission become clearer and more compelling? Mission is no longer something we just do overseas. It's working to see God's reign established everywhere.

But what does this way of looking at mission mean for churches and Christian organizations? Quite simply that God's purposes must become our purposes. Even as individual disciples of Jesus must place His purposes at the center of their lives, so must the community of Jesus.

In other words, every congregation and Christian organization needs to give priority to discerning how they are to advance the loving purposes of God. How? Here is one possible format:

(1)   Study Scripture together, seeking to discern as we did in chapter 3 what God's loving purposes are for His people and His world.
(2)   Begin to discern through group and individual prayer and active listening the specific ways the church or organization is called to work for His purposes in the community in which God has planted them.
(3)   Try to listen to the vision that God is already placing in the group or congregation. This involves not only listening to the leadership, but also creating ways to listen to the story God is birthing in every member.

(4)   As the vision for a congregation or organization begins to
       come into sharper focus, begin orchestrating all the church's
       or organization's time and resources around the loving pur-
       poses of God and participation in whole-life mission. This
       will probably mean discontinuing dying programs and start-
       ing new ministries that focus more outwardly on mission.

If we follow this format, we can discover God's vision both for
our individual lives and our congregations as well. As we discover
how we are to work for God's loving purposes in the world, mission
will move back to the center of our common life. You can be sure
that a growing share of our time and resources will be focused
outward in mission, and we will become churches for others. And
instead of seeking to maintain the present order, by the power of
God's Spirit, we will begin to see the world turned upside down
again.

A Christian agency working in urban mission once asked me to
critique their proposal for urban ministry. The entire document discussed meeting housing needs, employment needs, and nutrition
needs. I asked them, "What would happen if you succeeded in meeting every single physical need in an inner-city community? Would
you be home free? Isn't it possible you could meet all the needs
you're talking about and still have an essentially pathological community? Isn't our biblical purpose broader than just meeting physical needs? Aren't we laboring to see the reign of God established in
that community so that people start taking responsibility for one
another and change the conditions that cause the needs?"

Remember, God's redemptive mission is to restore everything
that was twisted in the Fall. He intends not only to reconcile individuals to Himself; He also intends that we be reconciled to one
another—and indeed that the very fabric of our society be transformed and the entire creation renewed by His loving initiative.

Wayne Bragg, an insightful consultant in international mission,
has vividly pictured God's vision of restoration and reconciliation
in a contemporary version of Isaiah's view of the future—written
specifically to his Christian brothers and sisters in Kenya. Picture, as you read this, God's loving intentions for all the people
of His world, including your own church and community:

For I create the land of Kenya to be a delight, and her people a
joy—

Luo,
  Maasai,
    Kikuyu
      Turkana,
        Kalenjin.
I will take delight in my people, and weeping and cries for help
from oppressors shall never again be heard in the land.

There, no child shall ever again die an infant, nor lack food or
health care.

No old man shall fail to live out his life; every boy and girl shall
live his and her hundred years before dying, and will live out the
years in respect and love with the family.

Men shall build houses and inhabit them, plant vineyards and eat
their fruit, plant millet, ground nuts, maize and sorghum and eat
thereof.

They shall not build for others to inhabit, nor plant to export for
others to eat; justice will reign in the land.

My chosen shall enjoy the fruit of their labor and leisure of their
efforts; they shall not toil in vain nor work for absentee landlords.

They care for the land I gave them, it blooms under their tender
care.

They shall rule themselves and share in the decision for the people as they see their own needs; no outsider shall impose his will or
plans on them.

Yet nation shall learn from nation, and tribe from tribe; none
shall exalt itself over the other.

They shall not toil in vain nor raise children for misfortune, for
they are the offspring of the blessed of the Lord, and their children
after them.

Before they call to me I will answer, and while they are still
speaking I will listen, for they are my people.

Their hearts are attentive to my precepts, they find delight in my
laws. My people hear the cries of the needy. They release the yoke of
the oppressed.

The man I care for is a man downtrodden and distressed, one
who reveres my words.

I will send peace flowing over Kenya like a river, and the wealth
of nations over her like a stream in flood.

The Lord shall make his power known among his servants, for
see, the Lord is coming in fire with his chariots like a whirlwind,
The Lord will judge by fire, with fire he will test all living men.

I myself will come to gather all nations and races, and they shall
come and see my glory.

For, as the new heavens and the new earth which I am making
shall endure in my sight, says the Lord, so shall your race, and your

name endure, and week by week on the Sabbath, all mankind shall come to bow down before me, says the Lord.[10]

Now, that vision is large enough to embrace the hopes and longings of all people. Our mission, "should we decide to accept it," is to become collaborators in God's loving initiative for all peoples.

In other words, an expanded understanding of God's redemptive initiative will necessarily expand the mission responsibility of His church in the world. We are invited by Him to become His agents, empowered by His Holy Spirit, to bring people to faith in Jesus Christ and see righteousness established in the earth. We are invited to struggle for social and economic justice for the poor. We are called to be peacemakers, working for the *shalom* of God not only in personal relationships, but in communities and between nations. We are challenged to bring wholeness to those who are physically, emotionally, and mentally disabled. We are reminded that as a kingdom people we are to work for the restoration and stewardship of God's good creation. We are commended to see the celebrative reign of God established in every dimension of our lives, churches, and society by the power of the Spirit of God.

acting out the compassionate purposes of God

What are some ways this broader vision for the mission of God's kingdom is finding expression in the world around us today? Let's look at some congregations that have developed their vision and moved mission to the very center of their common life. Note the broad range of ways God is using them to share life with those around them—actually changing their communities. These congregations can become models for all of us of ways we can put God's purposes first by giving top priority to whole-life mission.

sharing life in east london

Icthus Fellowship in East London is a remarkable gift to the church. One of the most rapidly growing churches in Europe (over

---

10. Wayne Bragg, "Social Transformation," in *Christian Response to Human Need*, ed. Tom Sine (Monrovia, CA: Missions Advanced Research & Communication Center, 1983).

thirteen hundred members in all), it is made up of a large network
of home groups. This burgeoning congregation, made up of West
Indians, Pakistanis, working-class Brits, Asians, and even a few
middle-class professionals tends to contradict the homogeneous
principle of some church planters. It is a dynamic model of biblical
reconciliation.

Roger Forster, the pastoral leader of Icthus Fellowship, tells
me this divergent cross section of East London society is relin-
quishing long-standing animosities. And in spite of their enormous
cultural differences, they are becoming sisters and brothers in
Christ together. They are becoming bonded together in jubilant
worship of the living God, the study of Scripture, and the celebration of the Eucharist. And they help one another find work and
housing and meet other basic needs. At the same time, they pray
God's Spirit supernaturally to deliver and heal those in need of
His touch.

This church meets in their small home groups twice a month
and in regional congregational get-togethers once a month. They
also come together monthly as an entire fellowship of over a thousand people. Icthus Fellowship is evangelizing and planting new
home groups and congregations in East London at a remarkable
rate. They are committed to a high level of church growth without
using God's money for building programs. They use homes,
schools, and existing churches for their meetings. People are
drawn by the vitality of their faith, the festivity of their worship,
the dynamism of their common life, and their commitment to help
those in need.

This unusual charismatic church is aggressively involved in
evangelism, church planting, discipling, healing, empowering the
poor, and working for peace and reconciliation all at the same
time. They are changing the character of East London and becoming a witness to the larger world . . . as they work for the whole-
life purposes of God.

sharing life through Jesus people usa

Over four hundred young people live, share, and minister together as a church and a community on the northside of Chicago.
Jesus People USA is both a church and a community in an inner
city area. Eighty of their members work full time at businesses
they own (such as remodeling) so the rest of the community can
spend their time in ministry.

These young people, many of them new converts, place mission at the center of their church and community life. Their approach to whole-life stewardship involves living with a common purse—all income is shared. And that means they can support themselves completely for only $200 per person per month. They live in apartment houses they own. By keeping their overhead low they are able to provide a broad spectrum of ministries to others. Let me mention a few.

Young people in your church probably know their band, called Resurrection. They also put out a magazine called *Cornerstone*. They feed two hundred fifty of their neighbors every day in what they call their Dinner Guest Program.

They work at evangelism and discipleship among young drug users on the streets. At the same time, they work with the poor to help them rehabilitate old apartment houses and gain ownership to their own apartments. And their worship services are an experience of the jubilation of God.

All of this is made possible because Jesus People has made a decision to live in community with the poor in a tough urban neighborhood. And their witness is having a powerful impact for the kingdom of God . . . as they orchestrate their entire lives around God's loving purposes.

sharing life in the mathare valley

Thousands of people every month migrate into the congested Mathare Valley outside of Nairobi. Cardboard boxes, shanties, and open sewers are home to over one hundred thousand refugees in an area three kilometers long and one kilometer wide! Predictably, this brutalizing environment spawns high levels of crime, drug addiction, alcoholism, and prostitution.

Rev. Arthur Kitonga realized that helping the Story of God take root in this troubled soil would require more than preaching the good news; it would require a compassionate demonstration of God's caring love, as well. In 1974, he and a small community of seven dedicated laymen answered God's call to evangelize the Mathare Valley. Out of their efforts the Redeemed Gospel Church was born, ministering to the full-range of human needs in the valley.

This rapidly growing Pentecostal church now has sixteen hundred members and over a hundred worship centers throughout Kenya. The church sends out teams to conduct two evangelism crusades monthly. This often results in planting new congregations that also minister wholistically in the villages in which they are located.

Slowly the Mathare Valley slums are being transformed by this shalom community God has planted in their midst. The people of Redeemed Gospel Church have concentrated their caring response to the special needs of families with children. For example, they provide nutritional and feeding programs for young children in order to combat malnutrition. They provide health education to increase the level of health and sanitation throughout the entire community.

World Concern, the Seattle-based Christian development and relief agency with which I work, recently stumbled upon this remarkable ministry. Committed to helping empower the church to enable the poor to become self-reliant, World Concern funded a job-training program the church had initiated. Here, instead of working alongside the church, World Concern is working through the church. Ninety students are being taught carpentry, leather-working, and sewing to provide them with marketable job skills and reduce the high unemployment in the valley. Rev. Kitonga said to thank American Christians "for helping us to hold up the banner of Christ."[11]

sharing life in a hispanic community

Rev. Manuel Ortiz, pastor of Spirit and Truth Fellowship, an independent Hispanic church in Chicago, declares, "We believe that the gospel extends not only to individuals but also to the systemic sin that exists in society. We've given the community an alternative—the kingdom of God."[12]

And indeed they are. They've started Humboldt Christian School, which offers a Christian education to over two hundred children in the inner city. They operate a thrift store, a family counseling center, and a legal counseling center. Manuel Ortiz is an agent for reconciliation between gangs, such as the Latin Kings and the Spanish Cobras. (Gangs are becoming a growing problem in many of our cities.)

No one has to teach poor people about the problems of social justice. The church periodically rallies together and marches on

---

11. World Concern's address is Box 33,000, Seattle, WA 98133.
12. "Claiming Turf in Hispanic Chicago," *Eternity*, June 1984, 25.

city hall or takes some other action to promote justice for their neighborhood.

Two years ago, the congregation of Spirit and Truth Fellowship divided into four separate groups meeting in homes. "Each house church is developing its own strategy for evangelism and discipleship. One house church has already doubled in size; another plans to send a missionary to Puerto Rico next year."[13]

Manny Ortiz is right. Our task as the people of God is not just meeting urgent human needs, as important as that is. Nor is our task simply bringing individuals to faith, as critical as that is. We are called to see an entire community live under the reign of God. We are called not only to be the shalom community of God, but to see the purposes of God begin to transform the fabric of life of entire neighborhoods.

sharing life in washington, d.c.

It's in community that we most clearly hear God's call on our lives and discover how our lives can be a part of His great drama. Church of the Savior in Washington, D.C., does a particularly good job of listening to God's call on their lives—collectively and personally. There's no Sunday-go-to-meeting Christianity for these folks; following Jesus is a whole-life proposition.

Years ago, this congregation felt God was encouraging them to break their one church of some one hundred and twenty members down into seven smaller churches. These people have no interest in simply maintaining a certain kind of culture for themselves and their kids. They believe God calls them to make a difference— work for real change—and they do.

Each of the seven congregations has a specific mission focus—a "calling." For example, there is the Potter's House Church. Their calling "begins within the Potter's House, a restaurant and bookstore in a poorer part of D.C., which offers hospitality, service, and a listening ear to all who come through its doors."

But Potter's House hospitality also includes running a health clinic next door for those in need. Last year they served over thirty-five thousand people, many of whom are Central American refugees. Almost half their staff consists of people from their congregation who donate time on a regular basis out of a shared sense of vocation.

---

13. Ibid.

Gordon Cosby, the pastor of Church of the Savior, reminds us,

> The teaching of St. Paul is clear (I Corinthians 12:1–31 . . .). Each
> person confessing Christ as Lord, living within the body of Christ,
> is given a gift by the Holy Spirit for the upbuilding of the Body. We
> can even say that the person himself, as his essence unfolds under
> the power of the Spirit, is a gift. He becomes more fully human,
> more fully Christian. If every member has discovered the unique
> treasure of his or her own being and is being received by the others,
> there is tremendous fulfillment and power.[14]

Becoming a member of a church such as this—one which places
mission at the center of congregational life—demands a little more
than just putting a name on a membership roster. To become a
member at Church of the Savior one has to commit to: (1) attend
worship weekly, (2) participate in a weekly mission support and
prayer group, (3) spend time every week in ministry to those in the
neighborhood, (4) give a graduated tithe of 10 percent and up, and
(5) spend an hour a day in prayer. They tell me that they aren't
having thousands join, but when members are added, there's a real
time of celebration.

Church of the Savior is having a greater impact than churches
many times their size because they have placed mission at the center and have found a nonbureaucratic way through small groups to
advance God's loving initiative.

sharing life through ministries of reconciliation

The stories of congregations involved in whole-life mission
could go on. All over the world, God's people are preaching good
news to the poor, release to the captives, and recovery of sight to
the blind. Let me share a few more snapshots of what whole-life
mission looks like in today's world.

Recently, messianic Jews who were being persecuted in Israel
for their faith in Jesus were rescued and protected by Arab Christians living in Palestine. George Fox College has established an
Institute for Peace to search for nonlethal ways to resolve international conflict and educate Christians in the ministry of reconciliation. And Mennonites have established programs to take up
where the criminal justice system leaves off—bringing together

---

14. Gordon Cosby, *Handbook for Mission Groups* (Washington, DC: Church of
the Savior), 2–9.

victims and offenders to promote restitution, reconciliation, and restoration for all parties.

A group of charismatic Catholics work with the poor who live near a garbage dump in Juarez, Texas. This group has believed God for all kinds of miracles. After Christmas, this group prayed for a little girl whose foot and hand had been paralyzed from birth. God healed her, and she has learned to run and play with other kids.[15]

And a Southern Baptist church in Houston has started a ministry among AIDS victims. Though this mission was not started as an evangelistic outreach, numbers of the dying have given their lives to God . . . and have discovered new life in Christ.

One story from Ireland gives particularly compelling evidence of the radical change that takes place when people come to live under the reign of God.

"Had I seen Jimmy on the street before I became a Christian, I wouldn't have hesitated to shoot him. Now he's my brother in Christ, and I would die for him," confessed Liam, a 26-year-old Catholic imprisoned for IRA terrorist activities. While in prison he participated in a series of IRA prison strikes which culminated in the 1981 hunger strikes that claimed the lives of ten IRA inmates.

> After 55 days on the hunger strike and in a coma, Liam was hours away from becoming the eleventh prisoner to die when his mother ordered that he be fed intravenously. While recuperating from the strike, he renewed a former interest in Christianity and started reading the Bible. Understanding he "cannot serve two masters," he realized he had to choose between the IRA political cause and Christ. He chose Christ.
>
> Soon after becoming a Christian, Liam took the brave step of leaving the Catholic tables and walking over to eat with Protestant inmates. He felt the love of God demanded this. He met Jimmy, a Protestant loyalist, and sympathizer with the Ulster Defense League cause. Jimmy and Liam began studying the Bible together with other Christian prisoners, and Jimmy committed his life to Christ. Jimmy and Liam are reconciled in Christ.[16]

---

15. Rene Laurentin, *Miracle in El Paso* (Ann Arbor, MI: Servant Publications, 1982), 14.

16. "In Christ, Reconciliation," *Jubilee International: A Newsletter of Prison Fellowship International,* July-September 1983, 4–5.

Prison Fellowship, which influenced Liam to follow Christ, is committed to reconciling the imprisoned not only to God, but to one another as well. In fact, their understanding of the mandate of the kingdom also motivates them to work actively for the structural reform of criminal justice systems all over the world.

We are invited to join thousands of Christians all over the world in working for the comprehensive purposes of God.

sharing life and enjoying the consequences

The spirit of sharing is the spirit of Christmas. And at least once a year we all learn the tremendous joy that comes from sharing life with others. And sometimes we are even surprised at how God uses our sharing to make a difference.

You could smell the savory turkey as soon as you opened the front door of David and Willow Teeter's home in Palestine. The huge turkey in the middle of the long buffet table was surrounded by salads, oranges, a mountain of rice, and plates of Christmas cookies.

This home had become not only a gathering place for a small cluster of Arab Christians, but also a "friendship center" where Muslim students dropped in from a nearby university. Surprisingly, the Muslim young people were particularly attracted to this Christian home at Christmas time. Every year they came by the dozens to participate in a Christmas feast that lasts seven days. Last year the Teeters served over one hundred sixty full meals plus snacks to their guests.

Each young person was encouraged to bring an ornament and come early to help decorate the tree. As they decorated the tree, Willow taught them the carol, "Joy to the World." After all the decorating and singing, they plugged in the lights. One of the Muslim students, a Bedouin from the Gaza strip, suddenly exclaimed, "Jesus the light of the world! Jesus the light of the world!" And he quoted several other verses.

The Teeters were astonished. They asked where he had learned these verses.

"From your library," he replied. He had been using their home as a study center.

By Christmas Day, the feast was nearly over and everyone had left. The small community of Christians began to celebrate Christmas by themselves with candles, songs, and prayers. In the middle of their Christmas sing-along, a knock came at the door. As they opened it, there stood some twenty Muslim young men. They were invited in. They listened quietly as the Christians continued singing their carols.

The next evening the same group of students came trooping in about seven in the evening. The first thing they did was to light the candles. They turned off the overhead lights, as had been done the previous evening. Then they said, "Tell us about Jesus. Start at the beginning." The conversation went on into the wee small hours of the morning.

Perhaps God's Story is reflected most compellingly and convincingly in our celebrations, play, and festivity. Remember, Jesus' ministry began at a wedding feast, and His Story will conclude in a wedding banquet that will be the celebration to end all celebrations.

how to move whole-life mission to the center of your church

As we seek to draw our friends and congregations into a way of life in which mission and sharing are put at the center of our life together, where do we begin? Let me outline a few steps you might try to nudge your church towards becoming a church committed to whole-life mission.

(1) Find a few other people in your church who share your vision for comprehensive biblical mission and prayerfully commit your common vision to paper.

(2) Locate some modest ways through ministry to others to begin giving expression to your vision with those people you've joined.

(3) Meet with key people in leadership in your church. Ask them to share their vision for mission. Then you and your colleagues share yours. Such dialogue can help move mission much more to the center of congregational life . . . particularly if you offer yourselves to help make their vision become a reality.

(4) Encourage congregational leaders to:
   (a) Identify the specific spiritual and physical needs in your neighborhood today, and anticipate those that are likely to be there in the next five years.
   (b) Through Bible study and prayer, try to discern God's vision for your congregation. How would He have you

participate in seeing His mission purposes realized in your neighborhood and in His world?

(c)   Audit as accurately as you can how much congregational time and money is presently being spent on yourselves, and how much is being invested in mission to those outside the doors of your congregation. Carefully evaluate all proposed building and expansion programs against the mission needs of the international Body of Christ.

(d)   Set a five-year goal to increase congregational investment of time and money in mission to at least fifty percent. (A Presbyterian church in Wabash, Washington, has set and reached this goal!) If your congregation decides to go ahead with a construction project, set a goal of matching a dollar for mission for every dollar used in construction.

(e)   Inventory the underutilized resources of time, building facilities, and financial resources in your congregation that could be more fully used in mission.

(f)   Create imaginative new forms of mission strategies to use congregational resources more effectively in order to implement mission vision and meet anticipated human needs in your immediate community and throughout the world.

(5)   Encourage the development of curriculum for all ages to help members learn to take mission seriously and become world Christians. Howard Snyder's *A Kingdom Manifesto,* John Stott's book, *Involvement,* and Donald Kraybill's *The Upside Down Kingdom* would be particularly good resources for adult study groups.[17] Also, a new adult curriculum on missions called "Adventures in God's Kingdom" is available from the Christian organization Harvest and can be ordered by calling 602-968-2600. Seek to challenge every member to take time regularly to share with those in need.

(6)   Initiate a program of congregation-wide prayer for a renewal of the Spirit of God and for the meeting of spiritual, physical, and relational needs of those in your neighborhood and the

---

17. Howard Snyder, *A Kingdom Manifesto* (Downers Grove, IL: Inter-Varsity Press, 1985); John Stott, *Involvement, Vol. 1: Being a Responsible Christian in a Non-Christian Society* (Old Tappan, NJ: Fleming H. Revell, 1985); Donald Kraybill, *The Upside Down Kingdom* (Scottdale, PA: Herald Press, 1978).

poor and forgotten people throughout the world. Pray to be
filled with God's Spirit so that you can be empowered to seek
God's purposes first.

(7)   Discern how you and your group, given your own sense of
vocational call, could fully participate in this more serious
approach to congregational mission, using your time and resources to become an incarnational model to others.

And the Conspirator God filled both hands with seed which Jesus
spread over Palestine like a lunatic farmer, giving the road and rock
an equal chance with the fertile field to go white with harvest. God
was taking root. The seed of God grew in secret and went the way of
wheat into the blood and sinew of unsuspecting people.[18]

Through these people God is changing the world with celebration and great joy. I encourage you and your church to join them
by placing sharing at the center of congregational life. And join
the joyful scattering of seed with thousands of others all over the
world.

for thought and discussion

*There are three questions you might reflect on as you think about
becoming more involved in a life of sharing and mission:*

1.   How is the community around your church likely to change in
the next five years? List some possible areas of increasing human need.
2.   What are specific ways your church is seeking to advance the
mission purposes of God? How could these purposes of whole-
life mission be given greater priority in allocation of congregational time and resources? How could they be moved much
more to the center of the congregational life?
3.   What are some creative new ways your congregation could
respond to the anticipated needs and implement God's loving
purposes? Ask yourself how God might use you to expand
your church's involvement in whole-life mission.

18. John Shea, "The Story Teller God," 200–201.

church directions
maintaining status quo
doing little to change
society

church priorities
less than 20% invested in mission
over 80% of time + money spent on those in the building

primarily self-serving

church directions
Putting God's mission purposes first...
working to change society

church priorities
Over 50% of time + money in mission to Others

Primarily other serving

traditional approach	whole-life mission approach
Unfortunately, many of our churches have no clear sense of direction. As a consequence, they simply settle for maintaining a certain environment for their kids. Their commitment is quite simply to maintain the institutional church and the cultural status quo. They don't expect anything to be changed in their community because of them. And change, if it actually did happen, would knock their socks off! They certainly don't work for kingdom change; their time and money is invested almost exclusively in facilities and programs that will benefit them and their families. Typically, no more than 20% of the members' time and money is ever invested in programs or ministries that touch those outside the building. God's larger purposes are largely ignored.	Then there are the churches—unfortunately, a minority—which take seriously God's call for His church to be an agent of kingdom change. They place the mission purposes of God—working for righteousness, justice, and peace—at the center of congregational life, not at the margins. They aren't maintaining anything; they are out to see the world changed by the power of God's Spirit. And they challenge the secular values of materialistic American culture at every turn. Typically, their commitment to kingdom change is reflected in new congregational priorities—even to the point of investing at least 50% of their time and resources in ministering to others! Without exception, these churches make a difference in their communities and in God's world. Thank God for congregations that place God's purposes first and become churches for others.

chapter eight

creating new possibilities

Creating! The Story of God begins with creation—with the spectacular, extravagant creativity of God. Before anything existed, God was, and out of nothing He created everything.

And our Creator has graciously gifted us, as His image bearers, with creativity. Though we are not able, like Him, to create something from nothing, we are able to imagine and bring into being a lavish array of new possibilities for ourselves and God's world.

Most important, we are invited, as God's children, to join Him in His task of re-creation—for the Bible makes it clear that He intends to make all things new.

Of course, when we place God and His Story at the center of our lives, He begins re-creating us. And He gives us the creative opportunity to fashion our entire lives around His purposes. But He also gives us the remarkable creative opportunity to join Him in seeing His world changed, too. And that's what this chapter—and this book—is all about.

The intention for this chapter is to help you learn to develop imaginative new possibilities for participating more fully in the Story of God—creating a way of life that will make a difference for you, for others, and for God's kingdom.

We will be exploring: (1) the meaning of creativity and the need for it in the Christian community, (2) common barriers to creativity and how to overcome them, (3) specific methods for creating new possibilities for our lives in the drama of God, and (4) some examples of those who have found innovative ways to collaborate with God in seeing the world changed.

In this chapter, we will be pulling together everything we have covered to this point. Have you begun to yearn for a life that is less stressful and more meaningful, less caught up in the rat race and more centered in the purposes of God? Have you discovered in the Story of God and our Christian past any models for your life? Have you begun to see new possibilities for whole-life discipleship and stewardship? Do you want to see your church move mission to the center of congregational life?

If so, write down some of the dreams you are beginning to have for your life, your church, and the world around you. In this chapter you will have the opportunity to unleash your imagination on those dreams, to create innovative new ways they can be realized in order to see God's loving purposes carried out in your life and His world.

creativity—an untapped resource

I conduct futures/creativity workshops with Christian organizations and churches all over the United States. And I have come to believe that creativity is one of the greatest untapped resources in the church today. I have seen remarkable things happen when people learn to use their imaginations in creating new possibilities for God's kingdom.

I cannot think of the word *creative* without remembering one bright sunny day in Estes Park, Colorado, where I conducted a day-long creativity session with the Sisters of Mercy.

As part of the workshop, the Sisters divided into groups to work on a "creativity task" I assigned them. Before they started, I challenged them to jettison their conventional approaches to living out their faith and solving their problems. I urged them to be creative, divergent, and "seriously weird" in imagining new possibilities. They didn't disappoint me.

After two hours of meeting together, the creativity groups streamed back into the lodge. As the first group got up to share, I saw a twinkle in their eyes. Their creativity task had been "to create an imaginative new approach to justice, education, and helping the poor."

I asked, "What do you have for us?"

They replied with enthusiasm, "The Traveling Solar Circus and the Mercy Clowns."

"What in the world is that?" I asked.

And they explained, "We plan to construct a circus tent with panels of all different colors. Then we are going to put solar collectors on the roof to run everything inside the tent.

"We will set up our tent in a small village in Honduras. The Sisters of Mercy will dress up like clowns. And through puppetry, mime, and dramatics we will teach the people of the village about literacy, sanitation, and community health.

"But that's not all. When we are done, we will move our tent—solar collectors and all—to an affluent suburban shopping center in Southern California. And the Sisters of Mercy clowns will use puppetry, mime, and dramatics to teach the upwardly mobile about social justice, the poor, and whole-life stewardship."

Now that's creative! That's the level of imagination we must have to burst out of the old wineskins of convention and create new and more effective ways to implement the vision of God in our lives and our world. We have scarcely begun to tap the imaginations God has placed within.

(And by the way, the Sisters of Mercy called me later and said they were seriously considering implementing aspects of their idea.)

defining creativity

But what do I mean when I speak of creativity? I am defining it as *the process of working in partnership with the Creator to generate new possibilities for our lives and world that are consistent with His redemptive purposes.*

This definition is important, because it is crucial that we recognize where our creativity comes from—our Creator, whose sheer inventiveness and imagination is astonishing:

> . . . God thinking up a giraffe, a cucumber, the overtone series, sexual reproduction, gravity, dolphins and strawberries. He is none of these and there were none of these for Him to copy. There was simply no information that He could gather outside of His own imagination that would give Him an inkling of what to make and how to make it.[1]

Because creativity originates with the Creator, a positive use of imagination requires acknowledging and working with Him.

---

1. Harold Best, "God's Creation and Human Creativity," (unpublished paper, Wheaton College, 1983), 8.

As Emil Brunner says,

> God the Creator, having created man in His image, has given him
> creative powers; where man acknowledges His Creator, he knows
> that he cannot create from nothing as God does, that therefore
> human creativity is a mere imitation of God's. . . .[2]

Brunner goes on to point out that if we seek to use our God-
given creativity autonomously apart from God, we will face
"the gravest consequences." But if we use our imaginations in
collaboration with His imagination, the possibilities for the
kingdom are unlimited.

Since we took the first bite of the apple in the Garden, we have
sought autonomy from God. We thought as we sank our teeth deep
in that forbidden fruit that we would know as God knows and be
as powerful as God is powerful.

We couldn't have been more mistaken. We have indeed used our
God-given creativity in autonomy from the Creator, and we are
experiencing the "gravest of consequences." Although some of humankind's new expressions of creativity add to the beauty and
bounty of all that God has created, others unfortunately reflect
the darkest side of human nature, threatening both human life
and creation itself. And in many ways, we have used our God-given
creativity to build a high-tech Babel for which we and those with
whom we share the planet are paying a very high price.

Harvey Cox asserts that the human creature,

> While gaining the whole world . . . has been losing his own soul.
> He has purchased prosperity at the staggering impoverishment of
> the vital elements of his life. These elements are festivity—the ca-
> pacity for genuine revelry and joyous celebration, and fantasy—the
> faculty for envisioning radically alternative life situations.[3]

But we also have the option of using our God-given creativity to
be collaborators in the inbreaking of God's kingdom. And if we
do, we will also discover a renewal of the festive, celebrative, joyful
aspects of life that God intended. That's what we are going to

---

2. Emil Brunner, *Christianity and Civilization* (New York: Charles Scribner's
Sons, 1948), 157.
3. Harvey Cox, *Feast of Fools: A Theological Essay on Festivity and Fantasy*
(Cambridge, MA: Harvard University Press, 1969), 9–10.

focus on in this chapter . . . learning to create with God, and in
the process rediscovering the joy and even fun that come with
creating new possibilities.

barriers to creativity

If creativity is so wonderful, why do so many of us in the
church seem to be so bound by convention . . . So stuck with
the same old ways of doing things? There are a number of reasons. Most of us have unconsciously erected barriers that block
our creativity and stifle our imaginations—and this is true both
of individuals and institutions. If we are to reawaken our imaginations, then, we must first identify and remove as many barriers as
possible.

One of the most important barriers is fear of change. Never has
there been a time when the church more desperately needed new
ideas for ways to advance God's kingdom more effectively. Unfortunately, many traditional approaches just aren't getting the job
done! We need new approaches to ministry, community, lifestyle,
and vocation. But at the same time there seems to be a firm resistance within the church, an inherent resistance to any type of
change. Someone has written that the seven last words of the
church are "We've never done it that way before."

As mentioned earlier, the agenda of most churches has much more
to do with maintaining the status quo and resisting change than
consciously positioning themselves to work for change in society.
Every denominational tradition tends to "sacralize" its conventional
institutional processes—to see them as sacred or inviolable, whether
they are effective or not. And, of course, we do the same thing in our
own lives.

We are conditioned by certain cultural expectations of what it
means to be Christian and what it means to be a church. We embrace these largely unexamined conventions as though they were
the gospel itself.

Now, resisting change is a very natural, human response. But
if we are going to learn to create with God, then we must be willing to relinquish our conventional approaches, understandings,
and expectations and fling open the windows of our lives to new
possibilities. While we can all affirm "Christ is the same yesterday, today, and forever," we need to realize that is not necessarily
true of our conventional ways of doing things. (Remember, we are

not looking for change for the sake of change. We are trying to discover creative new ways to see God's purposes realized in our lives and His world.)

How do we reduce the fear of change? By taking it slowly— trying a little selective change rather than sweeping revolution. By focusing on the benefits we will derive from creating new possibilities—and studying firsthand examples of others who changed and benefited from the change (we will be looking at some of these throughout this chapter). By internalizing the reality that only those who learn to do a little selective risk-taking ever experience what it's like to be fully alive. And of course, by spending significant time in prayer, asking for God's help and direction as we work to create new possibilities for His kingdom!

But resistance to change is not the only barrier to creativity. In many Christian traditions there is a deep distrust of imagination itself. Certain groups of our Christian ancestors, such as the Puritans, saw imagination as the "playground of Satan." While they placed high priority on the development of the intellect, they held imagination in high suspicion.

And many of us have inherited that attitude. Although we don't consciously think that imagination or creativity is sinful, we tend to discount them as trivial or unimportant.

One has only to examine the relatively small contribution Christians as a whole are making in the arts to raise the question as to whether we still distrust our imaginations or not. Quite frankly, I find very little emphasis in Christian day schools, colleges, or churches on developing the imaginative powers with which God has gifted us.

If we believe that God redeems us as whole persons, however, and that He intends to use us as whole-life disciples, it follows that He intends to use our imaginations and creativity as well as our intellects, our powers of communication, and our relational gifts.

It's time we embraced the reality that creativity and imagination are wonderful gifts from God. It's time we started enjoying them—and employing them much more fully to advance God's kingdom. I believe we need an absolute renaissance of Christian creativity. We need the Holy Spirit to blow through our imaginations, creating a whole generation of innovative ways to see God's dream come true in His world.

But this brings us to still another major barrier to creativity. It's the belief some people have that they aren't creative. People tend to think that imagination and creativity are selective gifts possessed by a small elite of artists, authors, and musicians.

Nothing could be further from the truth! I've found in over ten years of doing creativity workshops that *everyone* is gifted with creativity and imagination. Some, of course, have exercised their imaginations more than others . . . but God has given us all the capability of imagining and creating new possibilities. Those who feel they aren't creative simply need to exercise their "imagination muscles" more.

So even if you think creativity is for others, not for you, even if you're basically a little skeptical about your creativity and a little fearful of trying new possibilities, I urge you to read on. I believe you will find that "the water's fine." And I hope you will discover the joy and exhilaration of collaborating with the Creator in seeing all things made new.

pathways to creative living

I often find much more creativity in the secular society than I find in the church. For example, when I worked in the new business research division of the Weyerhaeuser Corporation, I worked with people who were committed to divergent thinking and creative planning. As a consequence, they were able to give birth to a range of new corporate ventures—such as fish farming on their forest lands. And years before the energy crisis they began using wood waste to heat their facilities.

In Sweden there is even a school for entrepreneurs, called the Foresight Group, which was established in 1980 to train people to come up with new answers, solutions, and ideas. As a result, a draftsman has started an eel farm in an abandoned section of the plant where he works. It will produce more than one hundred tons of eels annually.

A salesman in Sweden has designed an innovative way to fabricate concrete elevator shafts that can be installed without breaking down walls. There has been tremendous demand for the new product because Sweden, in the interest of handicapped people, has recently passed a law making elevators mandatory in buildings above a certain height.[4]

If secular society can come up with ideas like that, there is no reason Christians can't draw on the same innovative powers to

---

4. John Naisbitt and Patricia Aburdene, *Re-Inventing the Corporation* (New York: Warner Books, 1985), 67.

create new approaches to vocation, celebration, whole-life
stewardship and whole-life mission.

But how do people go about creating the new and innovative?
What are some of the creative methodologies we can use to create
with God? I'd like to suggest three possibilities: (1) "Many trails to
you!"—expanding your options; (2) venturing off the beaten path;
and (3) creating your own road home.

many trails to you—expanding your options

I have met a distressingly large number of Christians who limit
themselves to a depressingly narrow range of life options.

College students, for example, often think about vocation in
terms of a very narrow range of occupational choices. They limit
themselves to a very conventional array of timestyle and lifestyle
options that often have very little to do with the kingdom. And
frankly, I have found that the guidance programs in many of our
Christian colleges and the leaders of Christian ministry organizations on secular campuses usually do very little to help young
people explore nontraditional options in lifestyle, vocation, and
ministry.

But college students aren't the only ones who limit themselves;
most of us tend to get stuck in thinking of only a few possible
directions for our lives. And as a result, most of us live pretty
conventional, compartmentalized lives. Few have discovered the
adventure of significantly broadening their options.

The first step in creating new possibilities, then, is to make the
mouth of your creativity funnel as wide as possible. First, do research on your area of interest. Collect as broad an array of ideas
as you can think of—even those that may seem unlikely.

Roger Von Oech, a noted writer on creativity, helps us think
about how to expand our array of options by showing all the
possible answers to the question, "How do you keep a fish from
smelling?" The possibilities are much broader than what you
might think: "Cook it as soon as you catch it. Freeze it. Wrap it in
paper. Keep a cat around it. Burn incense. Leave it in water. Cut
its nose off."[5]

In working with college students who are interested in working

---

5. Roger Von Oech, *A Kick in the Seat of the Pants* (New York: Harper & Row,
1986), 31.

overseas, I find many limit themselves to traditional missionary roles. I have tried to help them expand their range of options to look at alternatives such as teaching in nonformal settings, teaching English as a second language, working in community health, training in small-scale technology or tropical agriculture, providing theological education by extension, or taking "tentmaking" occupations overseas (jobs to support oneself financially while working for mission).

Some friends and I are interested in creating a new rural Christian community. And I am trying to take the "many trails" approach in looking at the possibilities. Instead of limiting myself to the models of community I am already familiar with, I have been exploring as broad a range of options as possible.

On a recent trip to Europe, for example, I visited Cistercian abbeys, Benedictine monasteries, and Protestant lay communities. In the United States, I intentionally plan my trips so as to visit as many different communities as possible. And, of course, I read as much as possible, too. And I am discovering many more trails that lead to community than I had ever imagined.

Now, I realize not everyone has the opportunity to travel overseas. But there are many more creative models than you ever imagined right in your own region. And the reading materials on alternatives for Christians are abundant. Try your local library, bookstore—even your telephone book and newspaper, to seek out new ideas and see what others are doing. Don't exclude anything at this point. Exploring all the options will give you more to work with—and to pray about. Many trails to you!

venturing off the beaten path

If you're going to be creative, however, it isn't enough simply to expand your range of options. You're going to have to venture off the beaten pathways, too. Look for more than obvious answers. Seek out the divergent. Explore unlikely possibilities.

For example, a city in the Netherlands had a trash problem. Garbage was accumulating around homes and along buildings. The town was becoming an eyesore. The people of the town explored all kinds of options—more litter patrols, more garbage cans. But nothing worked.

So they started exploring off the beaten path. In one problem-solving session, someone suggested paying people for putting litter in trash cans. And while this idea wasn't economically feasible, it

became a springboard for considering some truly divergent alternatives, including this brilliant but offbeat idea, which was the one
that finally worked:

> The sanitation department developed electronic trash cans which
> had a sensing unit on the top which would detect when a piece of
> refuse had been deposited. This would activate a tape-recorder that
> would play a recording of a joke. In other words, joke-telling trash
> cans! Different kinds of trash cans told different kinds of jokes.
> Some told puns; others told shaggy dog stories, and soon developed
> reputations. The jokes were changed every two weeks. As a result,
> people went out of their way to put their trash in trash cans, and the
> town became clean once again.[6]

Venturing off the beaten path can result in some truly offbeat
solutions—but it can also involve simply doing something familiar
in an unfamiliar way.

For example, a Christian businessman and his family on the
East Coast wanted to find a creative way to invest their resources
in the advance of God's kingdom. And of course, there were all
kinds of traditional routes they could have taken—giving to local
mission organizations, sponsoring children overseas, giving to
their local congregations, and so on. But this family wanted to do
something a little different, and they wanted to have a little more
personal investment than just writing a check. So they got off the
beaten trail by exploring the possibilities of setting up a private
foundation—a more direct way to steward their resources for
God's kingdom.

This family discovered a creative way to set up what they call
"The Mustard Seed Foundation." They invited relatives to join
them in contributing to the foundation. Now they give small start-
up grants to Christian organizations that want to start innovative
programs of witness or service—and they are making a difference
for the kingdom.

Have you ever considered doing something familiar in an unfamiliar way?

---

6. Roger Von Oech, *Whack on the Side of the Head* (New York: Warner Books,
1983), 60.

creating your own road home

Beyond expanding the creative range of options and venturing off the beaten path, we also have the possibility of creating something that is almost totally new.

Now, when I talk about "creating your own road home," I am talking about both the process and the result. I am talking about getting "seriously weird" in imagining new possibilities for existing realities—turning what is tried and true on its ear and giving ourselves permission to be a "little crazy" in dreaming up what could be. Later on, we will explore creative ways to implement these ideas in the real world.

Creating something new is especially useful as a spark to the creativity process itself; trying to "go where no man has gone before" can be a big help in breaking free from the barriers to creativity.

Some groups use a creativity process called "synetics" to combine two totally unrelated items or concepts to create something entirely new. For example, what do you think of when you hear the term, "aerosol peanut butter"? Imagine all the possible uses (provided you can get it out of a can)—cake decorating, kid's lunches, catering, dental adhesive, an underarm deodorant? Has your imagination begun to take hold of the creative challenge?

Or look at something very ordinary in your life—for example, a seamstress's box of fabric scraps such as Velcro®, acrylic trims, and so on. What would happen if you broke loose from seeing these ordinary materials and looked at them from an entirely new perspective?

Let me share with you a letter to the San Francisco *Chronicle* in which the author did just that. Note the freshness and the fun:

I find your story in last Monday's *Chronicle* about the invention of Velcro® highly unlikely. I have been told by a reputable source that Velcro® is derived from the hide of Velcros, distant relatives to the Naugas. But now that Velcro® has become such a lucrative commodity, the Velcros are threatened with extinction. The wholesale slaughter of these helpless animals compounds the already difficult situation Velcros face in the wild. They easily stick to things, and during mating become literally stuck on one another and hence are easy prey to hunters.

For a long time Velcros were worshiped by the Acrylics, a primitive tribe of weavers who lived in their habitat. The Acrylics protected the

Velcros for religious purposes, but the commercial exploitation of the Acrylics for their weavings, and their subsequent fall from fashion favor, has forced the disintegration of Acrylic society. It is the same old story. We have seen it on every nature program on Channel 9. First come the explorers, then the traders and the missionaries. Finally, the designers and consultants, leading to the complete ruination of a noble people, the destruction of habitats and the extinction of their denizens.[7]

When we let ourselves be truly divergent and try for the truly new, any of us might be able to create an entirely new vocation for the kingdom of God. We are not limited to existing options, even those which are off the beaten path.

For example, look at how some Polynesian Christian young people living in Hawaii used some very familiar entertainment vehicles to create a wholly new vocation for the Story of God. They started a new group called Island Breeze to entertain at Hawaiian resorts.

They put together a program that presents authentic traditional dances from Maori, Samoan, and Tongan cultures. But they also work a number of Christian songs into their repertoire. Their show is entirely different from any I have seen in Hawaii, and there is no way for the audience to miss their clear Christian witness.

In addition to sharing their music, their culture, and their witness, this innovative group has created a ministry through which they use a generous share of their profits to: (1) bring other young Christians from the South Pacific islands to help them receive Christian education at Pacific and Asian University in Hawaii and (2) support Christian mission and ministry activities throughout Asia by working with Youth with a Mission.

With a little divergent imagination, these Hawaiian young people have really brought it all together. They are having a witness through their music, their lives, and their resources. They have created a new road home.

What are some new possibilities for your life if you: (1) seriously expanded your range of options, (2) checked out those alternatives off the beaten path, or (3) created whole new possibilities? This business of following Christ is a creative adventure that should use every ounce of our imaginations.

---

7. Bruce Skagen, San Francisco *Chronicle,* 13 May 1984.

unleashing your imagination

If you've stayed with me all the way through this book, you may be standing at a critical threshold in your life. You may have discovered that some of the tales to which you've given your life just won't bring you the kind of significant life you dream of. I imagine some of you want to begin taking greater charge of your life and are considering some creative new possibilities or even some serious risks.

But, as you know, changing the direction of one's life isn't easy. Considering any kind of change—not to mention risky new options—is scary business. But change and newness are also very exciting, and the kind of changes God intends to make in your life are only for the better. So I urge you to keep moving forward. The destination is definitely worth the journey!

What you will find—you may already be discovering it—is that the more we bring our life into alignment with the purposes of God, the more we find ourselves working *with* God's creation, not against it. You see, God only intends good for our lives. He intends that we discover a way of life not only in which we blossom and grow, but in which we enable others to flourish. Our God deeply loves us and wants us to experience life fully so that we might give it away.

So where are the handles? How can we actually begin to create whole new possibilities for our own lives, communities, and churches?

Let me outline two creativity processes you can try—one for individuals and one for groups. I call the individual approach "idea storming" and the group process "group storming." Both of these are variations on the idea of "brainstorming," which has proved itself over and over again in corporate and institutional settings. I have tried to adapt the standard brainstorming techniques to apply them specifically to Christians in search of new possibilities for life direction and kingdom mission.

idea storming for creative living

Idea storming only takes one to play. And all you need are a pad and pencil.

Remember, at the beginning of the chapter I suggested that you list new dreams and possibilities that have begun to fill your mind as you've worked through this book. Pick one that appeals to you—such as designing a less expensive house or creating a new celebration around a biblical theme.

If you didn't make a list, give yourself a minute to think of a problem or a challenge or an idea that has been on your mind—this will be your "creativity task." Here is a list of possible creativity tasks to give you some ideas:

(1)   Create a more festive and more sharing lifestyle for a suburban family.

(2)   Create a "tentmaking vocation" (a job to support you financially while working in ministry) for a single person who wants to work in the inner city.

(3)   Create a less expensive way to provide housing for a young couple just starting out.

(4)   Create a way to dramatically change your timestyle . . . freeing up more time for relationship, celebration, and ministry.

(5)   Create an innovative ministry to an area of need in your neighborhood.

Make your creativity task as specific as possible, and write it down at the top of your pad of paper. Now, invite the Spirit of God to flood your imagination and begin listing every possible idea that comes to mind regarding your task. Journey to the extreme edges of your imagination and drag into consciousness the most bizarre, far-out ideas you can come up with—write them all down.

At this point, be careful not to judge any of your ideas or discard any that "won't work" (or even those that "aren't creative"). That will come later. What you want to do now is unleash your imagination on the task and come up with as many ideas as possible.

After you have come up with as many ideas as you can, stop and survey the list. Circle what you feel are the three most compelling ideas on your list.

Now, turn to another sheet of paper. List the three ideas at the top of the page. Explore innovative ways you might cluster or combine the three ideas into a single, unified focus.

Visualize in your mind what that cluster of ideas might look like. Try to see them as a picture. Take another sheet from your page and draw a picture, either symbolic or literal, of your cluster of new ideas.

Don't worry if you're "not an artist"; the purpose of doing a picture is to help you look at the problem in new ways, not to produce a piece of art. Chances are you will find that thinking visually instead of verbally will help you see your ideas in a whole new light. You will probably notice that it helps your ideas feel more concrete.

Finally, on still another sheet, make a list of all the steps that would be necessary for your cluster of ideas to become a reality. Be sure to include three steps from chapter 6: (1) bringing your ideas before God in a time of listening and discernment, (2) doing active research, and (3) involving your community group in the prayerful decision of whether or not the idea is consistent with God's purposes for your life.

At this point, you may be through with the idea storming session. In idea storming, you can come up with as many ideas as you want on as many subjects as you want and have no obligation to implement any of them. Simply doing idea storming once a month will significantly broaden your approach to life and mission.

It is certainly possible, however, that you will want to go ahead with some of your ideas. If so, use your list of steps towards implementing your ideas. Spend time in prayer, do research, and draw others in on the decision. Then, if it is green light time, get your courage together and go for it!

group storming for creative mission

In this group process, simply have over a group of friends, or try this in place of a church committee meeting. If possible, have it in a home or another relaxed setting. Serve nachos or other delectables, dress casually, and try to create a relaxed, informal environment.

Develop a very specific list of creativity tasks, and focus on one task at a time. What these are will depend on the nature of your group. If you are a church committee, you might pick one of the tasks or challenges facing the committee. Or if you are a small group studying this book together, you may pick some of the issues raised in earlier sessions. Here are some possibilities:

(1)   How can we create a new approach for whole-life steward-ship for young marrieds?
(2)   How can we raise consciousness in our congregation regard-ing our responsibility for growing areas of human need in our community and the larger world?

(3)   How can we create new ministries that empower unemployed
       young people to become self-reliant?

If your group is large, break into smaller groups and allow people to work on the creativity task that interests them most. Groups
should be comprised of three to eight people—beyond eight people, groups tend to become unmanageable. Ask someone in each
group to be a facilitator and keep the group focused on their task.

Phase One—Idea Capture.   In the group, read over your creativity task again. Then begin suggesting possibilities. Select a
scribe and give him or her several large sheets of newsprint to
record everyone's ideas.

Now begin suggesting ideas and have the scribe jot them down
as they come up. At this point, no one should evaluate the ideas;
the purpose is to come up with as many as possible. Group members should be encouraged to be divergent and "seriously weird" in
the idea-capture phase . . . moving beyond the conventional and
familiar.

About forty-five minutes should be allowed for this part of the
process.

Phase Two—Idea Cluster.   After you have captured as many
ideas as you can from your group, ask participants to reach con-
sensus on what they feel are the three most compelling ideas you
have come up with. Ask the scribe to circle those ideas. Then begin
exploring imaginative ways you might be able to combine the three
ideas into some kind of a cluster or combination. How could they
be combined into a working whole?

Then expand the cluster idea, moving into specific goals and
strategies for implementing the cluster. Give your new cluster of
ideas an imaginative new name that is at least as creative as the
ideas you came up with.

If your group storming session involves more than one group,
prepare a stimulating three-minute presentation or skit to introduce your ideas to the larger group. Or if yours is the only group
involved, decide how you would present your idea to someone else.

This phase should take about twenty minutes.

Phase Three—Idea Communication.   If several creativity
groups have been involved, assemble all the groups together and
give each one the opportunity to share in three minutes a brief

summary of their group storming list and present their top idea
cluster. Encourage people to affirm one another and enjoy their
creativity as they share their ideas.

Now, whether your groups are large or small, allow time for
participants to: (1) discuss how they are feeling about their ideas,
(2) indicate if they are interested in seeing any of the ideas that
were presented actually take life and become a reality, and (3)
design a follow-up process to enable those who are interested in
seeing ideas implemented to actually do the necessary research,
prayer, and planning.

This final phase could take anywhere from thirty to sixty
minutes, depending on the number of creativity groups that
are involved.[8]

creativity for the kingdom

I guarantee that if you try unleashing your creativity on your
own or with a group of friends you will have a good time. And you
may even come up with some imaginative new ways to change
your own life or possibly even make a little difference in the world.
Then, of course, you need to develop ways to follow up on those
ideas that are particularly compelling. Creativity is involved with
implementation as well as ideas!

Let me share some of the more imaginative approaches I've
come across. Some of these came out of a creativity process like
the one I just described. Others came out of the fertile imaginations of those determined to give creative new expression to the
Story of God.

creativity for cooperative living

For example, once during a creativity seminar I gave a group
of American Baptists in Seattle an unusual task: "You have been
asked to help five imaginary Christian couples live together

---

8. If you actually implement some of your creative ideas, I would very
much like to hear about it. Or if you know of anyone who is involved in creative
new approaches to lifestyle change, celebration, community, or mission, please
drop me a note at: Box 9123, Seattle, WA 98109. We are developing a computer
file on Christian innovation to share with the larger church, and we want to
include models you are creating or are in touch with.

cooperatively to see what kind of time or resource you could free
up for the work of the kingdom."

I said, "Assume these ten people have incomes of $25,000 apiece.
They have five split-level homes with equity, five washers, five
dryers, ten cars, and no kids." I said, "Your task is to help them free
up resources for ministry by living together cooperatively without:
(1) leaving the middle class, (2) undergoing any sacrifice or deprivation, (3) doing anything "hippy-dippy" communal.

They came back an hour and a half later clearly excited. I said,
"What do you have?" And they explained that not far from where
these five imaginary couples lived was a marvelous old two-story
wooden schoolhouse for sale, plus some land. They calculated they
had enough equity in their five suburban homes not only to buy
the schoolhouse cash on the barrelhead but to rehabilitate it into
five separate condominium apartments, plus some common areas.
American privacy with a little creative cooperation!

I inquired, "How much did you free up?" They replied that in
this cooperative model these five Christian couples would be
able, without significantly changing their standard of living, to
free up $200,000 a year or the equivalent time for the work of the
kingdom.

Now, that's creative stewardship! And if we could ever learn to
make our lives totally available to the initiative of God, I think we
would be absolutely amazed at the resources that could be made
available to advance God's loving purposes among those in need.

creating a new look in interior design

How do Christians decorate their homes? Usually, the same
as non-Christians. The affluent do it with a lot of money and the
help of a professional decorator. Many of us in the middle do it
with plastic wall hangings from J.C. Penney and with varying
amounts of taste. And some of my friends who are into radical
lifestyles do it with orange crates and serious levels of ugliness.

Is that all there is? Can't our living environments reflect more
than our level of income? Can't they reflect our faith as well?

In our home we have attempted to decorate around the theme of
Jerusalem and what the city represents in the Bible—especially
homecoming, celebration, and festivity. We are making a replica of
a primitive sculpture of Christ's triumphal entry into Jerusalem
to hang over the mantle. We are developing large arched montages
of pictures that intersperse pictures of the Holy City with pictures

of people in jubilant celebration. Friends are doing some original art to help us carry out these themes.

We are attempting to create an interior environment that is festive, tasteful, and completed on a very low budget. But our primary purpose is for people to sense as soon as they step into our home the joy and celebration of our God. In whole-life stewardship, every area of our lives becomes a creative opportunity to give expression to the vision and the values of God's kingdom.

creating community at Christian colleges

Every time I speak on a Christian college campus, I urge the administration to consider creating an alternative Christian community on the campus in which faculty, students, and administrators live together, being the family of God to one another. Such a community could help all the students on the campus realize that there are alternatives to the rat-race lifestyles they are all too familiar with.

To my delight, I discovered that Beau and Rich Perkins have done just that at Houghton College, where Rich teaches sociology. Rich sees his Christian responsibility as being broader than the formal environment of the classroom. Several years ago, he and Beau decided that for them being whole-life disciples meant creating an alternative lifestyle community with students.

I have had the opportunity to talk to several of the students who have tried out this particular form of community while they were at Houghton. They told me this was one of the most important areas of learning during their entire college experience. They learned something of what it means to be family with the people of God, and what they learned is changing the direction of their lives.

creating families for others

Once, when I was addressing a Presbyterian church in Bellevue, Washington, I asked, "What in all candor really bonds American Christian families together? Isn't it the things we consume together—sitcoms, tennis lessons, and Big Macs®?"

And I added, "Whole-life discipleship mandates that we place ministry at the center not only of our individual lives, but of our family lives as well." And I said, "I have yet to see a church that has created opportunities for children to be involved in ministry opportunities with their parents."

I returned to that church some weeks later. A woman came up to me and said, "We are doing it."

"What are you doing?" I asked.

She said, "There are some senior citizens in our neighborhood who are bedfast and are going to lose their homes if someone doesn't help them with their chores. So I have started going once a week to help them with their chores. And my two preschoolers go with me. They don't just watch Mom work. They get right down and scrub the floor alongside me."

This remarkable woman had taken my passing comments on families for others and created a new whole-life stewardship opportunity for herself and her kids. What kind of children would we raise if they spent eighteen years being involved in that kind of active ministry with their parents instead of being indulged in the affluence of the Land of Evermore?

creating policy alternatives

Growing numbers of Christians are coming to realize that it isn't enough to work at the bottom of the cliff patching up those who are pushed off, but that we must also find creative ways to change policies and structures that are doing the pushing.

One of the most effective organizations working for creative change in this area is Bread for the World. With a staff of fewer than one hundred people and a membership of some forty-eight thousand, they are constantly involved in creating and proposing innovative legislation on behalf of the powerless.

For example, they were recently able to get a twenty-five-million-dollar appropriation to establish a Child Survival Fund. "The fund promotes four simple techniques: immunization, breast-feeding, growth charts, and oral rehydration. Used together, these techniques dramatically reduce infant and young child deaths. This means 250,000 kids are going to live because of one year's funding."[9]

Creativity in policy making can obviously have a significant impact on the world around us.

---

9. "Hunger Is No Longer Necessary," interview with Arthur Simon by Barbara R. Thompson, *Christianity Today*, 6 September 1985, 22. For information on Bread for the World, write: Bread for the World, 802 Rhode Island Avenue NE, Washington, DC 20018.

creating prayer letters to raise biblical consciousness

Evangelicals for Social Action has been concerned about the polarizing voices on the far right and the far left on issues of Central America, South Africa, and so on. They have a growing concern that American Christians learn how to discover a biblical response to contemporary issues that avoids becoming captive to the agendas of the right or the left.

In a particularly creative moment, they decided to use the prayer letter format to present both sides of the story in Nicaragua and South Africa. These two newsletters—one for each country—are called "Intercessors for Peace and Freedom." Frankly, these are the only publications I have found that try to look at both sides of those two very difficult situations from a biblical perspective, working with peoples inside the nations affected.[10]

creating random hospitality

At a creativity workshop at Brentwood Presbyterian in Los Angeles, workshop participants came up with a new way to celebrate hospitality. They are a large suburban congregation where a lot of folks don't know each other, so they found a way to get people connected. People who were willing to have others over for dinner simply printed up an invitation and randomly placed it beneath a pew somewhere in the sanctuary. During the morning worship the congregation was asked to check beneath their pews. Those who found invitations also found some friends in their congregation that they had never gotten together with before and enjoyed celebrating relationships with them.

creating a ministry of agricultural empowerment

And then there is the small home group from Bethany Presbyterian in Seattle who decided to sponsor some Laotian refugees. This small community of Christians has successfully sponsored over fifty people, working together to help them find housing, start a church of their own, and adapt to their strange new culture.

Adapting to the city has been especially difficult for these

---

10. If you would like copies of either "Intercessor for Peace and Freedom" or of the regular ESA newsletter, write: Evangelicals for Social Action, 312 West Logan Street, Philadelphia, PA 19144.

Laotians, who come from a rural tribal background. They had to be taught how to use the gadgets of an urban society that most of us take for granted—including the toilet.

The cultural differences between the refugees and their new home led to some funny experiences. For example, at one point Cal Uomoto, who headed the project, noticed that supermarket shopping carts kept appearing in the yard where the refugees lived. He got after the kids for bringing the carts home—but they still kept appearing. Then one day, as he was driving up the hill to the refugees' house, he saw to his amazement one of the men coming at him down the hill at a very rapid clip—in a shopping cart.

For all their efforts, however, the home group totally failed to enable the refugees to find employment. These rural people don't speak English, and they have very few skills that are marketable in an urban economy—they can't work at the counter in a fast food restaurant or pump gas at a service station. Months went by without turning up any jobs, and everyone was getting discouraged.

One day one of the Laotian men said, "We want to farm!" That had not occurred to anyone. So the group discovered another pathway and created a new alternative of employment. They rented twenty acres from King County and hired an agricultural coordinator to advise them on the specific needs of the region. (If you plant seeds two inches deep in Seattle, you will never see them again.) And they developed a strategy for marketing the produce in grocery stores, restaurants, and the Pike Street market.

If all goes well, these fifty people should be economically self-reliant in two years because a church cared enough to give not only a handout but also a hand-up.

So many churches when they do decide to help those in need simply give them food or clothing. And there's a place for that. But we need to create thousands of new ministries that empower the poor. We need churches to create new businesses with the poor, provide job training, enable people to achieve self-reliance and self-esteem and realize their own human dignity.

I should mention one thing that is making this Laotian farm project succeed—nine young people in this home group put this mission project at the center of their common and individual lives. They reduced their own personal lifestyle costs by living together cooperatively in three homes near the refugees. Only two of them worked for salaries; the remainder got part-time "tentmaking" jobs so they could free twenty to forty hours a week to work with the refugees. This is whole-life stewardship that makes a difference.

creating economic empowerment

Tragically, we in America are in the process of creating a permanent underclass of tens of thousands of young people who will live and die in the United States and never have jobs. And it's not because they are lazy or shiftless. Rather, they have gone to inner-city schools which are not doing a good job of teaching them to read and write. They have no job skills, and there is no place in the American economy for illiterate, unskilled people.

Tom Skinner Associates imaginatively responded to this challenge. They rented an empty building across the street from an inner-city high school in Newark, New Jersey. They put computers in the building and are using those computers to teach a small group of high-school people basic literacy skills. They are also teaching them to program and service the computers. Those young people are knocking themselves out to get in this program because they know if they successfully complete the program, they can break out of the cycle of perpetual unemployment.

By the way, do you have any idea what Skinner Associates has them use to program the computers? That's right—the Scriptures. Numbers of those young people are becoming Christians while they are developing job skills. We need a whole generation of new ministries that combine witness and empowerment for the kingdom of God.

creative Christian scrounging

Going through a creativity session with a group of participants in the Scupe Urban Conference in Chicago, I asked people to find something thrown away in the city and do something for the kingdom with it. When the group returned from their session, I asked, "What do you have?"

They responded, "Old tires thrown away on the streets. We are going to stack them nine tires high, fill the stack of tires with dirt and potato seeds. We water it from the top; the potato sprouts come out the side. When it's harvest time, we push over the tires, pick up the potatoes, and sweep up the dirt."

I said, "You're kidding."

They replied, "Nope. It's called vertical gardening, and it will work."

What are some underutilized resources that you could transform into tools for the kingdom? In the nineties, we are all going to learn to become creative scroungers if we're going to get the job done.

creative third-world mission

Dan Schellenberg is a Southern Baptist missionary who has found some marvelously creative ways to transform underutilized resources in Kenya into evangelism, discipling, and church expansion. He has created a whole range of imaginative new ways to enable those who are powerless in rural Kenya to become empowered. For example, he enabled Pastor Ngozi of Mbembani Church to live self-sufficiently and in the process have more time to spread the gospel and serve his congregation. Together, Dan Schellenberg and Pastor Ngozi planned a homestead for the pastor that actually generated enough income for Pastor Ngozi to become self-supporting.

The first thing they did was to build a water catchment system. Pastor Ngozi not only used the water to irrigate a new garden, but was actually able to sell water to others at the going rate.

The second phase was to build a silo to provide grain storage for the excess grain produced through irrigation.

Phase three was to build a $45 biogas digester using cow dung to produce methane gas for lights and energy. All of these steps not only give the pastor's family a buffer against famine, but provide a regular income from the sale of water, grain, and animals.

"Mbembani Baptist Church had six members when Ngozi became pastor and remained static as they struggled for survival. Now it has more than eighty members. During a recent six-month period he baptized forty. 'I have more time for Bible study, prayer, visitation, and evangelism now that I am free,' Ngozi says."[11]

Let me just mention a couple of other examples of creative mission. Bob Moffit has created an organization called Harvest that partners churches in the Third World with churches in the United States. In this people-to-people program, ministry flows both ways. Churches in the United States are partnering with churches in Latin America and Haiti. Together Christians are finding creative ways to make a difference.

A group of college students decided to create a whole new

---

11. "How the Ngozis Changed," *The Commission,* magazine of the Foreign Mission Board of the Southern Baptist Convention, December 1984, 55–59.

magazine on world mission. People told them they were crazy. But they took their small amount of cash and invested in the first issue. By living together cooperatively and raising their own support, they pulled it off. *World Christian* magazine is one of the most compelling, courageous publications on Christian mission today. It's amazing what God can do not only with our creativity, but with our courage, to advance His purposes.

Chavannes Jeune, whom I mentioned in the previous chapter, is head of the Institute for Rural Development for an indigenous Baptist denomination in Haiti. But Chavannes has also created a remarkable new ministry to kids in his country who are bonded servants. These are children who are locked in cycles of illiteracy, poverty, and virtual slavery. But Chavannes has set up a basic literacy program for them. It is held during the dinner hour to make use of churches and school buildings which are vacant at that time. High school students are trained as tutors and earn enough income by tutoring to pay their own tuition at high school.

The program uses the Creole New Testament to teach the children to read and write. They also learn basic math and personal hygiene and are taught job skills so that they can support themselves when they are liberated at age eighteen. Numbers of these children have come to faith in Christ and are looking forward with hope to the future as a direct result of Chavannes's God-inspired creativity.[12]

called to be creative

Within every image bearer of God is the creativity to imagine and create whole new ways—like those we have looked at—to participate in the adventure of God.

So don't limit yourself to tired tales and conventional options. Join those who are inviting God's Spirit to blow through their imaginations and give fresh expression to the Story of God.

We are a part of a magnificent story, a world-transforming history, and a community which will inherit the kingdom of God. Let's live as though we believed it.

Elizabeth O'Connor reminds us that

12. If you would like more information about this project, write Chavannes Jeune, MEBSH, Cayes, Haiti.

in every person is the creation story. Since the first day of our beginning, the Spirit has brooded over the formless, dark void of our lives, calling us into existence through our gifts until they are developed. And that same Spirit gives us the responsibility of investing them with Him in the continuing creation of the world. Our gifts are the signs of our commissioning, the conveyors of our transforming creative power.[13]

Let's join thousands all over the world who are discovering the secret of significant living, who are participating with the Spirit of the Living God in the continuing creation of the world and the inbreaking of the joyous, liberating, creative future of God.

for thought or discussion

1. Why do we need to break out of the wineskins of convention and create new approaches to life and mission?
2. What are some of your barriers to creativity—what in your life tends to hold you back from exploring new possibilities?
3. Try some of the creativity methods described in this chapter. What are some new ideas you come up with to make a difference in your own life, in your church, or among those in need in the world around you? Where do you plan to begin your creative journey with God?

13. Elizabeth O'Connor, *Eighth Day of Creation* (Waco, TX: Word Books, 1971), 17.

life links

confined to the conventional

Most Christians—and indeed most congregations—tend to confine their lives to a very narrow range of options as they look toward the future. They tend to stay within the safe shores of the familiar, regardless of whether this strategy brings the desired outcome. Individuals tend to limit their ministry, vocational, and lifestyle options to those with which they have been raised. Congregations tend to plan incrementally simply to do more of the same . . . whether it's effective or not. Unwittingly they smother their creativity and confine themselves to a very small cubicle . . . fearful of exploring beyond the conventional.

liberated to be creative

But a growing number of Christians are bursting out of the confining conventional boxes with which they have been raised—discovering the delight of creating a much broader array of ways to seek first the purposes of God in their lives and congregations. They are creating imaginative new approaches to whole-life discipleship—orchestrating their whole lives around the purposes of God. They are creating new ministries and new celebrations, and they are having the time of their lives. You are invited to join others in unleashing your creativity to express the joyful inbreaking of the kingdom of God.

begin now . . .

Beginning! Beginning any new initiative requires a deliberate choice. It won't just happen. The easiest thing in the world is simply to go with the flow—to avoid choices, risks, new beginnings—and live with the consequences and the regrets.

It was recently reported on *Good Morning America* that a group of people over ninety-five years of age were asked a single question: "If you could live your life over again, what would you do differently?"

Their responses varied, of course. But three answers dominated the results of the survey. "If I could live my life over again," they responded:

1. "I would take more time to reflect."
2. "I would take more risks."
3. "I would do more things that would live on after I die."

They're right, you know. The good life has nothing to do with mindless accumulation and frenetic scrambling. And those things that live on after we die are the things we give away. That's exactly what Christ told us—that it is only in losing life that we find life.

In this book we have argued that if we want our lives to have meaning and purpose, we must begin by abandoning the half-truths and full fictions to which we have given our lives. And we must begin by embracing a new story and becoming a part of a new venture that is quite literally changing the world.

Listen again to the compelling power of that story as John Westerhoff remembers it for us:

In the beginning, God had a dream of a world at one with itself; it was the world God intended at creation, a world of peace and unity, of freedom and equality, of justice and well being of all peoples.

We were created in God's image to enjoy God's dream, but with the capacity to say "yes" or "no" to it. And so the plot thickened. We humans didn't turn out as God had hoped. We were more interested in our own dreams than in God's dream. And so our human plight. Born with the capacity for right living, but seemingly inclined to live in estrangement from God, one another, nature, and ourselves, we continually frustrate God's dream.

But God is persistent. Having planted the dream deep within our conscience, God calls forth and raises up witnesses to the lost dream. God made a covenant with us so that forever we will experience the unswerving, patient pull of God toward the dream. God saved us from slavery, led us on a pilgrimage to a promised land, and gave us moral commandments to love God and neighbors so that we might live for God's dream. God raised up leaders to guide us and at last prophets to remind us of our covenant and to sketch a picture of what the world would be like if God's dream were realized.

Still, we frustrated God's dream by acting like all the rest of humanity. It is as if we were in bondage to the social, political, and economic systems we created. So God made a decision. God acted again, came to us in Jesus of Nazareth, the dreamer, story teller, doer of deeds, healer of hurts, advocate of the outsider, liberator of the oppressed; in Jesus, God shares our common lot and overcomes the principalities and powers that keep us from living the dream.

Good news has been announced. God's dream has begun; God's dream will come. Yet the dawn of hope is not yet the high noon of God's dream come on earth. Darkness still covers much of the earth and we still live as if this were the best of all possible worlds. But a new possibility exists. We have been given a new pair of eyes and with them the vision of dreamers returns.

We have been called into a visionary community to live risky, laughable lives of tomorrow's people, to live in and for God's dream, to witness to a world of peace and unity, of freedom and equality, of justice and well being for all people. We are called to accept the cost and the joy of discipleship, to proclaim in word and deed the good news of God's dream come true. God promises us courage and strength in the struggle for peace and justice; God forgives us our failures and lifts us up to new possibilities; God is present in our trials and rejoicing and hopes from this day forward.[1]

---

1. John H. Westerhoff III, *Inner Growth Outer Change: An Educational Guide to Church Renewal,* (New York: The Seabury Press, 1979) p. 135.

And from this day forward we have the opportunity by the power of God to begin over—to place God's dream and loving purposes at the very center of our lives. And if we do, we will discover a way of life with purpose that makes a telling difference in the world today . . . and will have a lasting impact tomorrow.

For whatever reason, God has chosen to work through ordinary people like you and me to change His world. And Jesus still stands at the edge of history inviting us to drop our nets and abandon our boats and join Him in the great adventure of seeing all things made new. What an incredible opportunity!

I have attempted in this book to show you some creative ways you can be much more a part of God's dream and His purposes. Now the ball is in your court. I urge you to spend some time in prayer as you conclude this book, listening to God, writing down what He is saying to you, developing some modest first steps. Then find one or two other people who are determined to put God's kingdom first in their lives and share with them the small initial steps you plan to take. Ask them for their prayers to hold you accountable for the changes God is calling you to make.

I am very interested in learning how God is drawing others into His kingdom initiative. I would enjoy hearing the ways in which God is calling you. And I am always looking for new creative examples of places where the kingdom is taking root. Why don't you drop me a note—Tom Sine, Box 9123, Seattle, WA 98109. I will reply to all letters.

Now, because this is a book about stories, I want to conclude it by telling you three brief stories that I hope will bring the central theme into sharp focus.

The first story concerns a pastor, Tim Dearborn, who was traveling in Bangkok, Thailand. One day Tim had trouble getting a taxi and wound up sharing a cab with a young man he didn't know. This young man was delighted to discover he was riding with a Christian pastor, and he quizzed Tim at length as to how he could spend his time promoting "a cause that couldn't possibly win."

Tim asked the young man what he meant, and he answered, "It is obvious that Christianity in your country is committed to self-interested living, always focusing on what your God can do for you. I am a Marxist," he continued, "on my way to India to organize fishermen to overcome their oppressive work situation." And then he added the clincher: "As a Marxist I would willingly lay down my life for the revolution, but to die for self-interest is a contradiction in terms."

The Jesus we follow didn't come calling us to a self-interested faith. Quite the contrary. As we follow Him through the pages of the New Testament we always find Him in one of two places— either with the Father in extended times of prayer, solitude, and worship, or with people in sharing, healing, and celebrating life. He didn't have time for anything else. He didn't even have a place to lay His head.

Jesus, our master, our model, and our Lord, was uniquely a man for others. And the reason Jesus was a man for others was that He was absolutely obsessed by God's dream for the future—a future in which the blind see, captives are set free, and God's reign is established in the earth.

Therefore, if we are to truly follow this Jesus, we must set aside our self-interested agendas and our egocentric piety and become a people for others, even as Jesus was a man for others. We must, like the Christ we follow, put God's other-serving purposes at the center of our lives, working with Him to see all things made new. And if we do, we will discover God will use our lives to make a genuine difference in His world.

All over the world, Christians are finding creative ways to be people for others, putting God's purposes first. And this brings us to the second story, about a small group of European Christians who wanted to see the light of the gospel shine more brightly in Eastern Europe. This group of Christians heard God's call to plant a church in a major East German city. But because they knew that traditional approaches to planting Christian faith wouldn't work in a Marxist society, they realized they must find ways to make God's other-serving love real to East Germans.

They began by asking, "What are the concerns and values of those with whom we are trying to share God's love?" And they answered their own question: "Germans care deeply about living things—forests, children, animals, beauty." So they intentionally set out to plant an innovative Lutheran church that would directly serve those they were trying to reach.

First, they purchased a tract of land right in the center of their selected East German city. They secured a grant from a West German foundation and used the funds to create a beautiful urban park on the land. They brought domesticated farm animals— sheep, rabbits, and so on—into the park and created something of a children's zoo. They erected a large greenhouse in the center of the park that served not only as a place to start new plants, but also as a setting for weekly art exhibits and public meetings. The people in the city have come to love their park and appreciate the caring spirit that built it.

That handful of Christians visited thousands of people in their high-rise apartments in this city, asking a question out of that same spirit of service: "How can we be of help to you and the community?" People in a communist society were surprised to see God's love so compellingly extended to them through the gift of the park and the caring lives of believers.

And, by the way, their efforts are making a difference. In only a few years of labor, hundreds have come to faith in Christ and they now have a congregation of over seven hundred believers. Where do they worship? In the park—in the large greenhouse—every Sunday.

When we determine to be people for others and place God's Story and loving purposes at the center of life, all of life becomes a creative opportunity to manifest God's jubilant kingdom. And that brings us to the final story—about a couple I know who found an imaginative way to manifest God's kingdom through their wedding celebration.

In a day in which young people (and their parents) often go into serious debt to get married, Terry and Patty created a refreshingly divergent approach. Not only did they keep the costs of the wedding to a bare minimum, having friends donate flowers and take the pictures, they had a wedding reception that those who attended will never forget.

In their wedding announcement, Terry and Patty wrote that they didn't want regular gifts for their wedding. Their note explained, "We have our health, each other, and opportunities to serve the Lord. We simply don't need a lot of things. Instead, we would appreciate it if you would give us turkeys, potatoes, or cranberry sauce."

Their bewildered families and friends complied with their wishes, but they didn't really understand until after the wedding, when they went downstairs for the wedding reception. . . .

Now, Patty and Terry work in a number of ministries at University Baptist Church in Seattle, including a Saturday feeding program for the elderly, poor, and street people in the University District.

As the homeless street people sauntered into the church basement for their usual meal that particular Saturday, however, they were amazed to find the room exploding with color—the entire basement was decorated with a huge array of flowers and balloons. Someone had found a string of old Christmas tree lights and made a heart on the wall. And instead of bearing the usual kettles of soup, the tables were laden with roast turkeys, mashed potatoes, cranberry sauce, and all the trimmings.

They asked what was going on, and Terry explained very simply, "My friend, Patty, whom you know, has become my wife. And we thought—who more appropriate to share our celebration with than you, our friends."

That day, over one hundred of Terry and Patty's friends from the streets, as well as their families and other friends, participated in a joyous celebration. Afterwards, Patty invited guests to take the decorations with them. Every doily, flower, and bit of decoration was carefully wrapped up and sent home with delighted guests, who packed them away as souvenirs.

Terry and Patty, like thousands of others, have discovered the secret of abundant living—that the good life of God is to be found in sharing, not in seeking life.

Remember how the story of God ends? A wedding reception! Listen to Jesus as He tells a parable of those who are unwilling to relinquish their self-involved lives to be a part of God's world-changing future:

The kingdom of heaven may be compared to a king, who gave a wedding feast for his son. And he sent out his slaves to call those who had been invited to the wedding feast, and they were unwilling to come. Again he sent out other slaves saying, "Tell those who have been invited, 'Behold, I have prepared my dinner; my oxen and my fattened livestock are all butchered and everything is ready; come to the wedding feast.'" But they paid no attention and went their way, one to his own farm, another to his business, and the rest seized his slaves and mistreated them and killed them.

But the king was enraged and sent his armies, and destroyed those murderers, and set their city on fire. Then he said to his slaves, "The wedding is ready, but those who were invited were not worthy. Go therefore to the main highways, and as many as you find there, invite to the wedding feast." And those slaves went out into the streets, and gathered together all they found, both evil and good; and the wedding hall was filled with dinner guests (Matt. 22:2–10, NASB).

Clearly, it isn't enough to believe in God, for even the devil believes. And it isn't enough to receive Christ into our hearts, as important as that is. We must realize if we want to have any part in God's final wedding celebration we must repent of our self-involved lives and our egocentric faith and seek His kingdom first, becoming persons for God and others.

As we place God's dream and loving purposes at the center of our lives and congregations, we will find creative new ways that God will use our lives to make a difference. Then and only then will we discover who we are called to be. We will discover the role God has for us to play in His world-changing drama. And we will discover a way of life more festive, compelling, and satisfying than anything this world can offer. Why in the world would anyone ever settle for more and miss the best?

Listen to the final description of the transcendent dream of God pictured for us in Revelation. For all of us who decide to accept God's invitation to that wedding celebration are headed for a future in which God's love makes all things new:

> And I saw a new heaven and a new earth; for the first heaven and the first earth passed away, and there is no longer any sea. And I saw the holy city, new Jerusalem, coming out of heaven from God, made ready as a bride adorned for her husband. And I heard a loud voice from the throne, saying, "Behold, the tabernacle of God is among men, and He shall dwell among them, and they shall be His people, and God Himself shall be among them, and He shall wipe away every tear from their eyes; and there shall no longer be any death; there shall no longer be any mourning, or crying, or pain; the first things have passed away." And He who sits on the throne said, "Behold, I am making all things new" (Rev. 21:1–5, NASB).

Welcome to life exploding with possibilities! Welcome to the adventure of working with our Creator Lord to see all things made new! Welcome to the wedding feast of God!

God has placed your future right in your own hands. You have the creative opportunity to find imaginative new ways to link your life with the purposes of God.

What are you waiting for? Get linked!

God is waiting to use your mustard seed to change His world . . . to help you discover a way of life with more meaning than you ever imagined . . . to use your life to make a difference for His kingdom.

About the Author:

Tom Sine is a "futurist" by profession, working in the areas of futures research and planning with major denominations and Christian organizations such as World Concern, where he has been a staff member and consultant for more than 10 years. He is also a prolific writer whose articles have appeared in periodicals ranging from *Sojourners* to *Family Life Today* and whose book, *The Mustard Seed Conspiracy,* won several awards and became a Christian bestseller.

A Presbyterian layman, Tom works with a broad spectrum of denominations. He is in wide demand as a speaker and served as coordinator for Wheaton '83, an international conference which gave the original impetus for this book. In addition to his speaking, writing, and consultation work, Tom holds creativity workshops for churches and other Christian groups.

Tom Sine holds the Ph.D. in American Intellectual History from the University of Washington and has served on the faculty of the University of Washington, Seattle Pacific University, and Fuller Theological Seminary. In addition, he has lectured widely at a number of colleges and seminaries, including Wheaton College and Westmont College.

For additional information on futures consultation, creativity workshops, or any of the issues raised in this book, write Tom Sine at PO Box 9123, Seattle, WA 98109.